AF529031

Education, Employment and Empowerment of Rural Women in India

Education, Employment and Empowerment of Rural Women in India

T. Sudha

GRP

GLOBAL RESEARCH PUBLICATIONS
NEW DELHI (INDIA)

© T. Sudha

First Published – 2011

ISBN: 978-81-89630-13-3

All rights reserved with the Publisher, including the right to translate or reproduce this book or parts there of except for brief quotations in critical articles or reviews.

Published by

GLOBAL RESEARCH PUBLICATIONS
4830/24, 1st Floor, Ansari Road
Darya Ganj, New Delhi-110002 (India)
Phone : 23245225. Fax : 91-11-23272135
E-mail: globalresearchpublications@gmail.com, grpindia@vsnl.net

CONTENTS

CONTENTS

FOREWORD

Empowerment is a heavy term that comprises the domains of State Market and Society. Hence, its conceptualization is quite a difficult task for researchers, particularly when they pursue the problem from a gender perspective. At the next level, they address the concomitant problem of measurement. Identifying the appropriate indicators of empowerment is the foremost step in this research. But in view of a lack of conceptual clarity and rigour, there seldom obtains consensus among researchers, in conferring meaning on different types of choices. I recall Kabeer's observation that indicators used to measure women's access to and control over resources have often failed to distinguish between different resources according to their degree of strategic value to women in a given context.

Dr. T. Sudha has gained appreciation of all those methodological problems, and it is evidenced by her comprehensive and well laid out chapter on review of literature. She defines Empowerment in terms of gender equality in decision making, and power of autonomy over resources as the indicators of rural women empowerment. Relating women empowerment to education and employment provides a convincing caveat for her study that education promotes women empowerment via employment. In order to lend theoretical support to her framework, she draws upon Amartya Sen's concepts of 'capabilities' and 'entitlements'. Empowerment is quantitatively assessed by her using Gender equality in Decision making (GEDM) and power of Autonomy over Resources and Mobility (PARM) at the empirical level.

The researcher has chosen two geographical locations–Salem and Thiruvarur, with contrasting performance in respects of female literacy. Thus, the sample households drawn from these micro settings lend scope for generalization of the empirical realities to apply to the entire India. Any research has dual ends to serve. Academically it should open up new vistas of research. Next it must pave way for rigorous discourses at the policy level, and help direct policy changes for the betterment of women. I have no hesitation to say that Dr. T. Sudha achieves these ends rather successfully in her work. Of course renegotiating gender relation and patriarchal institutions', is a long run process; but the scholars should continue to reiterate the task in their writings. This research points towards such a policy direction.

It is no surprise that this work does not exhaust all the possible interventionist strategies, for this would form by itself a separate area of research. But surely this work would hindle the thinking of researchers to explore these aspects in greater details in future.

I congratulate Dr. T. Sudha on her commendable piece of research. As her research supervisor, I find in her a promising scholar capable of objectivity and insightful inferences. I am sure she will gain still greater acclaim in future, making rich contribution to the multi–disciplinary tradition of gender economics.

I wish her Mother Grace in her Endeavours.

Annamalai Nagar

Dr. R. ELANGO
(Research Supervisor)

PREFACE

Empowerment of Rural Women is a much discussed subject, but conceptualization of empowerment is still under discourse. Earlier it has been discussed in terms of access to resources, and later on it has been defined in terms of control over resources and control of ideology. After the millennium year, empowerment has been defined in terms of gender equality. The present researcher defines empowerment not only in terms of gender equality, but also in terms of power of autonomy over resources, and studies the significant factors that influence the empowerment of rural women.

Women development is the most sensitized and multidimensional concept. Sociologists are defining it in terms of 'social inclusion', politicians in terms of 'empowerment' and economists in terms of 'entitlements'. Being an economist, the researcher has studied in terms of 'resources' (entitlements) and measures empowerment in terms of gender equality in decision making and power of autonomy over resources. But still, discourse is going on in defining empowerment as it is an interdisciplinary subject.

ACKNOWLEDGEMENTS

I wholeheartedly thank my Research Supervisor **Dr. R. Elango,** Professor and Head, Department of Economics, Dean Faculty of Arts and Director of Centre for Rural Development, Annamalai University for his constructive comments, and suggestions at every stage of this doctoral work. I am indebted to my supervisor for his involvement amidst his busy schedule.

I wish to express my sincere thanks to **Dr. N. Malathi,** professor of Economics, Annamalai University for her concrete ideas in designing this research work. I am also thankful for her unhesistant help at all stages of this work. I thank **Dr. T.S. Kalyani,** Professor of Economics, Annamalai University, for her continuous encouragement from the beginning of this work and her comments in writing this work.

I am thankful to **Dr. R. Sathiyamoorty,** Formerly Professor and Head, Department of Statistics, Annamalai University, for his directions in applying appropriate statistical tools. I wish to record my grateful gratitude to **Dr. D. Namasivayam,** Head, Economics wing, Directorate of Distance Education, for his valuable guidelines in applying statistical tools and in constructing tables. And my thanks are also due to **Dr. B. Mathavan,** Reader in Economics, Annamalai University, for his academic support. I thank **Dr. K. Saravanan,** Reader in Agricultural Botany, Annamalai University, who helped me in applying statistical tools.

I am thankful to **Dr. U.K. SudhaNayak,** Controller of Examinations, Sri Saradha College for Women, Salem for sharing her ideas in framing interview schedule. I am thankful to **Dr. R. Murugesan,** Professor, Center for Rural Development,

Department of Economics, Annamalai University, who gave guidelines in obtaining secondary data.

My thanks are also due to **Dr. N. Ramagopal** and **Dr. G. Ravi**, Professors of Economics, and **Dr. E. Selvarajan**, Reader in Economics, Annamalai University, for their instructions in strengthening this study. I thank **Mr. I. Ravi**, Lecturer (SG) in Economics and **Mr. P. Yuvaraja**, Programmer, Department of Economics, Annamalai University, for their assistance in operating SPSS package.

My special thanks are due to **Dr. M. Rajeswari**, Lecturer in Economics, Annamalai University, for her tiredless academic and moral support. I thank **Dr. K. Anbanandham**, Professor of English, for his scholarly suggestions regarding the language of this work.

I would like to to thank **Dr. D. Murugan, Mr. R. Asokan** and **Mr. P. Nalraj**, Lecturers in Economics, Directorate of Distance Education, Annamalai University and **Dr. K. Suriyan**, Lecturer (SS), Department of Sociology, Annamalai University, **Mr. K. Dhamodharan** Special Officer, Annamalai University and **Dr. K. Shafina Banu**, Reader in Economics, KNC College, Cuddalore, for their timely help. And I thank all the staff members of the Department of Economics, and Economics Wing, Directorate of Distance Education, Annamalai University, for their wishes.

I am thankful to **Mr. K.V. Arumugam**, Headmaster, **Ms. Selvi Priya,** Programme Assistant, G.H.S.S, Chittoor and **Mrs. Accammavarchese** Headmistress, **Mr. P. Mathiyazhagan**, PG Assistant, **Mr. K. Venkatachalam** P.E.T. Master, G.H.S.S. Vazhapadi. I thank **Mr. P. Thirulogachander** and **Mr. P. Kamaraj** Project Officers, Thiruvarur, **Mr.T. Mohan**, Accountant, Nagai Sweet Stall. Thiruturaipundi, **Mr. R.Varadharajan**, Advocate, Salem, and **Ms. L.Vimala**, Psychologist, Ramakrishna Hospital, Coimbatore, for their assistance in getting information from the sample respondents in the study area. Besides, I am thankful to the sample respondents who gave information. Without their information, this work could not have been done.

I thank **Mr. R. Prabhaharan**, Librarian, TIFR, Mumbai, who helped me in accessing study material from TISS, Mumbai and

I thank **Mrs. K. Dhanalakshmi,** Technical Assistant, Department of Economics, Annamalai University, for her assistance in getting study material and my thanks are also due to the staff members of the Library, Annamalai University., for their assistance in browsing study materials.

I thank the Research scholars in the Department of Economics **Mr. G. Kumar, Mr. D. Sridhar, Mr.A.Subburaman, Ms. K. Thamayanthi, Ms. S. Chandraleka,** and **Mr. M. Bharani** (Research Scholar in Philosophy) for their assistance.

On personal note I extremely thank my husband **Dr. E. Arumugam**, Senate Member and Reader in Philosophy, Annamalai University, and my daughter **Ms. A.R. Keerthana** for their kind co-operation and spontaneous encouragement and I am delightful to thank my parents- **Mr. P. Thambithurai and Mrs. T. Indirani** who motivated me to do this research work. Besides I dedicate this work to my well wisher **Mr. A.R. Ravichandran (late),** Assistant Public Prosecutor, Thanjavore. With their blessings, I am able to finish this work.

Last but not least, I am thankful to **Mr. M. Kamaraj,** Lecturer in Business Administration, Directorate of Distance Education, Annamalai University and his wife **Mrs. C. Deepa** and the staff members of Supreme Computer Centre for the neat execution of this work. I am thankful for their kind co-operation. I am also thankful to **Kannan Binding Works**.

T. SUDHA

ABBREVIATIONS

BC	—	Backward Communities
CV	—	Coefficient of Variations
FWPR	—	Female Work Participation Rate
GAD	—	Gender and Development
GDI	—	Gender Development Index
GEDM	—	Gender Equality in Decision Making
HDI	—	Human Development Index
HDR	—	Human Development Report
HRD	—	Human Resource Development.
HRD	—	Human Resource Development
MBC	—	Most Backward Communities
NSS	—	National Sample Survey
OC	—	Other Communities
PARM	—	Power of Autonomy over Resources and Mobility
RFL	—	Rural Female Literacy
RFWPR	—	Rural Female Work Participation Rate
SC	—	Scheduled Caste
UDHR	—	Universal Declaration of Human Rights
UFL	—	Urban Female Literacy
UNA	—	United Nations Agency
UNDP	—	United Nations Development Programmes
WAD	—	Women and Development
WID	—	Women in Development

1

INTRODUCTION

STATEMENT OF THE PROBLEM

This study focuses its attention on Education, Employment and Empowerment of Rural women in Tamil Nadu. Women play a key role in development, both in the context of the family and the society at large, including its economy and social system. Women are in a strategic position in human resource development.

Human development has been one of the major thrust areas since the Eighth Five Year Plan and consequently all the developmental efforts are being directed towards accomplishing this objective. Specifically the focus is on empowering both women and children besides mainstreaming them into the national development on equal footing along with their counterparts. The Ninth Plan too was expected to create an enabling environment with requisite policies and programmes, legislative support, exclusive institutional mechanisms at various levels, and adequate financial and manpower resources to achieve this objective (Banerji 2000).

Human Development Report (2004) views that the indicators of empowerment include access and rights to resources and economic opportunities and information (land, jobs, education, knowledge, health services, etc.) the division of labour and work load, access to services and institutions that supply them, involvement in household decision-making, political awareness and interest (voting, decisions about voting and relative representation in public decision-making bodies at community, state and national levels). In addition, intrahousehold decision-making receives importance among scholars as a commonly investigated indicator of women's empowerment (Kabeer 2001).

Gender Development

The UN-Agency working group on gender and development strives to increase effectiveness and efficiency amongst UN agencies to promote gender mainstreaming in the area of achieving gender equality. Its main interventions in the new millennium have been towards enhancing policy changes and promoting equal opportunities for strengthening women's decision making capabilities.

Gender backwardness is a term used to connote women's poor status measured by selected indicators in one sphere or area, denoting the opposite of gender development. The term gender development gained coinage while questioning the assumption of gender neutrality in development thinking and planning. Gender development focuses on enhancing capabilities for improving women's participation in development and ensuring that women share the benefits of development equally too. This may be further extended to mean that women must be recognized as individual entities with their own sets of rights. Discourses in gender and development, and the rôle of women in development in developing and less-developed countries have been instrumental in promoting education for women and shaping notions of social justice. In the first few decades after World War II, women were essentially confined to their reproductive roles as wives and mothers, as exemplified in the Universal Declaration of Human Rights (UDHR). These were mirrored in development theories in the 1950s and 1960s. Subsequently, feminist orientations induced a shift from welfare approaches to notions of empowerment, leading to the perception of women as rights holders.

Gender Mainstreaming: The Concept

The term "gender' is used to describe a set of qualities and behaviours expected from men and women by their societies. A person's social identity is formed by these expectations. These expectations stem from the idea that certain qualities, behaviour, characteristics, needs and roles are 'natural' for men, while certain other qualities and roles are 'natural' for women. Their "gendered" masculine and feminine identities are constructed through the process of socialization, which prepares them for the social roles they are expected to play. These social roles and expectations differ from culture to culture and at different periods in history. They can and do change. Gender relations in India (as everywhere else) are patriarchal-that is, they reflect and perpetuate a hierarchy where women are subordinate to men. Patriarchy makes women powerless in many ways by convincing them of their own inferiority to men; by demanding that they conform to certain stereotyped 'appropriate' roles and behaviour; by denying them control over their own bodies, lives and labour; by limiting their access to resources and by restricting their opportunities to participate in decisions which affect their own lives. These different forms of control often operate to strengthen each other, and have resulted in the exclusion and marginalization of women from social, economic and political processes. Women's subordination is reflected both in women's socio-economic condition (like their levels of health, income and education), and in their position, or degree of autonomy and control over their own lives. Gender equality cannot come about only through changes in women's condition. It requires transformation of the structures and systems which lie at the root of women's subordination and gender inequality. This transformation cannot be induced by external interventions. Women must themselves become active agents of change.

Gender equality therefore demands women's empowerment, a process that leads to greater participation in social and political processes, greater decision-making power and to conscious action for social transformation. The process of empowerment is not sectoral–it encompasses women's multiple roles and interests, and addresses the inter-relationships between them, leading to women gaining greater control over their own lives. Empowerment thus has many dimensions:

- Building a critical understanding of the causes and processes of disempowerment.
- Enhancing self-esteem and altering self-image.
- Gaining increased access to natural, financial and intellectual resources.
- Acquiring the confidence, knowledge, information and skills to understand and intervene in social, economic and political structures and passes.
- Increasing participation in and control of decision-making processes within and outside the family and community.
- Moving into new roles and spaces, which have hitherto been seen as exclusively male domains.
- Coming together to question, challenge and change unjust and iniquitous beliefs, practices, structures and institutions, which perpetuate gender inequality.

INDICATORS OF EMPOWERMENT

Many studies identified the indicators of empowerment (UNDP 1990; Karl 1995; Kishore and Gupta 2004; Rustagi 2004; Acharya and Ghimire 2005). The researcher sets her views in accordance with Acharya and Ghimire (2005) and indicates empowerment in terms of gender equality in decision making and power of autonomy over resources and mobility.

Gender Inequalities

The issue of gender inequality is ultimately one of disparate freedom (Sen 1992). Gender inequalities stem from relations of power and authority class, caste hierarchies and socio-cultural traditions, customs and norms. Empowerment may be defined as the process of transforming these structures and institutions, thereby ensuring equality. The causes of the persistent inequality between men and women are only partially understood. In recent years attention has been paid to inequalities in the allocation of resources at the household level, as seen in the higher share of education, health and food expenditures, boys receive in comparison with girls.

The decision-making process within households is complex and is influenced by social and cultural norms, market opportunities and institutional factors. There is considerable proof that the intrahousehold allocation of resources is a key factor in determining the levels of schooling, accorded household members. Gender inequality in family law can worsen women's bargaining position within and outside the household and affect household welfare and efficiency. Unless the disadvantages suffered by women are recognized and compensated so as to enable them to compete with men on an equal plane, realization of gender equality is difficult.

Promotion of gender equality and empowering women is one of the goals of UN General Assembly. (In 2000, it had set Millennium development goals). Tamil Nadu Human Development Report (2003) also states that as long as women are excluded from the development process, development will remain weak and lopsided.

Power of Autonomy Over Resources

Obviously empowerment is about power and about changing the balance of power. Power itself can be simply described as control over resources and ideology. The shift from addressing women's specific (Practical and strategic) needs through policy intervention in planned development (either WID or WAD) to gender and development (GAD) recognises the need for transforming power relations embedded in institutional structures to make possible a process of transformation and the realisation of equality empowerment.

"The empowerment process encompasses several mutually reinforcing components, but begins with, and is supported by, economic independence". Access to and control over productive resources are a necessary pre-requisite to greater awareness, of one self, of the facilities that society makes available to its members. Access to knowledge or issues like education, health, legal rights, and technological innovations are just some of the factors that help in developing the potential of an individual, thereby creating a level of confidence and self-image that further generates a desire to achieve greater control and participation in the decision making process.

When gender determines the access to resources and power to individuals, empowerment begins when the individual recognises and opposes the forces that deny such access. Power accrues to those who gain control over the distribution of resources. This control in turn confers the power of decision-making. In India women in general, poor rural women in particular, are relatively powerless with no control over resources and little decision making power. Often the decision is imposed on them. The prevailing ideology, which demands values of submission sacrifice and silent suffering often,

Fig. 1. Conceptual Framework

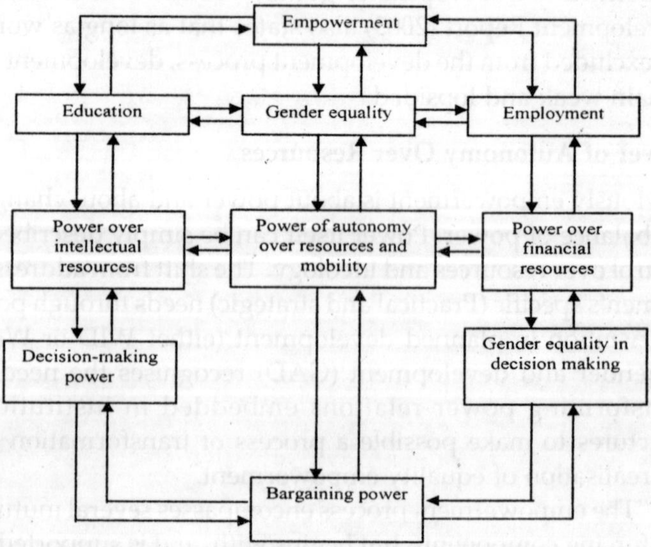

undermines their capacity and deprives them of their share of resources.

Women introduced the concept of 'empowerment' from the south at the International Women's Conference at Nairobi in 1985 as a counter project to the integration concept for advancing women. It aims at redistribution of social power and control of resources in favour of women based on development strategy. In India empowerment of women is one of the objectives of Ninth Five Year Plan and has become an integral part of the development strategy.

In short, empowerment includes access not only to education and resources, but also to basic needs and services, freedom and ability to make decisions about their own life options.

Women's Issues - A Global Scenario

Women and development as a subject entered the international scene around 1970 and from then on the "hidden" economic and social contribution of women began to be uncovered. The declaration of the "International Women's Year" by the United Nations General Assembly in 1975 could be considered a turning point regarding the place, role and position of women in a society

To recognize the role of women in economic development and to enhance the status of women all over the world, four International Conferences on women have so far taken place in addition to numerous sessions on women and development in various International conferences. The first conference took root in Mexico in 1975, the second one was held in Copenhagen in 1980, the third one took place in Nairobi in 1985 and the fourth one occurred in September 1995 in Beijing. Besides, in the World summit that took place in Copenhagen during 6th to 12th March 1995 on "poverty and unemployment," the role of women for the economic development of any country had been duly highlighted.

In the Fourth World Women's Conference (Beijing, 1995), it was realised that "women's literacy was essential for making women able for taking decisions in society for health and education of the families." It further appealed for eliminating discrimination between men and women in the field of education as well as for making 'basic education' available for all women essentially till the end of this century.

Women's Issues – A National Scenario

In the wake of the declaration of the International Year of Women 1975 and the Women's Decade (1976-1985), Women's Status and Development, for the first time, had begun to occupy a high place on the political agenda of the country. The Indian Parliament passed a unanimous resolution "to initiate a comprehensive programme of legislative and administrative measures aimed at removing, as far as possible, the economic and social injustices, disabilities and discriminations to which Indian women continue to be subjected". In 1976 the first move towards the formation of a National Machinery for Women's Development was made; a Women's Welfare and Development Bureau was set up in the Ministry of Social Welfare to act as a nodal point in the Government of India for women's development. The next decade saw the coming into existence of Cells for Women's Development in the Ministries of Labour and Rural Development. A National Committee of Women was set up during the beginning of this period, which was short lived. In 1985, a new Department of Women and Child Development was formed, out of the erstwhile Ministry of Social Welfare and placed, significantly, under the Ministry of Human Resources Development. In 1988, a National Perspective Plan for Women, for the period up to 2000 A.D., was drawn up.

Status of Rural Women

Gender inequality has been predominantly seen in rural areas as compared to urban areas. Village people believe that it is sons, not daughters, who inherit their family name and wealth, sons not daughters, who will care for them when they are old; thereby they invest less in women and more in men.

In rural and poor families, daughters-in-law are the main workers of the household, they cook, clean, and care for children and for old people. Public space and work outside the home are secondary; even employed women turn over the earnings to their husbands. Girls are socialised to be mothers, wives and workers under other's authority. Women are always depicted as weaker than men, which in turn justifies 'protectiveness' and reluctance to let women go out of the house (Gail Omvedt 2005).

In rural areas, a woman has little autonomy from her family and husband. Within poor households, women are the poorest of the poor. They have less access to money in the family than their husbands. Other access factors have clear and obvious gender dimensions. In literacy and education, girls and women lag behind men in every developing country. Social and cultural norms work against women in accessing the limited facilities that are available, and women globally suffer from an overload of demands on their tune for more than men. Lack of contextual information use skills also has a gender dimension, since women's location gives them fewer opportunities to broaden their range of comprehension.

Gender equality is seen as only a goal, a social desirability to which many people think they should be seen to agree, surely, that is a step forward in non-discrimination. But rural women still lack a critical mass of people who are willing to launch public action for women's equality of access to livelihood opportunities (equality in employment/ self employment and control of property and assets) and equality of reward or pay in work.

Women at Home

Home or household is the base on which the economy revolves. And no doubt the home has its positive or beneficial influence on economic habits, and the impact in the reverse direction is also immense. The bondage between home and women is more intense than that between men and home and this relationship is fundamental to any analysis of women's role in the economic field.

Despite this existence of intra-household disparities in health and educational status, decision-making power, in access to resources, discriminatory practices in feeding and health care, etc. have been increasingly pinpointed in research.

Assessing Women's Status

Wieringa (1999) describes a measure called the Gender Equality Index that is in the process of being developed by researchers at and around the Institute of Social Studies at The Hague. The measure aims to provide a measure of the status of women based on the power differences between men and women in any society. It consists of eight dimensions, each of which is to have indicators that are culturally relevant. The dimensions are gender identity (reflective of gender ideology such as rigidity of sexual division of labour and tolerance of transgender practices), autonomy of the body (as reflected in incidence of gender based violence, and control over sexuality and reproduction), autonomy within the family and household (as reflected in freedom to marry and divorce, decision-making power within the household), political power (in terms of decision making in municipalities, unions, government, and proportion of women in managerial positions), access to social resources (such as health and education), access to material resources (such as lands, houses, credit), employment and income dimension (in terms of gendered wage differentials, relative distribution of paid and unpaid labour), and time use (particularly relative access to sleep and to leisure).

In assessing the status of rural women in Karnataka, Batliwala *et al.* (1998) use a conceptual framework that focuses on women's access to and control over, resources that confer power at individual, household and societal levels. Seven broad parameters are studied: women's control over their labour and income, women's access to public resources, women's control over private assets and resources, women's control over their bodies, women's control over their physical mobility, women's access to and control over political spaces, and women's access to right and legal redress. Gender identity is not directly assessed, but is reflected in some behavioural practices as well as through studying some attitudes.

The Need for Empowerment

Women must be empowered to participate in the design and implementation of key decisions that shape their lives (HDR, UNDP, Oxford University Press, Delhi, 1995). Gender and gender relations in society define women's position and degree of empowerment. In discussions of women's empowerment, emphasis is often placed on women's decision-making roles, their economic self-reliance, and their legal rights to equal treatment, inheritance and protection against all forms of discrimination.

MEANS OF EMPOWERMENT

Education and employment are the two sides of a coin, which empower rural women. Education paves the way for GEDM and PARM relates to employment. Formal employment may have more PARM than informal employment. Women who are in informal employment in rural areas could not attain GEDM and PARM as compared to urban areas. Feminisation of poverty is the special feature of rural areas. Rural Women are employed not to kill their leisure time but to earn their livelihood.

Education, and gainful employment are all potential sources of women's empowerment. Not only are all of these sources of modernising influences, but each can also be a channel for information and a catalyst for behaviours associated with increasing women's access and control over resources.

Education has the potential of empowering women in several different ways: by equipping them with the awareness and knowledge required to make beneficial life choices, by increasing their ability to access resources and services, by enabling them to become informed consumers and citizens, by inculcating a feeling of self-worth, and by increasing their ability to challenge and make accountable those who hold power and authority, among other things. Education is also likely to enhance women's economic independence by equipping them with skills necessary to avail of paid employment opportunities, thereby also making their economic contributions more visible. At the national level, educating women results in improved productivity, income and economic development as well as a better quality of life, notably a healthier and better-nourished population (World Bank 2001).

Investing in women's education expands their choice in labour market and other income-generating activities and increases the rate of return on a household's most valuable asset–its labour. In the last few years, there has been a significant increase in the percentage of women participating in economic activities, although this involvement is still limited in many developing countries. The significance of receiving adequate compensation is to be viewed in terms of the economic independence it gives to women. It becomes a route for an improved power base and greater resourcefulness. Once established, the status of women rises leading to greater say in decision- making.

Fig. 2. Education, Employment and Empowerment and its indicators GEDM and PARM

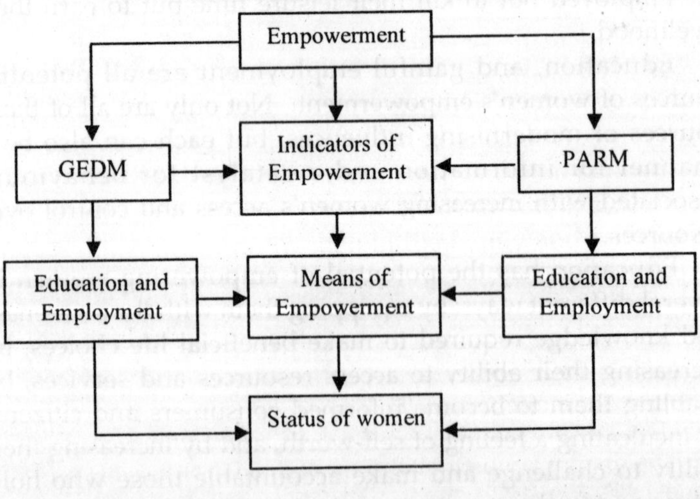

Thus, the entire effort of empowering women is to help them to exercise their rights in decision-making at all levels and in every sphere, both within and outside homes as equal partners along with men, spell out a major strategy for the empowerment of women.

The interrelationships among education, employment and empowerment conceptualized from the angle of the present study is depicted in Fig 2.

With both wage labour and own-account production, women have greater prestige in the family and also have a greater control over how their income is spent, which is what Amartya Sen's theory of household bargaining as cooperative conflict would predict. Women are able to direct more of the household income towards their own and their children's well being and even control or reduce wasteful consumption.

RATIONALE OF THE STUDY

Tamil Nadu is relatively a middle-income state (fifth among major states) and it has the credit of impressive attainments in human development indicators. Further its gender sensitive policies are also quite commendable. In short, Tamil Nadu may be considered as a model of a middle-income state that has tried to enhance the needs of the poor, vulnerable and marginal population of the state.

The family in most parts of contemporary Tamil Nadu is largely patrilineal, that is lineage and inheritance is from father to son, and patrilocal, that is women are brought as brides into the family of the male. The head of the family is normally a man unless by death, divorce *(de-jure)*, sickness or migration when a woman assumes headship. In the past, most women in Tamil Nadu married a close kin within close distance from their natal family, and this practice is still common but slowly declining. As a result of this practice, women in Tamil Nadu have greater access to support from the natal family, and a greater say in decision-making as compared to women born elsewhere, for example northwest India (Dyson and Moore 1983).

But these observations are not in conformity with certain other objective data on the relative position of women in Tamil Nadu as compared to that of other states. For example half of the Districts in Tamil Nadu have low female literacy, and Rural

Female Literacy is low as compared to Urban Female Literacy. Education is a stepping-stone for employment and empowerment. Since low RFL literacy affects the empowerment status of women, the present researcher intends to pursue still further, accommodating all factors in play in determining women empowerment.

The present study takes up to analyse empowerment status of women. A few studies have analysed education and empowerment and a set of another few studies have examined employment and empowerment. Very few studies are on education, employment and empowerment. Little attempt has so far been made to explore empowerment with GEDM and PARM at various leaves of education and employment status. To fill this gap the researcher has made an attempt to study Education, Employment and Empowerment of Rural women in Tamil Nadu.

PLAN OF THE STUDY

The first chapter deals with gender issues at national and international level, significance of women empowerment, indicators of women empowerment and means of empowerment. The second chapter presents the setting of the study and the area profile. The third chapter focuses on review of related literature based on theoretical studies and empirical studies. The fourth chapter gives the research design of the study. The fifth chapter describes the socio-economic characteristics of the respondents and their perceptions on education, employment and empowerment. The next three are analytical studies on GEDM, PARM and empowerment (VI, VII, VIII). The last chapter summarises the findings of the study and presents policy implications, besides indicating the scope for further research.

2

THE SETTING

This study has chosen Tamil Nadu as the empirical setting in which the question of women empowerment is subject to a close analysis. In particular two districts, Salem and Dharmapuri, constitute the study area. This chapter presents the economic, social and demographic features of the state and districts. This profile will enable the scholar to appreciate the micro factors at work behind the phenomenon of empowerment in latter chapters in due recognition of the broad empirical setting.

Tamil Nadu State is situated at the South Eastern extremity of the Indian Peninsula bounded on the north by Karnataka, and Andhra Pradesh, on the east by Bay of Bengal, on the south by the Indian Ocean and on the west by Kerala State. The State can be divided broadly into two natural divisions: (a) the coastal plains of South India and (b) the hilly western area.

The state is divided into 30 administrative districts and 385 community development blocks. The urban part of the state comprises 6 Corporations, 104 Municipalities and Cantonments, 611 Town Panchayats, 111 Census towns. The rural part comprises 385 Panchayat unions and 12,618 village Panchayats with a population of 1000 to 2000 and 10% of the village Panchayats have population below thousand.

The provisional population of India is 1,027,015,247 comprising 531,277,078 males and 495,738,169 females. The population of Tamil Nadu stood at 62,110,839 comprising

31,268,654 males and 30,842,185 females. The population of Tamil Nadu constitutes 6.05% of the Indian Population. It ranks 6th among the states/union territories. The density of population per sq. km is 478 in 2001 as against 429 in 1991.

STATUS OF HUMAN DEVELOPMENT IN TAMIL NADU

Tamil Nadu's human development achievements have been largely due to its educational heritage. The literacy rate has been increasing progressively, and the government has invested forcefully in the rural education infrastructure. This has resulted in a growth in years of schooling to 6.4 years which is much higher than the national average of 5.5 years making Tamil Nadu a close third to Kerala (8.1) and Maharashtra (7.1). Tamil Nadu is also the first state in the country to make computer education available at the secondary and high school level.

Tamil Nadu's HDI (2001) was 0.657 as compared to 0.571 for India. It is also well placed in the South Asian context and fares better than some of the neighboring countries of India. According to the Planning Commission, Tamil Nadu ranks third among the 15 major States of India, though of few specific indicators it lags behind some States. Within Tamil Nadu there are gaps and variations in the inter-district HDI, but its level of achievements suggests that high standards of literacy and health can be reached despite low per capita income. Even so, improvement of income levels would ensure improved literacy and health status. GDI is important for comparing the stages of gender development and assessing the extent of gender equality. In this area, Tamil Nadu's achievement is better than the attainment of the country as a whole, while within the state there is a symbiotic correlation between human development and gender development indices. This reinforces the view that human development is not an end in itself; rather it is necessary to create an overall improvement in the condition of the people.

LITERACY IN TAMIL NADU

Tamil Nadu has a rich heritage in education. Though the early Christian missionaries used English as the medium of instruction, the national movement spurred education in the vernacular from 1910 onwards. Leaders like G.K.Gokhle championed educational development in the villages. By 1920 local bodies were given the power to raise funds for education making it possible to introduce compulsory primary education in selected areas. By 1941, Tamil Nadu's literacy rate was almost comparable to the all-India position, and by 2001 Tamil Nadu reached the third position among the major States of India.

While the overall literacy rate had gone up from 62.7 per cent in 1991 to 73.47 in 2001, male literacy level grew even more from 73.75 per cent to 82.33 per cent in the same period. Equally encouraging was the growth in the literacy rate for females, which went up from 51.33 per cent in 1991 to 64.55 percent in 2001. The ratio of male literacy to female literacy also came down from 1.4 in 1991 to 1.27 in 2001, indicating a narrowing of the gender inequality ratio in the State. Despite this, wide disparity exists in the districts where gender and social groupings appear to make a difference. This gender discrimination, evident in almost all districts, and the low level of rural literacy rates need careful analysis and appropriate strategies.

The availability of schools in Tamil Nadu is more than required criteria of every 300 people having a primary school within a distance of 1 km. In fact, the declining birth rate makes it necessary to undertake a national average of 40, but variations across the districts need to be narrowed. For example, in the Nilgiris the pupil-teacher ratio is 30 while in Villupuram it is as high as 57. This imbalance requires greater teacher management skills, together with devising appropriate transfer policies, especially in the remote areas. Incentives have to be designed to reward teachers who perform well, and headmasters need to play a more positive role in teaching as well as in administration.

Goals on Education by Tenth Five-Year Plan

1. Universalisation of primary education by the year 2005, with special efforts for girls and disadvantaged groups.

2. 100 per cent retention of all enrolled children till age 14 by 2007
3. 100 per cent access to a school within a km. by 2007.
4. Raising of literacy rate from 73.5 per cent in 2001 to 80 percent in 2007.

Literacy rate in Tamil Nadu state as per 2001 census is 73.47% as against 62.66% in 1991 census. This shows the good growth rate in literacy. This growth rate is in tune with all India growth rates and literacy population is 65.38% in 2001 census as against 52.1% in 1991 census.

EMPLOYMENT IN TAMIL NADU

The working population of Tamil Nadu, 24.2 million in 1991, had increased to 27.8 million in 2001. However, statistics reveal that the proportion of workers to the population had actually declined during the 40-year period of 1961-2001 from 41.7 per cent to 44.8 per cent, though there was an upward trend between 1981 and 2001, from 41.7 per cent to 44.8 per cent. What is disturbing is that the number of marginal workers increased from 1.4 million in 1991 to 4.1 million in 2001. This implies that the increase in the worker participation rate (WPR) was the result of an increasing number of marginal workers rather than main workers. The higher rate of worker participation in the rural areas, as compared to the urban areas, has been a disquieting trend, though the urban WPR accelerated at a faster rate when compared to the rural WPR during the period 1981-2001. A positive feature was that female WPRs, in both rural and urban areas, increased at a faster rate than male WPRs with the result that total female workers increased from 31.4 per cent in 1981 to 34.7 per cent in 1991.

Goals on Employment by the Tenth Five-Year Plan

To bring down unemployment rate as measured by current daily status from 12.05 percent in 1999-2000 to 6 per cent by 2007 and to near zero by 2012.

Employment – Sector wise

In sectoral terms, the primary sector is the major provider of employment. Though the proportion of main workers in this sector decreased from more than 60 per cent in 1961 to about 50 per cent in 1999-2000, it is still the largest contributor to employment. In 1999-2000 the secondary sector accounted for 23.6 per cent of employment. This scenario could change in future when the secondary and tertiary sectors, in both rural and urban areas, account for larger employment growth as the rate of growth of the primary sector decreases. A gender-wise analysis illustrates a similar pattern, where male and female primary sector employees were steadily declining and increasing in the secondary and tertiary sectors. There had been a significant increase in the share of tertiary sector employment for females from 13.7 per cent in 1993-4 to 16.5 per cent in 1999-2000.

Agriculture continues to be the primary source of bulk employment, though this is not reflected in the income generated from the sector. Agricultural income declined over the period 1993-94 to 1999-2000 from percent to 18.16 per cent, whereas the share of income from the secondary and tertiary sectors improved in the same period. In per capita terms, this means that the average output per worker in the primary sector increased only marginally compared to the other sectors. This has wider implications of distribution of income and consumption. Since employment in the secondary and tertiary sectors is concentrated in the urban areas, high differentials in per worker output could create an acute rural-urban divide in the state. Remedial measures in the agricultural sector are, therefore, necessary in both physical and monetary terms. Diversification of agriculture capital would greatly mitigate the problem. Another feature of this sector is casual labour, which also increased from 32.9 per cent in 42.7 per cent in 1993-94. A host of factors was responsible for this increase though the transformation of the agrarian sector appears to have reduced the demand for casual employment. This resulted in inter-sectoral mobility of labour and a high level of income instability. Employment in the organized sector accounted for 8.7 per cent of the total workforce in the state in 1999-2000.

GENDER ISSUES IN TAMIL NADU

The performance of Tamil Nadu with respect to female literacy, female IMR, female life expectancy and fertility shows that the status of women in Tamil Nadu is higher than in other states, barring Kerala. However, while women have made improvement in absolute levels of literacy, enrolment and life expectancy, their position *vis-a-vis* men have remained unchanged or even worsened in many ways. This implies general lack of concern for gender issues in society.

In most parts of Tamil Nadu, society is patrilineal where inheritance goes from father to son. Women rarely head households and their historical role has been that of a domestic and reproductive member of a family. The secondary position of women in Tamil Nadu is reflected starkly in the extent to which they have control over their labour and wages. The workforce of the state finds that more women engaged in agriculture than in manufacturing or services. The value placed on women's work is less than that of men, and even in the service sector domestic work, nursing, teaching or secretarial jobs are set aside for them while the high-end tasks are performed by men. The same is true in the manufacturing sector where women work as beedi workers, as manual labour for cotton textiles, fish, food processing and the match industry. They do intermittent jobs at extremely low wages, for long hours under unsatisfactory working conditions. They face sexual harassment and intimidation. In rural areas, women laborers are harassed more than men and few have leadership positions in unions.

Girl child labour is significant part of the rural work force. The 1991 census revealed the presence of over 606,000 child laborers in the main and marginal worker categories, with a large majority being girls. In the rural areas, 10 per cent of girls in the age group 5-14 years were workers as against 4 per cent of male children. In the urban areas, the situation was better with 2.4 per cent of boys. Often it was seen that the dropouts' at school were child workers at home and about 50 per cent of girls in the age group 10-14 years belonged to this group.

It is evident that if women were to play a bigger role in decision-making process, especially in elected offices, it would make an impressive advance to their position in society. In Tamil Nadu, though differences in vote participation among men and women have not been considerable, gender difference is sharp in achieving positions of power through elections. The percentage of female members of parliament has been consistently below 8 per cent (The all-India position was higher in 1984 at 9.09 per cent, but it came down to 2.5 per cent in 1996). These statistics reveal a distinct gender bias and reflect a relatively lower position of women in society.

Growth in Women Population

Female population mirrors the great disguised potential of the country. It may be noted that even though the annual growth of female population also fell in tune with the trend in male population, the growth of females obtained at a level higher than that of males. The size of female population, which was 204 lakhs in 1971, increased to 308 lakhs in 2001.

Sex Ratio

Sex ratio is defined as the number of female population to 1000 male population. The sex ratio in Tamil Nadu, which has been declining over the decades, saw some significant improvement in 2001. The 1991 census reveals that in as many as 25 out of 30 districts, an adverse sex ratio was observed.

It is clear that in as many as 15 out of 30 districts the sex ratio was above 1000 in 2001. The sex ratio had turned in favour of females in Nilgiris, Karur, Tirichirapalli, Perambalur, Ariyalur, Nagapattinam, Thanjavur, Virudhu Nagar and Kanniyakumari in 2001 as compared to the adverse sex ratios over the last three decades. There is an improvement in the sex ratio in some of the districts prone to female infanticide. Salem's sex ratio had improved from 925 to 929, Dindigul 976 to 986, Madurai 964 to 978, Theni 964 to 979. However,

Dharmapuri defies any positive change. It sex ratio (938) has been deteriorating since 1951(979).

Female Work Participation Rate

The degree of empowerment of women can be seen through the parameter, "Work Participation Rate". It is gratifying to note that the work participation rate for the female had increased from 33.55 per cent in 1981 to 38.50 per cent in 1991 against 59.24 per cent and 58.28 per cent for male during the above period in rural areas. In urban areas it rose from 11.97 per cent to 13.10 per cent for female and from 51.25 per cent to 52.78 per cent for male in urban areas.

As per census 2001, the estimated number of female workers is 96.6 lakhs as against 82.4 lakhs in 1991 and 63.4 Lakhs in 1981. However, as per NSS estimates, the estimated number of female workers in 1999-2000 was 107.25 lakhs. The female work participation rate, which had increased from 37.9 per cent in 1987-88 to 39.3 percent in 1993-94, indicates a decline during 1999-2000 (35.2%) The number of female workers in the subsidiary status had comedown from 16.49 Lakhs in 1993-94 to 7.62 Lakhs in 1999-2000. It may be mentioned that in Tamil Nadu, like in rest of the countries, females dominate the subsidiary status work counting for about 85 per cent.

While the female workers in the subsidiary status urban areas came down from 2.84 lakhs in 1993-94 to 1.99 lakhs in 1999-00, by 30 per cent, in rural areas it had declined at a steeper rate (58.7%) from 13.64 Lakhs to 5.63 lakhs.

Tamil Nadu Corporation for Development of Women Ltd.

The Tamil Nadu Corporation for Development of Women limited, 1983, aims at empowering and uplifting the poor women above the poverty time. The Corporation's main objectives are to focus on empowerment of women, encourage entrepreneurship among women, identify trade and industries suitable for women, undertake marketing activities for products manufactured by women and encourage women to form Self-Helf Groups through giving training and extending credit facilities. The Mahalir Thittam started in 1997-98 is directed towards empowerment of women and capacity building of poor woman in rural areas through self-help Groups. As of March 2001 about, 68268 groups were formed under this programme enrolling 11.84 lakh women. The total savings came to Rs.7391 Lakhs.

Social Security Schemes

The Government has been implementing a number of social security schemes including Marriage Assistance Scheme, Widow Marriage Scheme, Old age pension, Accident Relief Scheme and Distress Relief Scheme to tide over the financial contingencies.

Women Participation in Social and Political Spheres

The system of universal franchise has been in vogue in India. It gives much leverage to the women in participating in political process and body politic. The 73rd and 74th constitutional amendments have provided ample scope for women in participating in developmental activities undertaken by the Local Bodies. These provisions have really empowered the women by way of taking decisions, operating and keeping accounts, conducting meeting including Gram Sabha, planning for development at village level and interacting with people. It is worth noting that the Reservation Policy allocating 30 per cent of the seats for women to legislature and Parliament would give a much-needed shot in the arm for the women.

SALIENT FEATURES OF THE STUDY AREA

Two districts in Tamil Nadu namely, Salem and Tiruvarur, have been selected for this study. Salem is the district, which has RFL below the state average, and Tiruvarur is the district, which has RFL above the state average. Similarly, Salem has high FWPR than the state average and Tiruvarur has low FWPR than the state average.

Salient Features of Tiruvarur

The District is situated between 10 20′ and 11 07′ of the Northern Latitude. The District is bounded on the East and

North by Nagapattinam District and on the South by Palk Strait and on the west by Thanjavur District. The District is predominantly in Agriculture. Out of the total Geographical area of 2097.09 sq.km. the net area under crop is 123853 hectares. Cauvery is the chief river of the district.

According to the 2001 census, the population is 1169474 of which 580784 are males and 588690 are females. The 2001 population census reveals that 76.6% of total population is literates. In the field of education, there are 7 arts and science colleges, two engineering colleges and 1056 schools for General Education. Though industrially backward, Tiruvarur District having fertile land area is a part of the rice bowl of Tamilnadu. It occupies fifth rank among the districts RFL of Tamil Nadu.

In this district (Thiruvarur) two blocks such as Valangaiman and Tiruvarur blocks have been selected according to rural female literacy rate. In Tiruvarur block RFL is high and FWPR is low (it is also the head quarter of the district). In Valangaiman rural female literacy is low and FWPR is high.

Salient Features of Salem

Salem is one of the biggest districts of Tamil Nadu. This district is surrounded by Dharmapuri district at its north. Erode and Namakkal districts in the south, Villupuram district in the east and Western Ghats in the west. The district headquarters is centrally situated in the district. This district is surrounded by numerous hills. Shervaroy Hills and Kalrayan hills are bigger in size and they adorn the district's with natural beauty and forest wealth. Salem district geographical area is 5205 sq. kms.

While Salem district occupies the 9th rank among the districts in Tamil Nadu in regard to size, the population of Salem district occupies 4th rank among districts in Tamil Nadu. As per 2001 census 53.90% persons are in rural areas and the remaining 46.10% persons are in urban areas. Scheduled Caste and Scheduled Tribe in the district constitute 15.8% and 3.5% respectively. The density of population as per 2001 census is 580 persons per sq.kms. Female infanticide exists in higher rate in this district (1223 per year), which shows the low status of women. It occupies twentieth rank in RFL of Tamil Nadu.

The number of education institutions is high as compared to Thiruvarur district. There are twenty-seven Arts and Science Colleges, 9 Engineering Colleges and 2012 Schools for general Education.

In Salem district, two blocks namely Edapadi and Vazhapadi have been selected for the study. Rural Female Literacy rate is low and FWPR is high in Edapadi and RFL is high and FWPR is low in Vazhapadi. Two districts exhibit contradictory parameters such as sex ratio, RFL, RFWP, etc. (Table 1). Moreover, Salem is an industrially advanced district and it has high per capita income (above Rs.15,000 whereas Tiruvarur is an industrially backward district with low per capita income (below Rs.10,000). The study has been undertaken to assess empowerment status of women at different levels of education and employment status.

Table 1
Socio-Economic Indicators of Tamil Nadu

Districts	*Tamil Nadu Literacy Rate*	*Tamil Nadu Rural Literacy Rate*	*Tamil Nadu Rural Female Literacy Rate*	*Tamil Nadu Sex Ratio*	*Tamil Nadu Sex Ratio Rural literacy*	*Gender Development Index*	*Human Development Index*	*Female Work Participation Rate*
Thiruvallur	76.5	68.36	57.96	970	733	0.651	0.654	17.81
Chennai	80.1	k	k	951	k	0.766	0.757	19.30
Kancheepuram	77.6	67.74	58.69	961	754	0.71	0.712	21.74
Vellore	73.1	68.12	57.26	997	726	0.655	0.658	23.61
Dharmapuri	59.2	55.42	44.79	938	647	0.582	0.584	25.69
Tiruvannamalai	68.2	65.47	52.8	996	676	0.608	0.612	23.90
Villupuram	64.7	61.83	49.72	983	663	0.582	0.587	22.83
Salem	65.7	58.1	46.11	929	611	0.625	0.626	26.76
Namakkal	67.7	63.31	51.63	967	671	0.631	0.636	34.94
Erode	65.5	58.3	46.7	971	650	0.656	0.658	33.45
The Nilgiris	81.4	76.89	67.18	1015	796	0.686	0.685	35.22
Coimbatore	77.0	65.1	56.16	959	741	0.697	0.699	25.41
Dindigul	69.8	64.83	52.85	986	685	0.638	0.641	28.96
Karur	68.7	63.07	50.27	1000	671	0.641	0.647	31.40
Tiruchirapalli	79.2	70.57	59.27	1000	730	0.671	0.671	22.03
Perambalur	65.9	63.76	51.41	1007	681	0.592	0.596	35.01
Ariyalur	64.9	63.08	49.63	1007	656	0.629	0.63	24.81

Contd.

Districts	Tamil Nadu Literacy Rate	Tamil Nadu Rural Literacy Rate	Tamil Nadu Rural Female Literacy Rate	Tamil Nadu Sex Ratio	Tamil Nadu Sex Ratio Rural literacy	Gender Development Index	Human Development Index	Female Work Participation Rate
Cuddalore	71.9	66.26	53.36	985	669	0.643	0.654	18.97
Nagapattinum	76.9	74.79	65.7	1014	791	0.652	0.654	19.10
Tiruvarur	76.9	74.69	65.47	1013	791	0.633	0.637	19.45
Tanjavore	76.1	71.34	61.13	1020	761	0.629	0.63	20.86
Pudukottai	72.0	68.98	57.04	1015	719	0.615	0.618	19.77
Sivaganga	72.7	67.4	55.34	1035	728	0.635	0.64	19.14
Madurai	78.7	68.24	56.05	978	692	0.661	0.661	20.70
Theni	72	66.59	54.26	979	676	0.628	0.628	32.39
Virudhu Nagar	74.2	69.31	57.54	1011	721	0.649	0.651	34.85
Ramanathapuram	73.1	69.16	58.65	1033	768	0.626	0.629	18.28
Thoothukkudi	82	78.13	70.66	1049	886	0.703	0.703	26.32
Tirunelveli	77	73.02	64.04	1042	821	0.656	0.658	36.81
Kanyakumari	88.1	86.72	84.11	1013	954	0.708	0.711	19.02
State	73.5	66.66	55.84	985	720	0.654	0.657	24.99

Source: Computed from the secondary data, Census of India, 2001.

Table 2
Socioj Economic Indicators of Selected Blocks of Tamil Nadu

	Salem District		*Tiruvarur District*	
Socio-Economic Indicators	*Edapadi Block*	*Vazhapadi Block*	*Tiruvarur Block*	*Valangaiman Block*
Density of Population per sq. km.	639	367	588	464
Total population	320,766	171,857	1,169,474	94,474
Number of Females per 1000 males	880	968	1010	1012
Percentage of Scheduled Castes to total Population	8.6	22	41.8	40
Percentage of scheduled Tribes to total Population	0.008	6.7	0.20	0.07
Rural population	127,464	136,800	932,231	83,193
Percentage of Workers to total workers	55.6	54	35.5	43.6
Percentage of Female workers to total workers	22	11	25.9	33.05
Percentage Literacy	35.0	52.7	64.9	61.5

Source: Census of India 2001.

3

REVIEW OF LITERATURE

This chapter is designed to review the past studies that are relevant to education, employment and empowerment of rural women. It is pertinent to mention that women empowerment has been emerging as an important issue for a long while. One may notice that the issues on women empowerment has captured the attention of policy makers, academicians, economists and researchers on gender issues. Many scholars have attempted to analyse women empowerment dealing with socio-economic factors, which are at play. It is also noticed that the availability of literature in the field is quite vast, especially on the aspects of women education, employment and empowerment. This chapter reviews those works under two broad divisions namely theoretical and empirical studies respectively. The review provides the necessary theoretical insights and empirical facts to help prosecute the present study.

THEORETICAL STUDIES

Before analysing the empirical relationship between women's education, employment and empowerment, a discussion of the relevant theories is useful. It is important to understand the different avenues through which gender equality in decision-making and power over resources and freedom of mobility might have an impact on empowerment. The inequalities concerning women are a very complex social phenomenon and therefore, on the basis of theoretical assumption, no aspect of it must be excluded from analysis (Jain 2006).

Women's subjugation seemed inextricably tied to their economic status. During the last few decades, there has been a tremendous concern on women's economic interests. Development literature and the role of international agencies, including the UN bodies, spurred by the women's movement, national and international, have identified some major issues: unequal treatment in the labour market, unequal access, control and ownership of productive resources like land, credit, technology, education, skills; inequitable work burdens; invisibility and under valuation of women's subsistence production in third world countries in data systems; the link between women's unpaid work and paid work, the inequitable distribution of consumption resources within the household; absence of a focus on women in national policies or if at all there is a focus, in a limited, narrow perspective and finally the relevance of all these not only to development issues such as fertility control, children's well being and productivity of the economy but most of all their contribution to women's autonomy, agency and freedom (Krishnaraj 2001).

Gender in Classical Economics

In the classical thought, women's wages and conditions of their employment first drew attention. Adam Smith devoting hardly a page to women in his scholarly time (Smith 1776) rationalized gender roles. While he recognized that women work for her wages, he argued that men's wages must be enough to raise a family and that the material conditions of families require the care of children by mothers and hence women's reproductive role is important for the good of society.

John Stuart Mill (1879) advocated egalitarian economic reforms, which would promote women's economic autonomy. Women's lower wages, he pointed out, were unrelated to productivity and were the result of custom and prejudice. He said that restrictions to women's employment arose from their economic dependence as wives and mothers, which imposed a double day and led to patriarchal power in the family. However he did not see the productive contribution of women's work at home but saw it as production of utilities. Mill, though by far the most progressive thinker of his time, in line with many others including some feminists with socialist ideas, did not perceive the contradictions in capitalism and liberalism which espoused individualism and free entry in the market along with prevalent sexual division of labour.

Alfred Marshall (1907) propounded the human capital theory. He contended that the productivity of workers would improve, if given education by the state, which would improve their wages. He linked infant mortality to women's employment; mothers must be given motherhood skills. Women's lower wages were because of custom. But Pigou (1952) addressed the issue of unequal wages from purely an economic angle. He said wages were unfair if they were below marginal productivity or if they were lower than their reward in similar labour elsewhere in the economy. He observed that women's wages in some place or occupation may be fair relative to women's wages elsewhere but may be unfair compared to men's wages in that occupation.

Gender in Marxian Economics

The Marxist school placed social structure as the determinant factor and the individual agent as conditioned by it, thus acknowledging interdependencies and the existence of a conflict of interests. Insofar as it makes a distinction between the ideological superstructure and the material base, it has the problem of explaining the relative autonomy of the superstructure; Feminists point out how in the Marxist theory of capitalism, while gender gets attention, it has limitations because it fails to theorize the problem of women's unpaid labour, sexual division of labour and the role of gender ideology which even in the event of women moving into paid labour under socialism do not disappear.

Discourse on power frequently includes reference to both Marxist and post-modern positions. In Marxism, power operating in the social formation is ultimately grounded in the economic power of the dominant class. In a post-modern analysis, power is no longer seen as a rectified possession, but as capillary, that is exercised in every moment of social life. In this construction, power is conceptualized as a generative, productive phenomenon, as well as repressive (Morley 1995).

The Marxist doctrine of women's socialized labour and the management of the 'double burden' was men and women found refuge as citizen in the home, the household and family became the locus of resistance to state power in the communist countries and was not perceived as a locus of gender conflict (Metcalfe and Afanassieva 2005)

Gender in Institutional Economics

Institutional economics admits the role of power and institutional processes explicitly but unlike the Marxist school, goes beyond class analysis and does not give primacy only to the 'public' sphere. For these reasons feminists have found the Institutional School more friendly to gender analysis. Feminist work falls in this genre (Waller and Jennings 1990).

Gender in Feminist Economics

Feminism and feminist theory developed rapidly after the 1960s. Here Marxist feminists began to note the inadequacy of Marxist theory to explain gender subordination even though

Fig. 1. Feminists Views on Gender

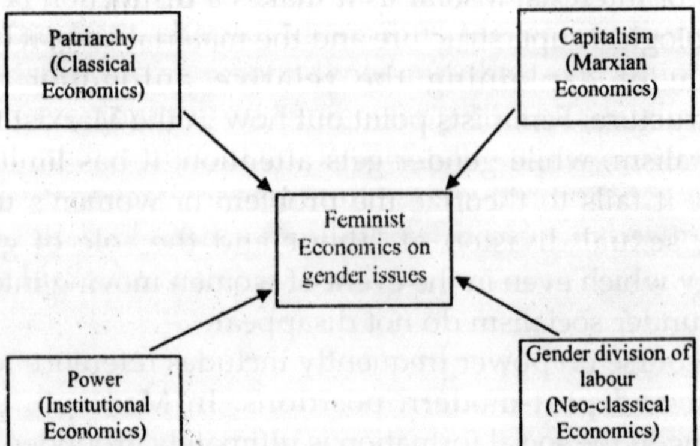

it was the first to pay attention to it. These feminists used categories and tools from the Marxist toolbox. These efforts for the first time shifted the focus to 'domestic labour' as the terrain, which was the site of women's exploitation. This direct focus on sexual division of labour and its impact was a pioneering step.

Feminist discussion on gender issues is centered on patriarchy, capitalism, power and gender division of labour which is depicted by a flow chart.

Gender in Household Economics

In the 1960s there came up the New Household Economics. The division of labour between men and women was explained in a model that imitated the market model. The best-known architect of this theory is the Nobel laureate, GaryBecker (1971). In a hypothetical two-person household, a man and a woman through exchange of market work and household production, maximise each person's own utility as well as total utility of the household. Assuming both can do both types of work, women's returns from the market were lower because they were less skilled. Their returns from domestic labour were more because they had the expertise. Likewise men were better at wage work and less equipped for domestic work. The best solution was therefore where men did more market work and women did more non-market work. The model had this merit that for the first time, it analysed the household as a productive unit where domestic labour was equated to home production of goods and services. Secondly, it did not take the household as a composite glued together unit. The trouble was that it did precisely what feminists were protesting against – the justification of status quo

Gender in Neo-Classical Feminist Economics

Collier (1991) locates four distinct processes, based on underlying 'social conventions', that account for why women face differential constraints upon economic activity. The first is discrimination outside the household-in labour and credit markets. The second is that role model (in production) is gender-specific, i.e., girls copy women, while boys copy men. If men initially take up a new economic opportunity, it may be diffused over the male population by a mechanism that will not transmit it to the female population. The third is that within the household, rights and obligations between husband and wife are asymmetric, such that women have little incentive to increase their labour input. The final element is the 'burden of reproduction,' with its attendant demands or women's health and time.

Palmer views that the social aspects of gender impose their own definitions of correct exchange, which tend to reflect bargaining power and status, and inevitably mean that the terms of trade are biased against women. This can be described as an asymmetry of obligations and responsibilities between women and men.

Gender asymmetries in rights and obligations in terms of 'social convention' the mode provide an extremely static picture. These asymmetries are not simply given by society, as the term 'social convention' seems to imply. They are in fact constantly created and re-created through the everyday relations between men and women; those with power against those without power actively mobilize them. Women's obligation to use their incomes savings to feed the family in some social settings is not just a social given. It is through conjugal conflicts underpinned by power asymmetries that the more powerful household member (adult men) are able to shift these responsibilities onto women while they maintain personal control over other income flows.

Gender in Feminist Critical Economics

Feminist economics seeks to move beyond a gender disaggregating of roles and activities to emphasize the power relations underpinning the gender division of labour (Folbre 1986; Kabeer 1994). Questions are asked about how social institutions and norms shape or constrain individual 'choices' in ways that perpetuate gender inequalities.

Feminist economics challenges the conceptualization of the gender division of labour in neo-classical micro economics, particularly 'new household economics', as the outcome of free choices of economic agents specializing according to their innate comparative advantage. From the neo-classical perspective, gender differentiation is depicted as generally rational, efficient, and mutually advantageous to men and women, with women undertaking unpaid domestic labour because of their preferences and skills. The neo-classical perspective does not attempt to explain how such skill differentiation comes about.

Discourse on Gender Versus Patriarchy

The first attempt to comprehend the unequal social situation of men and women concentrated on the concept of "patriarchy". Walby (1990) defines patriarchy as "a system of social structures and social practices in which men dominate, oppress and exploit women". This concept descriptively draws attention to ways men discriminate and exploit women. It helps illuminate the unfavorable position of women in relation to men, and it unquestionably also has explanatory power concerning several inequalities, for example in the family or communicative processes.

But patriarchy fails as a general explanatory principle. It does not take into account the multiple causes which influence women's situation. Explanation by patriarchy supposes intentional acts of suppression and the homogeneity of men. It makes the role women play in reproducing their unfavorable situation invisible. Patriarchy as a universal principle of explanation does not take into consideration the unintentional consequences of human actions or the routines of everyday life. On the other hand, it also does not differentiate between inequalities based on the explicit intention of discriminating against women and those gender-neutral inequalities where other groups can replace women with still lower access to life chances.

Because of these objections, feminist scientists tried to develop more inclusive and comprehensive approaches, which were similar in one respect; they attempted integrating gender into Marxist theory as a central category by combining the role of women and men in the productive and reproductive spheres and in the division of labour (Hartman 1981; Beer 1990). Because of this background, they concentrated on specific social phenomena, especially the mutually reinforcing disadvantages in work and the family. They took it for granted that there is one general explanation for all inequalities: a combination of men's domination over women and of capitalists over workers (e.g. patriarchy and class in "feminist dualist" theories).

The most important critique of these theories is that this concept of two mutually reinforcing discriminatory mechanisms cannot explain improvements in the situation for women in specific fields. These are areas, which, up to now, have had far-reaching consequences with their participation in social life. From a theoretical point of view, Wright's work (1995) is representative of the attempt to explain discrimination against women in the context of class theory. He distinguishes between a direct and a mediated class relation. The first refers to direct access to the production sphere via employment, while the second type of relation refers to the distribution of resources resulting from employment.

The mediated class relations are the ones which link class members who are not integrated into any employment with the production process via the institution of the family. In this way, gender is recognized as an autonomous influencing factor, which may modify access to life chances; however, extensive areas of gender-specific inequalities remain outside the scope of this theoretical framework. Such inequalities are, for example, hindered access to education; disadvantages regarding social interaction, control over reproductive behaviour and the power structure of this institution is determined by the dominance of men.

Work by Kreckel (1992) is a further step in the analysis of gender inequalities, integrating them both with class theory and the analysis of the political system. It proves that any kind of inequality is dependent on the power structure of society. Groups and also domains in life suffer disadvantages when they are at the periphery when it comes to allocation of power and access to dominant groups and institutions.

Fig. 2. Theoretical Views on Gender

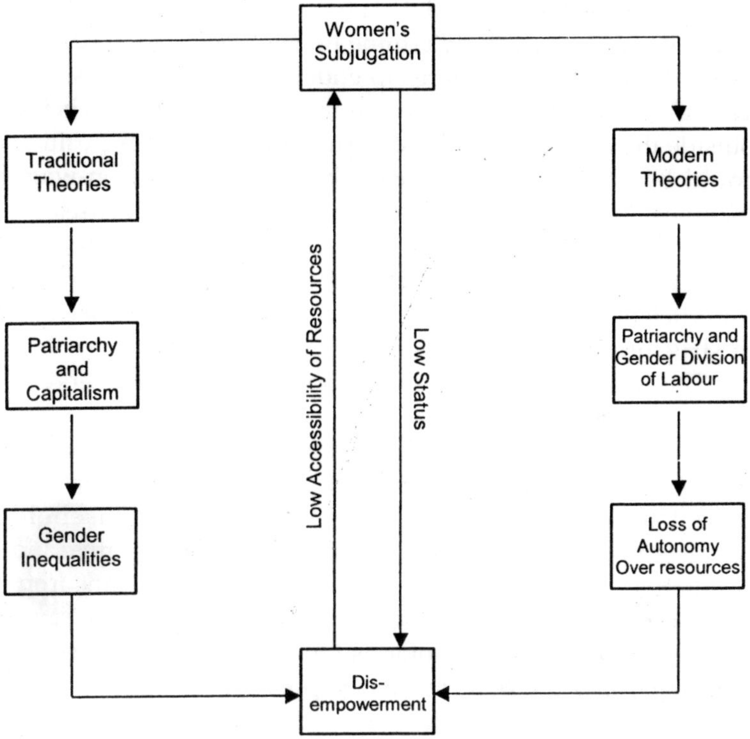

The dominance in the class structure is only one dimension (even if an important one) of the political center influencing the distribution of social goods. The contrast of periphery and center makes it possible to also take into consideration the women's movement that tries to influence unequal distributions. In this model, women are not passive victims of patriarchal power but actors in the political arena.

Bargaining Model

In the late 1980s, what is known as the game theoretic model was introduced to account for the fact that exchange between economic agents is a process of bargaining. 'Bargaining theory with Nash solution' caught the attention of feminist economists, because it facilitated the unpacking of what happens inside the household. The determinants of bargaining might be factors which determine the well being each partner could attain if their relationship ended–the fall back position. The fall back is the maximum attainable levels of well being outside the relationship. The determinants of fallback position could be women's skill level, other assets, and non-wage incomes. The advantage of the model is that it focuses on external, structural factors, which produce unequal opportunity. In a way it combines the neo-classical concern for efficiency with the Marxist concern for confliction aspects of structure.

The allocation of income and labour between members can be analysed through how they bargain and with what resources. Why women's bargaining power is limited can be demonstrated. Amartya Sen (1983, 1990) popularised this model to emphasize the dual nature of the household partnership. Household partnership is at once cooperative and conflicting. It is cooperative because each member gains from the common pool as if she or he was alone, but at the same time it can be confliction sofar as the interests of the partners vary regarding the shares from the pool.

Given the fact that gender has social meanings, there may not exist a perfect correlation between an individual's economic contribution to the household and his or her decision-making power. Social power of men implies that women's social resources outside the household are limited. Feminists also contest the notion of a common household pool as the standard model especially in the third world (Fapohunda 1988). There may be different streams of allocation: some to the common pool and some for the individual's expenditure. Each member may have greater or less rights to draw from the common pool. In many ways the model was an advance over the earlier home economics. The home economics model defines tastes and preferences in a joint household function. The bargaining model disaggregates tastes and preferences by household member and shows how the individual's influence over the expenditure of household income varies according to the bargaining power of the members.

Bargaining power of members in the household depends upon 'capabilities' and 'entitlements' of the members. In mainstream development discourse, notion of 'capabilities' and 'entitlements' propelled development of embrace human agency and freedom, beyond its essentially economic connotation. These articulated a precise agenda for women as in Drezee and Sen's (1991) capabilities theory, which centrally advanced women's right to education that would benefit them as individuals rather then merely fulfill larger social goals. This perspective demanded the construction of spaces, both intimate and public, within which notions of equality and inequality become pertinent, where individuals progress beyond passivity to evolve as socially useful and influential begins and enjoy 'real freedom' (Dreze and Sen 1991; Sen 1999) considering the complex situations within which gender inequities dwell. Nussbaum expands the theory comparative use to a 'threshold of capabilities' without which human functioning is impossible, capturing the essential purpose of social goals.

The model focuses on process internal to the household-accrual of income of different members, intra-household transfer, allocation of income to goods and services by each individual member. Thus, it is able to show different economic goals of members. It allows for both shared and competing preferences. It incorporates effects of constraints into the formation of economic goods of the household and variation in economic goods according to type of household.

Studies were carried out on differential allocation between men and women within households with respect to income, work burdens, nutrition, health, mortality, morbidity, fertility decisions and education (Krishnaji 1987; Sen 1995). Many doctoral research works on women's education and employment began to include the intra-household dimension. Bina Agarwal (1994, 1997) uses this model successfully to include the specific contours of social and cultural configurations in South Asia and has thus enriched this model to argue for land rights to women and for women's management of natural resources. From these studies, the advantages of bargaining model can be obviously understood. Hence, the research applies this model to study education, employment and empowerment and rural women in Tamil Nadu.

EMPIRICAL STUDIES

Empirical studies can be grouped under three heads:

(i) Studies on Gender Inequalities

(ii) Studies on Women's Educational Benefits.

(iii) Studies on Education, Employment and Empowerment

Gender Inequalities

Gender inequality exists in most parts of the world, from Japan to Morocco, from Uzbekistan to the Unites States of America. However, inequality between women and men can take very many different forms. Indeed gender inequality is not a homogenous phenomenon, but a collection of disparate and interlinked problems. Amartya Sen (2001) discusses seven dimensions of inequalities; mortality inequality, natality inequality, basic facility inequality, special opportunity inequality, professional inequality, ownership inequality, household inequality. Based on these dimensions gender inequality arises and affects empowerment of women.

Causes for Gender Inequality

The ideology of gender inequality is inculcated in both men and women from birth, before they can think for themselves, religion, mythology, social and cultural labour and superstitious behavioural training, seclusion, veiling, curtailment of physical mobility, distribution of work, dietary discrimination and rewards and punishment all are used to socialize girls to accept and participate in their own oppression (Batliwala 1993). Gender disparity could be seen in terms of histological advantages. Even in the womb, the male foetuses have a lower rate of miscarriage than their female counter parts, says Waldron (1983).

Yadav (2000) states that the quality and quantity of women's work is governed by a host of social, religious and traditional factors. It results in constraining women from taking up occupation and education and thereby gender discrimination has been raised. Becker (1981) views that gender division of labour is the root cause of gender discrimination.

Gender discrimination caused by cultural traditions reserves the best food for men or feeding men first or devoting more time to the care of boys than to girls when children fall side. Shortage of food in the household offers poorer nutritional status to the girls than to the boys. Although women usually bear primary responsibility for safeguarding family health and often find health care for others in the family, they may have difficulty in obtaining health care for themselves. Sometimes women need a male relative's permission to seek health care (World Bank Report 1992).

Patriarchy is the main reason for gender discrimination in the family. (Jyothi Rani 1991; Nandini Azad 1998). Furthermore, women themselves cause gender discrimination. Female infanticide, child marriage, dowry deaths and so on continue to be a part of the Indian women's life. These problems are due to women themselves.

Gender Quality and Gender Specific Polices

Human Resource Development Programme should include empowerment strategies such as educating girls and women, facilitating their involvement in economic activities through development of their entrepreneurial and income earning and access to credit, involving women in policy formulation and decision making, encouraging socio-cultural change by exploring gender issues and promoting the effective implementation of equal rights legislation. Cart (1997) is of the same view that an organization is needed to remove structural inequalities inherent in the gender system.

Many researches suggest that gender specific policies with emphasis on activities and resource beneficial to women may help in providing equal opportunities and reaping the benefits of development. These policies would enhance women to take decisions in their life and the socio economic status of women can be improved (Kawabatta 1995; Agarwal 2001; Venkata Subramaniam 2001; Shelly 2004).

Women's Educational Benefits

Education will address the historical, socio-economic and political factors, which have acted to define the poor in general, and poor women in particular. Education is a dynamic process of learning in which women gain access to meaningful information, engage in critical reflection and act as a collective to transform the material and social conditions of their existence in some way. Education literacy enables people to become more active participants. With education individuals and societies have more responsibilities and choices (Keller 1992).

Education and Decision Making Power

Education is strongly related to decision making on accessing own health care, ability to set aside money for own use and mobility (Sengupta and Johnson 2003; Singh 2004). Malhotra and Mather (1997) view that education is critical in determining women's decision-making impact on financial issues, but not on social and organizational matters. Education is related to increased decision making on economic issues in the household: very strongly in Malaysia, Thailand and Pakistan more moderately in Philippines and not at all in India Jejeebhoy (1996) observes that education is more closely related to decision-making, autonomy, mobility indicators in Tamil Nadu. The effect of education (primary and secondary) is positive on women's decision-making authority (Kritz and Makinwa – Ade busoye, 1999).

Education is immaterial in defining control over finances or household decision-making, but does increase women's freedom of movement (Bloom 2001). There is another view that education is positively related with women's decision making, control of resources, and autonomy except mobility with which it is negatively associated (Balk 1997). Many studies find a positive relationship between education and women's decision-making power (Kishor (1995) and Govindasamy and Malhotra (1996), Kritz and Makinwa – Adebusoye (1999)). Women with higher schooling are more likely to say that their opinion has weight in household decisions, and they are also more likely to think that women should have decision-making input on matters both within and outside the customary female domain. In India based on the National Family Health Survey-II (NFHS-II) reports a strong and consistent positive relationship between women's schooling and their input on health care decisions for themselves and their ability to set aside money for personal use (Sengupta and Johnson 2003).

In Indonesia, Asian Marriage Survey demonstrates a strong and positive effect of girl's education on their decision-making input in the selection of a spouse (Malhotra 1991). In contrast, Education does not lead to greater decision-making power in certain specific settings is well-demonstrated by the three studies in the State of Uttar Pradesh, India (Jeffery and Jeffery 1994; Jejeebhoy 1996; Hindin 2000). Agnihotri (1999) says that even without education women are liberal and enjoying the power of autonomy in decision-making. Niraula and Morgan (2000) have stated in another way that education has strong effects on women's freedom of movement but has no effect on their decision making capacity.

Education and Freedom of Movement

Jejeebhoy and Sathar (2001) opine that secondary schooling is associated with higher autonomy in Punjab, U.P. and T.N. Primary schooling is moderately associated with higher autonomy only in Tamil Nadu. There is another view that education is immaterial in defining control over finances or household decision-making, but does increase women's freedom of movement (Bloom 2001). Hollos (1998) is of the same view that less educated women who have more independence and autonomy than educated women.

Studies on Asia and the Middle East countries reported a positive relationship between, women's education and their freedom of movement. But, Balk (1997) finds a strong negative association between women's education and their mobility.

Studies by Kishor (1995) and Govindasamy and Malhotra (1996) in Egypt, Sengupta and Johnson (2003) in India, find support for a positive relationship between education and not just decision-making, but also mobility.

Other studies based on primary data, which found a null or conditional relationship on decision-making in specific settings, find that for mobility the relationship to education is more clearly positive. Bloom (2001) and Jejeebhoy (1996) report a positive impact of schooling on aspects of women's mobility. Similar findings are also reported by Niraula and Morgan (2000) for Nepal. Education does not increase women's autonomy on decisions regarding household purchases, wife working outside home, fertility and other household decisions (Hindin, 2000).

Education and Gender Equality

Greater prosperity, modernization and more widespread education for girls have reinforced patriarchal structures by defining an economically dependent role for women relative to their husbands. (Vlassoff 1994). The gender gap in education grew with girls having lower level skills and lesser access to higher paying jobs (Green Halgh 1985). The effect of women's education on gender relations is minimal because of the power of gender ideology and practice, lack of economic opportunities for women, and the largely irrelevant content and poor quality of education. (Vlassoff 1994).

Vlassoff (1994) argues that greater prosperity, modernisation and more wide-spread education for girls have actually reinforced patriarchal structures by defining an economically dependent role for women relative to their husbands. Moreover, it is only in theory that education is seen as a means of financial independence for girls; in practice, girls are educated to secure a husband, not to get a job.

Education and Natality Equality

Parents prefer boys to girls since boys provide more security than girls (Amartya Sen 1990). Recent research in India shows that higher levels of education have a significantly stronger effect as compared to primary education in lowering the entrenched preference for sons. Studies suggest that it is only at high levels of education that women are successful in rejecting gender-biased norms, or finding alternative opportunities, roles and support structures than those afforded by giving birth to sons (Bourne and Walker 1991; Basu 1992; Govindasamy and Ramesh 1996; Pande and Astone 2001).

A preference for sons reflects women's acceptance of gender role that ascribes a higher status to males than females. Son preference reinforces and is reinforced by women's economic and social dependence throughout their life cycle and implies not just recognition but also an acceptance of the higher status ascribed in the culture to mothers of sons.

Education and Time Allocation

For women participating in the labour force, education has a negligible effect on time allocation in domestic work. For women not participating in the labour force, education has a strong negative effect on time allocation in her domestic work, says Khandekar (1988). Higher female education reduces the amount of time spent in all non-market activities except teaching children, which is positively associated with education (Malathy, 1994; Newman 2001).

Education and Absence of Home Violence

Severe and ongoing domestic violence has been documented in almost every country in the past decade. On one hand it reflects gender asymmetries in power relations and on the other challenges to gender ideology. Violence towards women may be considered a sensitive index of their wellbeing and status.

Educated and uneducated women report different forms and precipitating factors for violence, and higher levels of education are associated with lower reported physical or psychological violence (Sen 1999; Visaria 1999; Duvvury and Allendorf 2001).

The extent to which women are willing to report violence may be influenced by education (Visaria, 1999; Koenig, 2003). Moreover, the direction of this bias is not certain. If violence is more stigmatized among the educated, then educated women may be more likely to under-report violence. On the other hand, educated women may be more willing or able than uneducated women to recognize and vocalize violence, perhaps because of greater exposure to the issue (Duvvury and Allendorf 2001).

Koenig (2003) found in Bangladesh that education remained strongly and negatively associated with domestic violence even when community level variables of education, autonomy and credit-group membership were included. In contrast, other studies in India and Bangladesh show that atleast some part of the protective effect attributed to education is due to women's participation in community level organization, whether they are credit-based groups (Schuler, Hashemi *et al.* 1994) or activist organizations involved in campaigning against violence (Sen 1999).

Some research in India (Rao 1997; Block and Rao 2000) and in Sierra Leone (Coker and Richter 1998) finds no evidence that education protects women from violence. Moreover, Bloch and Rao (2000) view that wife's education does not have a significant impact on whether the wife gets severely beaten. Thus, any negative or positive relationship of violence with women's education may at least partly reflect education related differences in reporting rather than in actual experiences of violence.

Education, Employment and Empowerment

Tapen (1998) opines that education provides information about health and nutrition, reproductive and sexual rights, family planning decision, gender quality, environmental awareness, religious objectives, political consciousness, economic opportunities, women's rights and legal provisions, production and consumption patterns, etc. which definitely empower women in a complete sense

Education is a fundamental right to women. The educational policies should link education to empowerment, says Ramachandran (2002), Berhman (2003). Dreze and Sen (1991) are of the view that education is likely to increase their role in household decision making which in turn increase the level of empowerment. Education is an investment, which enhances the skill and credentials of women by increasing their knowledge. Moreover, it increases the freedom of women to to choose their career, whatever they prefer (Barua 2002). Right education is one of the most important means of empowering women with knowledge, skill and self-confidence. (Neelima 2001; Agarwal 2001; Singh 2001).

Sundaram (2000) is of the view that education to rural women is highly essential to increase their earning activities. Learning by doing and earning is the apt way of empowering the rural women in India. Moreover employment with education augments financial position of women which in turn leads to economic independence. Thereby the productive and creative energies of women should be properly utilized and streamlined by education (Seth 2001).

Education is an investment in opening up employment opportunities – access to credit, land ownership and power to decision-making and thereby empowerment is achieved. Sharma (1991) says that education is the potent instrument of empowerment, which refers to capacity building. Education is the major determinant to make the women self-reliant and pursue their goals and achieve their success in diverse fields, which they like. Careful planning on the part of women education will result in enhancing the empowerment of women (Jayanthi 2001). Educated women are the forerunner in making awareness among the other women in the society, says Manonmoney (2000). Education equips women to assess their position and to participate in all socio-economic activities (Keller 1992).

Education and Employment

Women with education and employment make for themselves in society by the flowering of their personality while retaining their essential womanliness. Their mental orientation is more prepared than a typical household. In the event of working outside, the traditional division of labour has been rearranged to meet the situation. Nair and Siddagangamma(2000) are of the view that the low rate of employment of women is due to low level of female literacy. Agarwal (2001)states in another way that education and employment are the significant factors that influence women's empowerment.

Women's education increases labour market participation and provides better employment opportunities for women and hence raises their incomes (Cameron *et al.* 2001). Khandeker (1988) finds a positive relationship between women's education and labour force participation in Bangladesh and also finds that the husband's education is likely to reduce his wife's labour force participation rate because of the positive wealth effects of potential earnings.

Female labour force participation is governed by the reflection of economic hardship and suggests that the female labour force participation widely differs among the states, which is due to the differences in the rate of female literacy. Education is a marginally significant determinant of female labour force participation of labour market work and earnings (Psacharopulos 2002). Probability of participation in wage work increases with post-secondary education less so with lower levels of education (Mammen and Paxson 2000; Kingdom and Unni 1998).

Tertiary education increases the probability of being in the labour force (Cameron *et al.* 2001). Duraisamy (2002) views that graduate and above increases probability of women entering regular salaried government or private sector or wage work. Thus, primary schooling has no effect on earning for women (Tansel, 1993). Education is associated with better earnings for women; its effect varies with level of education. It is evidently seen from the study conducted in Ethiopia, Uganda and Cote de' Ivoira by Appleton, Hoddinott and Krishnan (1999).

The returns to school for both men and women increase with each level of education and are higher for women than for men (Aromolaran 2002; Duraisamy 2002; Berhman, 1995). On the contrary Esim (2001) states that education has positive effect on earnings of both female and male self-employed, but impact on men's earnings is greater. The impact of schooling on earnings is positive and significant for females in the formal sector, but not in the informal sector and domestic sectors (Mammen and Paxon, 2000).

Employment and Power Over Resources

Employment has given women an opportunity to shoulder responsibility, play new roles, react with new people, face new situation, etc. (Lalitha Devi 1982). Many studies reveal that female earnings in the household by employment status would increase the power of financial management and decision making (Kalpagam 1991; Dixon-Muller 1993; Rowlands 2000; Agarwal 2001). Not only can employment be a source of economic independence, but also it can help to give women a sense of self-work.

Empowerment Strategies

Empowerment is an active multidimensional process that enables women to realize their full identity and powers in all spheres of life (Laxmidevi 1998; Suguna 2001). The dimensions of empowerment are self-perception, perception of the women in the society, economic independence, decision-making, innovativeness and attributes towards group action, communication and desire to improve living conditions (Devadas *et al.* 1989). Empowerment aims at changing the values and direction of systematic forces, which marginalize women and other disadvantaged sections in a given context. It is a process of challenging existing power relations and of gaining greater control over the sources of power (Batliwala 1993; Sharma 1991).

Indicators of Empowerment

UNDP (1990) measures women empowerment in terms of choice, such as the choice to live long healthy life, to have better education, access to resources needed for a decent standard of living. Karl (1995) measures in terms of collective awareness building, capacity building and skills development participation and greater control and decision making power and action to bring about greater gender equality.

Sydney Schuler and Syed Hasheme (1996) measure on the basis of sense of self and vision of future, mobility and visibility, economic security status, decision making power within the household, ability to interact effectively in the public sphere and participation in non-family groups. Lalitha (1997) is of the view that empowerment means equality of work and wages, autonomy over reproductive life, access to ownership of land learning, access to bank credit and market, safe water and energy. Iyyampillai and Theresa (2001) assess women empowerment in terms of decision making process, political awareness, psychological strength, provision of credit and education are the factors that determine empowerment.

Rustagi (2004) identifies women empowerment in terms of employment, education, health survival, safety and participation in private and public decision making. Kishor and Gupta (2004) and Acharya and Ghimire (2005) identify empowerment in terms of gender equality and freedom of ability to influence decision making process at all levels.

Gender issues in terms of power relations and inequality have received much attention only among feminist economists. Besides efforts taken by Gary Becker and Amarthya Sen, others have registered a good spread effect. Sen's cooperative conflict model of household dynamics (1990) treats women as decision maker influence by endowments, Perceptions, etc. No researcher affords to neglect the theory of capabilities and entitlements while discussing the term 'empowerment'. In Sen's model bargaining power varies through differential capacities of men and women, and it can be increased by wage, work and other support system.

The following issues have emerged on the basis of the literature reviewed:

- Gender inequalities can be reduced by increasing bargaining power of women.
- Bargaining power can be restored and obtained by capabilities and entitlements.
- Education and employment are the entitlements of women, which augment their bargaining power.

- Bargaining power paves way for power of autonomy over resources and mobility.

These issues have been examined by many researchers on gender studies. However, an integrated approach to the question of empowerment and its indicators, relating it to the levels of education and employment status, is a novel attempt. The present researcher has made an attempt to study education, employment and empowerment with reference to the chosen indicators of Gender Equality in Decision Making (GEDM) and Power of Autonomy over Resources and Mobility (PARM). Thus, the study is probing into the bi-dimensional relationship of relating the effects of education and employment on empowerment on the one hand and relating the effects of education and employment on the indicators of empowerment on the other. Being inspired by the theoretical and empirical literature, the researcher intends to pursue his study, with two indicators, GEDM and PARM. Conceptually, the two indicators are needed together for empowerment of women.

4

RESEARCH DESIGN

This chapter presents the research design of the study. The review of literature made has provided the basis for conceptualising the research issues and drawing up the survey design for the proposed empirical study. Besides presenting the objectives and hypotheses the systematic approach of the scholar to the task of sampling and scaling are detailed here. The transition from a theoretical conceptualization to an empirical study, involves operationalising the concepts and delimiting the scope of the exercise. The scholar attempts the same while presenting the limitations of the study.

OBJECTIVES

1. To juxtapose the socio economic characteristics of the respondents and the corresponding levels of Empowerment and its indicators namely Gender equality in decision making and Power of autonomy over resources and mobility (GEDM and PARM)
2. To assess the Gender equality in decision making and Power of autonomy over resources and mobility (GEDM and PARM) of the respondents according to educational levels and employment status.
3. To examine the empowerment status of rural women in relation to their educational levels and employment status.

4. To find out the most influential factors that determine rural women empowerment and its indicators (GEDM and PARM)
5. To suggest policy measures to empower the Rural Women.

HYPOTHESES

Many researchers have suggested that access to income earning opportunities alone may not be sufficient to facilitate women's empowerment within the household. It is the levels of earnings in combination with having control over resources lead them to the path of empowerment. The studies of Youssef (1982) Sen (1990) Mahomud and Johnson (1994), Kabeer (1999, 2000) etc. suggest that economic contribution by women is found to be related to their status in a society. Further, more women who perceive that their earnings constitute a substantial proportion of total family earnings, are more likely to be empowered than other employed and unemployed women. Being inspired by these views the first hypothesis is drawn up as,

> There is an association between rural women's income and empowerment; female income and GEDM; female income and PARM;

Women work not because of economic necessity, but because they want to have economic independence, individual status, or to have intellectual satisfaction. Economic independence makes women conscious of their rights. Besides, working outside home and coming into contact with other people have broadened their outlook and mental horizon which brings equality in the family. Thus, power of autonomy is more required than GEDM to achieve empowerment. Many researchers argue infavour of women's economic independence (Kalpagam 1991; Dixon-Muller 1993; Rowlands 2000; Agarwal 2001). Hence, the second hypothesis is phrased as,

> PARM excels over GEDM in influencing the empowerment of women;

Education is related to increased decision-making on economic issues in the household, which brings gender equality. Education is also likely to enhance women's economic independence by equipping them with skills necessary to avail of paid employment opportunities there by also making economic contributions more visible. The studies of Jeejee bhoy (1991) Malhotra and Mather (1997), Kritz and Makinwa-Adebusoye (1999), Sengupta and Johnson (2003), expressed the positive relationship between education and GEDM, PARM and empowerment. This leads to the third hypothesis:

> There exists significant positive correlation between education and empowerment; employment and empowerment;

Rustagi (2004) says that it is only education rather than employment which makes Kerala gender neutral in character. She finds negative correlation between employment and empowerment in her study at Kerala. This finding has prompted the researcher to formulate the fourth hypothesis as,

> Social factors are more dominant than the economic factors in deciding the extent of rural women empowerment, GEDM and PARM

CONCEPTS AND OPERATIONAL DEFINITIONS

Levels of Education

The levels of education can be grouped into six heads– illiterates, primary school education, secondary school education, high school education, higher secondary school education and above higher secondary school education. Those who are not able to read and write and who never gone for any formal institution are called illiterates. The levels of education has been classified as upto five years of schooling, six to eight years of schooling, nine to ten years of schooling, eleven to twelve years of schooling and more than twelve years of schooling. These have been categorized as Primary School Education, Secondary School Education, High School Education, Higher Secondary School Education and Above Higher Secondary School Education respectively.

Employment Status

Women who are engaged in paid work and income generation activities are defined as employed women. It includes all types of employment viz., private and public, organized and unorganized and self employed and wage employed activities. The women who employed atleast 100 days are taken for this study (according to NSS report). The present study takes 120 employed women comprises 28 wage employed women from organized sector (Teachers–12, Nurses–7, Typists–2, Clerks–3, Office Assistants–4); 72 wage employed women from unorganized sector (Agricultural labourers–20, domestic servants–6, sago factory labourers–9, Brick layers–18, Care takers of live stock–6, care takers of poultry–3); 18 self employed women from unorganized sector (Petti shop owners–4, Tailors–5, Fish vendors–2, Vegetables vendors–3, Book binders–2, Owners of poultry–2) and 2 self employed women from organized sector (2 Doctors)

Empowerment

For the present study rural women empowerment is operationally defined as gender equality in decision-making in the family and power of autonomy over resources and mobility of women. To measure empowerment of rural women the total score values of GEDM and the total score values of PARM are taken. For GEDM 25 items are given and for PARM 25 items are given. Totally 50 items are considered to measure empowerment of rural women. From the highest score value (150), one could observe high level of empowerment and from the lowest score value (50) one could observe the low level of empowerment.

Gender Equality in Decision Making (GEDM)

It is defined that men and women in the family should have equal power in taking decisions in the household chores. Likert's three point scale is adopted to measure GEDM. The 25 items given for GEDM includes decision maker, managing financial resources, account holder, power of withdrawal of money, decisions regarding children's education and children's marriage, power to employ servants, asset holder, possessing highest level education, decision on spacing of child, medical intervention for family planning, gender preferential treatment, assisting household activities, purchasing of groceries and vegetables, purchase of land and other properties, physical resources for liquidity, child care responsibility, preference for professional education, decision on family budget, leisure activities, gift made to others; rest hours, working hours, assisting children's academic work, reading magazines and newspapers. Each item is measured by three responses–men, women and both. The scores given for the responses are 1, 2 and 3 respectively. Since the study is for women empowerment, the score value for women is given higher than men. If the total score for any respondent is the highest score value 75 it means gender equality is prevailing in that household. If the total score is 25, the equality is skewed for men and for the total score of 50, the equality is skewed for women.

Power of Autonomy over Resources and Mobility (PARM)

This signifies that women should have control over financial, physical, intellectual and human resources and control of ideology. They should also have freedom of movement. Under PARM 25 items are considered. The 25 items are viz., Spending money for personal needs, purchasing durable goods, purchasing jeweler, freedom to spend mother side, Freedom to cultivating crops, Purchasing land, expressing desire in higher studies, Power to mortgage, voting rights, Choice of spouse, Decision on vote schedule, freedom to Watch TV, Freedom to cook, Freedom to keep money, Freedom to sell lands, Freedom to invest, Disposal of property from others, and Borrowing from others. For each item three responses are given viz., without permission (WOP), with permission (WP) and not allowed to do independent household chores. If some of the cases are not applicable to the respondents, the score value for that item is given as zero. The score given for WOP, WP and NA are 3, 2 and 1 respectively. From the highest score value (75) one could observe full autonomy over resources and mobility of women and the lowest score value (25) assigned for least autonomy over resources and mobility.

METHODOLOGY

The researcher has carried out a pilot study during 2004 - 2005 by using well-structured interview schedule and has adopted proportionate random sampling to collect information from 50 respondents. The respondents had been classified in to four categories viz., illiterates with formal employment, illiterates with informal employment, educated with formal employment and educated with informal employment. However, the pilot study revealed that the classification of respondents could be done as per the levels of education, to lend greater precision to the analysis. The schedule was later modified accommodating the changes for the present survey for further analysis Accordingly, the respondents have been classified in to twelve categories with various levels of education and employment status and the present study adopts disproportionate random sampling to compare the extent of empowerment with different levels of education and employment status.

This study is mainly based on primary data. Secondary data are used only for the selection of Districts and Blocks in Tamil Nadu. The choice of districts has been based on the criterion of education, specifically with reference to Rural Female Literary, Tiruvarur, enjoys the status of one of the five top districts whereas Sales ranks one of the bottom five districts in respect of this criterion. Hence they are chosen to facilitate comparison. Following the same procedure, two blocks in each of the districts are selected and the respondents are selected on the basis of levels of education and employment status.

The secondary data sources are Tamil Nadu Human Development Report 2003, Tamil Nadu Economic Appraisal 2004 and Census report of India 2001. (Table 1 and 2). Selection of districts, blocks and samples in different stages are given in Flow Chart

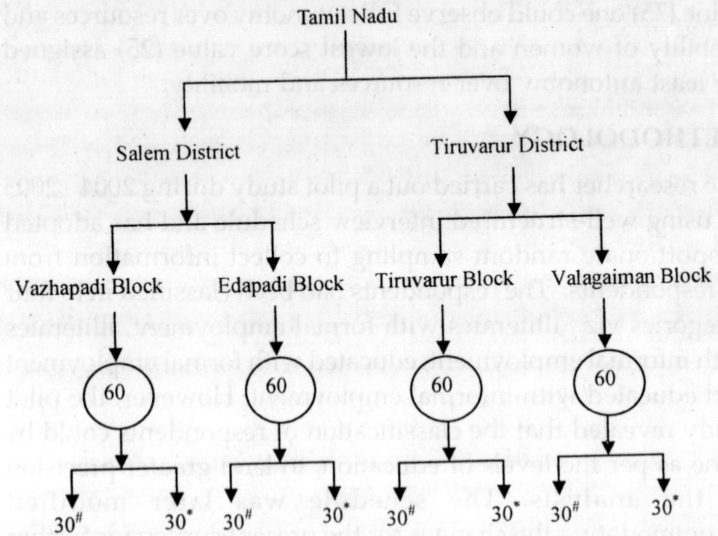

Note:

\# *Employed (30):* Comprises 5 illiterates, 5 primary education, 5 secondary education, 5 high school education, 5 higher secondary education and 5 above higher secondary education.

* *Unemployed (30):* Comprises 5 illiterates, 5 primary education, 5 secondary education, 5 high school education, 5 higher secondary education and 5 above higher secondary education.

According to levels of education and employment 240 sample respondents are identified. The sample respondents are classified into twelve categories as stated below. From each category 20 samples are taken for the study. They are interviewed by the researcher by using a well structured interview schedule.

These samples can be grouped under two heads viz., Education and Employment.

Sampling Design (240)

Employment status

Employed	-	120
Unemployed	-	120

Level of Education

Illiterates	-	40
Primary	-	40
Secondary	-	40
High school	-	40
Higher secondary	-	40
Above higher secondary	-	40

Period of Study

This study takes up the information regarding economic status such as income, Saving, Expenditure, borrowing and asset structure of the family and the social status such as education total years of schooling in the family size, Family type, Age of the respondents and Age difference between husband and wife and perception of the respondents in the context of education, employment and empowerment during 2005–2006.

Statistical Tools

Percentages and Chi-square analyses with Tschuprowe's co-efficient* are used to bring out the association of socio-economic variables with levels of GEDM, PARM and Empowerment. Descriptive statistics viz., Average ($\overline{X}$), Standard Deviation (s) co- efficient of variation are used t2o analyse levels of GEDM the levels of education and employment status with socio economic variables which help the researcher to assess the levels of GEDM, PARM and Empowerment of rural women. Pearson correlation co-efficient is used to bring out the relation between education, employment and empowerment and its components. In order to study the relationship between exogenous variables and each of the Indigenous variables ie., GEDM, PARM and women Empowerment, the data are subject to correlation and path analysis#.

However, the path analysis[1] undertaken in this study differs slightly from usual applications. It is not used here to eliminate logical alternative models. Rather, it has been employed in this study to assess the relative importance of various variables and its proposed linkages in the model. The causal linkages of the model on independent and dependent variables have been assumed to be fixed. The causal order assumed for the variables under study is taken from deductive theory and not derived from the data of the present study. Thus, the approach to causal modeling as followed is the present study avoids some problem raised by Mukherjee.[4] The problem of multi-collinearity, highly correlated independent variables–has received extensive treatment.

Levels of GEDM, PARM and Empowerment (Categorisation)

The levels of GEDM, PARM and Empowerment are determined on the basis of $\overline{X}$(average) and s (standard deviation). When the score values for these levels lie below $\overline{X}$-σ, the level is considered to be low; lie between $\overline{X}$-σ, and $\overline{X}$+σ the level is considered to be medium; when the level is more than $\overline{X}$+σ, the level is considered to be high.

Based on the above scoring procedure the level of empowerment is low when the respondents obtain below 90 ($\overline{X}$-σ = 89.7) and medium when the score value lies between 90 and 117 inclusive of both limits ($\overline{X}$-σ = 90, $\overline{X}$+σ = 117) and high when they obtain more than 117. GEDM is low when the respondents obtain below 41 ($\overline{X}$-σ = 40.8) and medium when the score value lies between 41 and 57 inclusive of both limits ($\overline{X}$+σ = 57) and high when they obtain more than 57. PARM is low when the respondents obtain below 45 ($\overline{X}$-σ = 45.1) and medium when the score value lies between 45 and 64 inclusive of both limits ($\overline{X}$+=σ =64) and high when the score value is more than 64.

DELIMITATION

This study is delimited to relate levels of education to empowerment and it does not relate the degree of empowerment to various levels of employment. This study covers only the sample respondents of married women and it assesses the empowerment of rural women in the family and not that out side the home.

REFERFNCES

1. The path analysis is widely used in social sciences. For instance, Richard Breen, Path analysis: an example: Journal of Agricultural Economics, Vol. XXX IV, No.3, Sep. 1983; pp.407-417; Alwin D and Hauser, R, 'The decomposition of effects in path analysis', American Sociological Revising, vol. 40;1975, pp. 37-47; Duncan, O. D, 'Path Analysis: Sociological Analysis' American Journal of sociology, Vol.72, 1966, pp.1-86; Funny, J.M, 'Indirect Effects in

Path Analysis,' Sociological methods and Research, Vol. 1, 1972, pp.175-186; Geary, R.C, The method of path coefficients and OLS Regression, The Economic and sociological review; Vol.7, 1976, pp.249-263; Grene, V, 'An Algorithm for total and indirect causal effects', Political methodology, vol.4, 1977, pp 369 – 381; Johnston, J, Econometric methods' London: McGraw Hill pub.1972; Lewis Beck, M.S., Determining the importance of an independent variable, A Path Analysis solution social science Research, Vol.3, 1974, pp. 95-107, Scully J.J, 'The influence of family size on efficiency of farms. An Irish study; Journal of Agricultural Economics, 1962, Vol-15, pp 116-121.

2. Richard Breen, *Op. cit*, p.417.
3. Glisson, C.D and Man – Knong Mok, H incorporating nominal variables in Path Analysis: A cross cultural example with human service organization; Journal of Applied Behavioral science, Vol.19, No:1, 1983, pp. 95-102.
4. Mukharjee, B, Mass Media and political modernity; Agra, Bhargava Bode House, 1979, p.45.

NOTES

*** T-Coefficient (Tschuprow's co-efficient)**

When data regarding two qualitative characters are given as a contingency table based on manifold classification, the independence of these two attributive characters can be tested using the chi-square test for independence of two attributes. But there are some conditions which should be satisfied by the data for the use of the chi-square test. These conditions include the cell frequencies not less than 5, etc. But if such conditions are not satisfied by the data, an alternative approach based on descriptive statistical methods is to compute Tschuprow's 'T' value. It is computed using the formula

$$T^2 = \sqrt{\frac{\phi^2}{\sqrt{(r-1)(c-1)}}}$$

$$\phi^2 = \frac{\chi^2}{N}$$

It takes values between 0 and 1. If the value of T is high such as 0.7 or 0.8 etc. a high degree of association between the two characters can be thought of. If the value of T is close to zero, then it is indicative of low or no dependence between the two characters. It is a descriptive method and does not involve the test of hypothesis.

The stepwise regression analysis is used to locate significant independent variables (explanatory variables) on GEDM, PARM and Empowerment of women. The path analysis is applied in order to find out the direct and indirect effect of explanatory variables on the dependent variable(s) of GEDM, PARM and Empowerment of women.

Analytical Pattern–Path Analysis

This analysis is based on some of the assumptions such as that relations are linear and additive (the causal assumptions are shown in the path diagram), the residuals are uncorrelated with the variables in the model and with each other, the causal form is one way and the variables are measured on interval scales and also measured without error.

The path analysis is a means of decomposing statistical relationships between variables in a structural equation model in order to distinguish that part of the relationship consisting of what the investigator believes to be causal effects from that part which is spurious or irrelevant. It does this in the light of theoretical prior assumptions about the causal relationship between the variables expressed in the form of a structural equation model. The researcher can point out at least three advantages of this form of analysis over the more conventional regression analysis. Firstly, by forcing us to specify a model of the inter-relationships between the explanatory variables we make use of their inter-correlations to obtain better estimates of the effects of these variables, on the dependent variable. On the other hand, in a simple regression, in which all the exogenous variables are presumed to be independent, these correlations are considered troublesome, rather than useful; The larger the correlations, the less adequate the classical 'partial differentiation', interpretation of the co-efficients becomes'. A corollary of this is that by necessitating the specification of a model, we are obliged to make use of theory–however simple to justify the model. Secondly, the method allows to assess which of variables in the model have the strongest causal relationship with the dependent variable, and finally, we can model the specific ways in which this casual (direct/indirect) relationship brought about and assess the relative strengths of each of these. In other words, not only can we compare one variable's effect with that of another, but we can compare for any single variable, the magnitude of the different effects it has[2].

5

ANALYSIS OF HOUSEHOLD CHARACTERISTICS OF RURAL WOMEN

Having conducted a field survey as far the survey design described in the previous chapter, the researcher presents the socio-economic profile of the study population in the following pages. The socio-economic and demographic background of the respondents is necessary to understand Women's empowerment. This will enable us to have an idea of the study area, and about the ranking of an individual by the society she lives in, in terms of her material belonging and cultural possession. In this chapter socio-economic and demographic factors that affect the levels of GEDM, PARM and the empowerment are clearly analysed. Besides, the perceptions of the respondents on education, employment and empowerment are also presented. From that perspective, one can correlate the levels of GEDM, PARM and empowerment with reference to Education, Employment and Empowerment.

SOCIO-ECONOMIC STATUS AND LEVELS OF GEDM, PARM AND EMPOWERMENT

Empowerment on the basis of two indicators–GEDM and PARM-is ranked at low, medium and high levels. The respondents at the high level of GEDM reflect that they have an equal say in decision-making and the respondents at the high level of PARM reflect that they have a control over resources and financial autonomy and the freedom of movement.

It is seen from Table 1 that one–sixth of the respondents is at a high level of empowerment. Among the indicators–GEDM and PARM, the respondents at high level of PARM out numbers the high level of GEDM. It shows that the respondents have higher a PARM than GEDM, and one could note that it is because of the high level of PARM that rural women get empowerment.

Age and Community

Age not only determines an individual's physical and mental maturity, but also depicts her experiences. Table 1 presents the age and community-wise distribution of the respondents. Nearly half of the respondents belong to the age group of 25-40 years. They are more or less equally distributed at the low and the medium levels of empowerment and it is observed from Table 1 that only one-fifth of the respondents belong to the age group of 25-40 years and they are distributed at the high level of empowerment. While taking GEDM and PARM, there exists a variation in the distribution of the respondents. The respondents who belong to the age group of 25-40 years are more or less equally distributed at the medium and the high level of GEDM and PARM, and it is observed that one-fourth of the respondents are at the high level of GEDM and PARM. Thus, it is found that the over-all empowerment is low as compared to GEDM and PARM among the respondents, belonging to the age group of 25-40 years.

Community is an important variable of an individual's ascribed status. The Indian society is hierarchically divided based on community, and this is more true of the rural areas. The position of a caste in the hierarchy is independent of its economic status. It determines the social status too. Agarwal (1997) notes that the bargaining position is not just determined by inter–household factors but exogeneous factors linked to the areans of market. Bargaining position of women determines the level of empowerment. It is interesting to note that the respondents who belong to MBC are highly distributed as

Table 1
Distribution of the Respondents According to Levels of GEDM, PARM and Empowerment by Age and Community

	Categories	N	Levels of GEDM			Levels of PARM			Levels of Empowerment		
			Low	*Medium*	*High*	*Low*	*Medium*	*High*	*Low*	*Medium*	*High*
Age	Below25 years	46	32(23.0)	7(13.2)	7(14.6)	27(20.2)	10(20.4)	9(15.8)	25(24.0)	14(15.1)	7(16.3)
	25 to 40 years	102	56(40.3)	22(41.5)	24(50.0)	59(44.0)	18(36.7)	25(43.9)	43(41.4)	40(43.0)	19(44.2)
	Above40 years	92	51(36.7)	24(45.3)	17(35.4)	48(35.8)	21(42.9)	23(40.3)	36(34.6)	39(41.9)	17(39.5)
	N	240	139(100)	53(100)	48(100)	134(100)	49(100)	57(100)	104(100)	93(100)	43(100)
Community	OC	34	17(12.2)	11(20.8)	6(12.5)	17(12.7)	7(14.3)	10(17.6)	11(10.6)	14(15.0)	9(20.9)
	BC	75	37(26.6)	17(32.0)	21(43.8)	40(29.8)	15(30.6)	20(35.1)	28(26.9)	32(34.4)	15(34.9)
	MBC	85	57(41.0)	14(26.4)	14(29.2)	49(36.6)	15(30.6)	21(36.8)	42(40.4)	30(32.3)	13(30.2)
	SC	46	28(20.2)	11(20.8)	7(14.5)	28(20.9)	12(24.5)	6(10.5)	23(22.1)	17(18.3)	6(14.0)
	N	240	139(100)	53(100)	48(100)	134(100)	49(100)	57(100)	104(100)	93(100)	43(100)

Source: Computed.
Figures in parentheses are percentage to column total.
N j Number of sample respondents, GEDM plus PARM equals Empowerment

compared to BC. One-third of the respondents are MBC. Among them, half of them are at the low level of empowerment. At the high level of empowerment, the respondents who belong to BC are highly distributed. The same observation is noted at GEDM also. But while taking PARM the respondents belonging to MBC are highly distributed at the high and low level. Since MBC respondents have the low GEDM, they are distributed least in number at the high level of empowerment. It is observed that the BC respondents have a high GEDM and hence they are highly distributed.

Type and Size of Family and Age Difference between Husband and Wife

Table 2 presents the distribution of respondents according to the type of family, size of family, and the age difference between husband and wife. Now the tendency towards nuclear families is increasing not only in urban areas but also in rural areas. This is observed in the study. Three-fourth of respondents are from the nuclear families. They are highly distributed at the low and the medium levels of empowerment. One-sixth of the nuclear families respondents are at the high level of empowerment. Regarding GEDM and PARM, the nuclear families respondents are highly distributed at the low levels. One-fifth of nuclear families' respondents are more or less equally distributed at the medium and the high level of GEDM and PARM. GEDM is low as compared to PARM for the respondents who belong to nuclear families and there by distribution is least at the high level of empowerment.

The size of the family has influenced the bargaining power of the women (Amartyasen 1991). In Tamil Nadu the Family Planning Programmes are successful and most of the families have small-size families. Half of the respondents have small size families. Less than half of them are at low level of empowerment and one-fifth of them are the high level of empowerment. The respondents from small sized families are more or less equally distributed at the low and the medium level of empowerment. In contrast, they are equally distributed at the medium and the high level of indicators of

Table 2
Distribution of the Respondents According to Levels of GEDM, PARM and Empowerment by Type and Size of Households

	Categories	N	Levels of GEDM			Levels of PARM			Levels of Empowerment		
			Low	*Medium*	*High*	*Low*	*Medium*	*High*	*Low*	*Medium*	*High*
Type of Households	JOINT	65	38(27.3)	15(28.3)	12(25.0)	38(28.4)	14(28.6)	13(22.8)	28(26.9)	27(29.0)	10(23.3)
	NUCLEAR	175	101.00(72.7)	38.00(71.7)	36.00(75.0)	96.00(71.6)	35.00(71.4)	44.00(77.2)	76(73.1)	66(71.0)	33(76.7)
	N	240	139(100)	53(100)	48(100)	134(100)	49(100)	57(100)	104(100)	93(100)	43(100)
Size of Households	SMALL (1-4)	122	74(53.2)	24(45.3)	24(50.0)	68(50.7)	23(46.9)	31(54.4)	51(49.0)	47(50.5)	24(55.8)
	MEDIUM (5&6)	64	33(23.8)	15(28.3)	16(33.3)	36(26.9)	16(32.7)	12(21.0)	28(27.0)	27(29.0)	9(20.9)
	LARGE (7&above)	54	32(23.0)	14(26.4)	8(16.7)	30(22.4)	10(20.4)	14(24.6)	25(24.0)	19(20.5)	10(23.3)
	N	240	139(100)	53(100)	48(100)	134(100)	49(100)	57(100)	104(100)	93(100)	43(100)
*Age Difference**	BELOW 5	71	34(24.4)	19(35.9)	18(37.5)	36(26.9	20(40.8)	15(26.3)	27(26.0)	29(31.2)	15(34.9)
	5 - 10	108	66(47.5)	23(43.4)	19(39.6)	59(44.0)	18(36.7)	31(54.4)	49(47.1)	38(40.8)	21(48.8)
	ABOVE 10	61	39(28.1)	11(20.7)	11(22.9)	39(29.1)	11(22.5)	11(19.3)	28(26.9)	26(28.0)	7(16.3)
	N	240	139(100)	53(100)	48(100)	134(100)	49(100)	57(100)	104(100)	93(100)	43(100)

Source: Computed.
Figures in parentheses are percentage to column total.
N j Number of sample respondents, GEDM plus PARM equals Empowerment
* - Age difference between husband and wife.

empowerment. Even though the distribution of respondents at the low levels of GEDM and PARM is high, they are less in numbers while observing the over-all empowerment.

Nearly half of the respondents have 5-10 years of age difference with their spouses. One-fifth of them are at the high level of empowerment. The respondents at the high level of GEDM is low (1/5) as compared to the respondents at the high level of PARM (more than one third), and hence the distribution of the respondents at the high level of empowerment with 5-10 years age difference with their spouses is also low.

Levels of Education and Employment

Education is considered an important variable not only for widening mental behaviour, but also for helping a person to make use of rational and scientific approach to different problems. It is a known fact that literacy rate in India, with the exception of Kerala, is very low and this is more true in the rural areas. Table 3 clearly shows that the higher the levels of education, the higher will be the levels of empowerment. Besides, GEDM and PARM are also high at the higher levels of education.

Women are competing with men on an equal footing and have entered into occupations which were considered the domain of men. The employed women enjoy higher level of empowerment than the unemployed women. At the lower levels of empowerment, the unemployed women are highly distributed. The distribution of respondents is more or less same at the high levels of GEDM, PARM and empowerment Lalitha Devi (1982) views that employed women have an extent of freedom in spending family income, an extent of freedom in decision making of the family, an extent of help received in discharging household responsibilities, an extent of deviation from the observation of traditional customs and behaviour. The employed women are at higher levels of empowerment. The employment status thus influences the levels of empowerment.

Table 3
Distribution of the Respondents According to Levels of GEDM, PARM and Empowerment by Levels of Education and Employment

	Categories	N	Levels of GEDM			Levels of PARM			Levels of Empowerment		
			Low	*Medium*	*High*	*Low*	*Medium*	*High*	*Low*	*Medium*	*High*
Education	Illiterates	40	30(21.6)	6(11.3)	4(8.3)	34(25.4)	2(4.0)	4(7.0)	29(27.9)	7(7.5)	4(9.3)
	Upto High School	120	75(53.9)	29(54.7)	16(33.3)	70(52.2)	24(49.0)	26(45.6)	58(55.8)	46(49.5)	16(37.2)
	Above High School	80	34(24.5)	18(34.0)	28(58.4)	30(22.4)	23(47.0)	27(47.4)	17(16.3)	40(43.0)	23(53.5)
	N	240	139 (100	53(100)	48(100)	134(100)	49(100)	57(100)	104(100)	93(100)	43(100)
Occupation	Unemployed	120	74(53.2)	27(51.0)	19(39.6)	67(50.0)	27(55.1)	26(45.6)	57(54.8)	49(52.7)	14(32.6)
	Employed	120	65(46.8)	26(49.0)	29(60.4)	67(50.0)	22(44.9)	31(54.4)	47(45.2)	44(47.3)	29(67.4)
	N	240	139(100)	53(100)	48(100)	134(100)	49(100)	57(100)	104(100)	93(100)	43(100)

Source: Computed.
Figures in parentheses are percentage to colun·n total.
N - Number of sample respondents, GEDM plus PARM equals Empowerment

Total Family Income and Female Income

The total family income comprises income earned by all the family members, irrespective of gender. Table 4 shows that when the total family income is low (below Rs.50,000), the respondents are highly distributed at the high levels of empowerment and when the level of income increases from Rs.50,000 to Rs.1,00,000, the respondents are highly distributed at the low levels of empowerment. The same result is observed at GEDM and PARM too. It is further noted that at the higher levels of income (above 1, 00,000), the respondents have a high GEDM and not PARM, and hence they are distributed among the least members at the high level of empowerment.

The women who perceive that their earnings constitute a substantial proportion of total family earnings are more likely to be empowered than the other employed and unemployed (Youssef 1982; Sen 1990; Mahmud and Johnson 1994). It is interesting to note that when the female share in the total income increases, the level of empowerment also increases. At the higher level of empowerment, the respondents with a high share of the total income are highly distributed. The respondents with the lowest share are highly distributed at the low level of empowerment. There exists a positive relation between female share in total income and the level of empowerment. But the converse exists in the case of relation between total family income and levels of empowerment.

Total Expenditure and Female Share in Total Expenditure

Expenditure in a family is based mainly on the income earned by its members. Other factors such as the number of dependents and pattern of expenditure have varied influence in the expenditure pattern on their domestic requirements. Table 5 indicates that when the level of total expenditure in the family increases, the level of empowerment also increases. The respondents are highly distributed at the high level of empowerment, while the total expenditure in the family is above Rs.50,000. Similarly when the female share in the total expenditure increases, the respondents are highly distributed

Table 4

Distribution of the Respondents According to Levels of GEDM, PARM and Empowerment by Income Status

	Categories	N	Levels of GEDM			Levels of PARM			Levels of Empowerment		
			Low	Medium	High	Low	Medium	High	Low	Medium	High
Total Income	BELOW Rs.50,000	67	35(25.2)	14(26.4)	18(37.5)	19(14.2)	20(40.8)	28(49.1)	21(20.2)	21(22.6)	25(58.1)
	Rs. 50000 j 1,00,000	96	65(46.7)	19(35.9)	12(25.0)	62(46.3)	18(36.7)	16(28.1)	49(47.1)	40(43.0)	7(16.3)
	ABOVE Rs.1,00,000	77	39(28.1)	20(37.7)	18(37.5)	53(39.5)	11(22.5)	13(22.8)	34(32.7)	32(34.4)	11(25.6)
	N	240	139(100)	53(100)	48(100)	134(100)	49(100)	57(100)	104(100)	93(100)	43(100)
Female Income	Nil Earnings	95	58(41.7)	21(39.6)	16(33.3)	52(38.8)	20(40.8)	23(40.3)	43(41.4)	41(44.1)	11(25.6)
	BELOW Rs.25,000	108	69(49.7)	19(35.9)	20(41.7)	74(55.2)	20(40.8)	14(24.6)	56(53.8)	41(44.1)	11(25.6)
	ABOVE Rs.25,000	37	12(8.6)	13(24.5)	12(25.0)	8(6.0)	9(18.4)	20(35.1)	5(4.8)	11(11.8)	21(48.8)
	N	240	139(100)	53(100)	48(100)	134(100)	49(100)	57(100)	104(100)	93(100)	43(100)

Source: Computed.

Figures in parentheses are percentage to column total.

N - Number of sample respondents, GEDM plus PARM equals Empowerment

Table 5
Distribution of the Respondents According to Levels of GEDM, PARM and Empowerment by Levels of Expenditure

	Categories	N	Levels of GEDM			Levels of PARM			Levels of Empowerment		
			Low	*Medium*	*High*	*Low*	*Medium*	*High*	*Low*	*Medium*	*High*
Total Expenditure	BELOW Rs.25,000	49	34(24.5)	8(15.1)	7(14.6)	21(15.7)	13(26.5)	15(26.3)	22(21.2)	14(15.1)	13(30.2)
	Rs. 25000 j 50,000	107	63(45.3)	27(50.9)	17(35.4)	73(54.5)	16(32.7)	18(31.6)	54(51.9)	44(47.3)	9(20.9)
	ABOVE 50,000	84	42(30.2)	18(34.0)	24(50.0)	40(29.8)	20(40.8)	24(42.1)	28(26.9)	35(37.6)	21(48.9)
	N	240	139(100)	53(100)	48(100)	134(100)	49(100)	57(100)	104(100)	93(100)	43(100)
Female Share	Nill Contribution	108	64(46.0)	25(47.2)	19(39.6)	61(45.5)	22(44.9)	25(43.9)	50(48.1)	45(48.4)	13(30.2)
	BELOW Rs.25,000	90	60(43.2)	15(28.3)	15(31.3)	58(43.3)	18(36.7)	14(24.5)	46(44.2)	34(36.6)	10(23.3)
	ABOVE Rs.25,000	42	15(10.8)	13(24.5)	14(29.1)	15(11.2)	9(18.4)	18(31.6)	8(7.7)	14(15.0)	20(46.5)
	N	240	139(100)	53(100)	48(100)	134(100)	49(100)	57(100)	104(100)	93(100)	43(100)

Source: Computed.
Figures in parentheses are percentage to column total.
N - Number of sample respondents, GEDM plus PARM equals Empowerment

at high level of empowerment, but not at the high levels of GEDM and PARM. The household expenditure depends on women's earnings, on the ground that women are likely to have greater access and control over resources if they are primary earners in a household (Kishore and Gupta 2004). When the female share in the total expenditure is nil, they are at low levels of empowerment and also at the low levels of GEDM and PARM. When GEDM and PARM are low, the level of empowerment is also low.

Total Savings and Female Savings

The capacity to save is an important indicator of economic empowerment. The higher savings may be expected to lead to the higher levels of empowerment. Not only the total savings, but the female savings is an indicator of the levels of empowerment. The rural women keep their accounts in private and public financial institutions. Chit fund is the most likely institution to them. Besides, SHG is an institution to save the money of the rural women. Table 6 shows that when the level of total saving increases, the levels of GEDM and PARM increase and the levels of empowerment also increase. When the total saving is low, the level of GEDM and PARM is low, and the empowerment is also low. It is also observed that when the female saving is nil, the level of empowerment is low due to low GEDM. The absence of female savings reduces gender the equality in decision-making and hence the level of empowerment is found to be low.

Total Borrowings and Female Borrowings

The major sources of borrowings for the respondents are the private sources like moneylenders, friends and relatives, and institutional sources like National Banks, SHGs and different Welfare Schemes of Government. Table 7 shows the level of total borrowings in the family and female borrowings. When the total borrowing in the family is nil, the respondents are highly distributed at all levels of GEDM, PARM and empowerment. Similarly when the female contribution to the total borrowings is nil, the respondents are distributed at all

Table 6

Distribution of the Respondents According to Levels of GEDM, PARM and Empowerment by Levels of Savings

	Categories	N	Levels of GEDM			Levels of PARM			Levels of Empowerment		
			Low	Medium	High	Low	Medium	High	Low	Medium	High
Total Savings	Nil Savings	38	33(23.7)	3(5.7)	2(4.2)	24(17.9)	7(14.3)	7(12.3)	26(25.0)	8(8.6)	4(9.3)
	Below Rs. 25000	107	65(46.8)	24(45.3)	18(37.5)	66(49.3)	23(46.9)	18(31.6)	48(46.2)	50(53.8)	9(20.9)
	ABOVE Rs.25000	95	41(29.5)	26(49.0)	28(58.3)	44(32.8)	19(38.8)	32(56.1)	30(28.8)	35(37.6)	30(69.8)
	N	240	139(100)	53(100)	48(100)	134(100)	49(100)	57(100)	104(100)	93(100)	43(100)
Female Savings	Nil Savings	97	75(54.0)	13(24.5)	9(18.7)	57(42.5)	20(40.8)	20(35.1)	55(52.9)	36(38.7)	6(14.0)
	BELOW Rs.25,000	96	47(33.8)	25(47.2)	24(50.0)	64(47.8)	18(36.7)	14(24.6)	40(38.5)	40(43.0)	16(37.2)
	ABOVE Rs.25,000	47	17(12.2)	15(28.3)	15(31.3)	13(9.7)	11(22.5)	23(40.3)	9(8.6)	17(18.3)	21(48.8)
	N	240	139(100)	53(100)	48(100)	134(100)	49(100)	57(100)	104(100)	93(100)	43(100)

Source: Computed.

Figures in parentheses are percentage to column total.

N - Number of sample respondents, GEDM plus PARM equals Empowerment

Table 7

Distribution of the Respondents According to Levels of GEDM, PARM and Empowerment by Levels of Borrowings

	Categories	N	Levels of GEDM			Levels of PARM			Levels of Empowerment		
			Low	*Medium*	*High*	*Low*	*Medium*	*High*	*Low*	*Medium*	*High*
Total Borrowings	Nil borrowing	94	52(37.4)	25(47.1)	17(35.4)	48(35.8)	19(38.8)	27(47.4)	33(31.7)	43(46.2)	18(41.9)
	Below Rs. 10,000	43	29(20.9)	3(5.7)	11(22.9)	29(21.7)	10(20.4)	4(7.0)	23(22.1)	17(18.3)	3(6.9)
	Rs.10,000 j 50,000	54	34(24.4)	12(22.7)	8(16.7)	37(27.6)	9(18.4)	8(14.0)	32(30.8)	14(15.1)	8(18.6)
	Above Rs.50,000	49	24(17.3)	13(24.5)	12(25.0)	20(14.9)	11(22.4)	18(31.6)	16(15.4)	19(20.4)	14(32.6)
	N	240	139(100)	53(100)	48(100)	134(100)	49(100)	57(100)	104(100)	93(100)	43(100)
Female Borrowings	Nil Borrowings	182	106(76.3)	43(81.1)	33(68.7)	106(79.1)	34(69.4)	42(73.7)	83(79.8)	69(74.2)	30(69.8)
	Borrowings	58	33(23.7)	10(18.9)	15(31.3)	28(20.9)	15(30.6)	15(26.3)	21(20.2)	24(25.8)	13(30.2)
	N	240	139(100)	53(100)	48(100)	134(100)	49(100)	57(100)	104(100)	93(100)	43(100)

Source: Computed.

Figures in parentheses are percentage to column total.

N - Number of sample respondents, GEDM plus PARM equals Empowerment

levels of GEDM, PARM and empowerment. Level of borrowings has no significant influence on the levels of GEDM, PARM and empowerment.

Total Property and Female Property

Property is the most important determinant of empowerment of women. When women possess more assets, they will have higher levels of empowerment. The acquisition of property decides the level of empowerment and therefore the government insists on Women's Property Rights. It is observed from Table 8 that when the total asset structure in the family is low, the respondents are highly distributed at the low level of empowerment, GEDM and PARM and *vice-versa.* There exists a positive relation between the total structure in the family and the levels of GEDM, PARM and also the levels of empowerment. On the other hand, when the family's asset structure increases, the respondents are highly distributed not only at low levels of GEDM, PARM and empowerment, but also at the high levels of GEDM, PARM and empowerment.

Earner–Dependent Ratio and Sex Ratio

It is noticed from Table 9 that two-third of the respondents have more dependents in their families and one-third of the respondents have fewer dependents. Amongst them more than half of them are at the low level of GEDM, PARM and thereby they are at the low level of empowerment. At the high level of empowerment, the respondents with the less dependents' families are spread at a higher rate, and almost the difference between the less dependents and more dependents is nil at the high level of PARM, whereas the difference is high at the high level of GEDM. Thus, it is found that the higher the dependents, the lower will be the level of empowerment, and the lower the dependents the higher will be the level of empowerment.

India is the second largest country in terms of female population. But one of the study areas (Salem) has the lowest sex ratio in Tamil Nadu due to female infanticide. A decline in the proportion of women in the population of many

Table 8

Distribution of the Respondents According to Levels of GEDM, PARM and Empowerment by the Levels of Property

	Categories	N	Levels of GEDM			Levels of PARM			Levels of Empowerment		
			Low	*Medium*	*High*	*Low*	*Medium*	*High*	*Low*	*Medium*	*High*
Total Assets Structure	Below Rs.50,000	74	51(36.7)	10(18.9)	13(27.1)	47(35.1)	16(32.6)	11(19.3)	41(39.4)	25(26.9)	8(18.6)
	Rs. 50000 - 200000	34	23(16.6)	7(13.2)	4(8.3)	21(15.7)	7(14.3)	6(10.5)	15(14.4)	15(16.1)	4(9.3)
	Rs. 200000 - 400000	34	21(15.1)	8(15.1)	5(10.4)	22(16.4)	4(8.2)	8(14.0)	16(15.4)	14(15.1)	4(9.3)
	Above Rs.400000	98	44(31.6)	28(52.8)	26(54.2)	44(32.8)	22(44.9)	32(56.2)	32(30.8)	39(41.9)	27(62.8)
	N	240	139(100)	53(100)	48(100)	134(100)	49(100)	57(100)	104(100)	93(100)	43(100)
Female Assets	Nil Property	18	13(9.3)	2(3.8)	3(6.3)	11(8.2)	4(8.2)	3(5.3)	9(8.7)	6(6.5)	3(7.0)
	Below Rs.100000	76	40(28.8)	20(37.7)	16(33.3)	36(26.9)	18(36.7)	22(38.6)	28(26.9)	31(33.3)	17(39.5)
	Above Rs.100000	146	86(61.9)	31(58.5)	29(60.4)	87(64.9)	27(55.1)	32(56.1)	67(64.4)	56(60.2)	23(53.5)
	N	240	139(100)	53(100)	48(100)	134(100)	49(100)	57(100)	104(100)	93(100)	43(100)

Source: Computed.

Figures in parentheses are percentage to column total.

N - Number of sample respondents, GEDM plus PARM equals Empowerment

Table 9

Distribution of the Respondents According to Levels of GEDM, PARM and Empowerment by E/D Ratio and sex Ratio

	Categories	N	Levels of GEDM			Levels of PARM			Levels of Empowerment		
			Low	Medium	High	Low	Medium	High	Low	Medium	High
E/D Ratio	Less Than One	80	43(30.9)	20(37.7)	17(35.4)	37(27.6)	15(30.6)	28(49.1)	29(27.9)	28(30.1)	23(53.5)
	More Than One	160	96(69.1)	33(62.3)	31(64.6)	97(72.4)	34(69.4)	29(50.9)	75(72.1)	65(69.9)	20(46.5)
	N	240	139(100)	53(100)	48(100)	134(100)	49(100)	57(100)	104(100)	93(100)	43(100)
Sex Ratio	Less Than One	146	89(64.0)	33(62.3)	24(50.0)	85(63.4)	29(59.2)	32(56.1)	66(63.5)	57(61.3)	23(53.5)
	More Than One	94	50(36.0)	20(37.7)	24(50.0)	49(36.6)	20(40.8)	25(43.9)	38(36.5)	36(38.7)	20(46.5)
	N	240	139(100)	53(100)	48(100)	134(100)	49(100)	57(100)	104(100)	93(100)	43(100)

Source: Computed.

Figures in parentheses are percentage to column total.

N - Number of sample respondents, GEDM plus PARM equals Empowerment

countries the world over has been witnessed over the years (Krishnaraj 2000; Das Gupta and Bhat 1997). This is especially so in societies with a strong cultural tradition of son preference [strong male preference]. This is common not only in India but also in other Asian societies-Japan, China, South Korea, etc. More than half of the respondent's families have a large number of male members which shows lowest sex ratio (less than one). Amongst them more than half of the respondents are at low level of GEDM and PARM and less than half of them are at the low level of empowerment. It is found that whatever be the sex ratio, they are equally spread at the high level of GEDM and the high level of PARM and empowerment is captured by the respondents whose families have more number of male members. Hence, it is observed that the sex ratio in the families determines the level of GEDM, PARM, and empowerment.

Income Earner and Control over Expenditure

It is observed from Table 10 that more than half of the respondent's families have male as well female income earners. It is surprising to note that when the income is earned by the female alone, no one is found at the high level of GEDM. When the income is earned by the male and female more than half of the respondents are in the low level of GEDM. Two-third of the respondents have male and female, income earners. It is found that when the income is earned by both male and female, they are highly spread not only at the high level of GEDM, PARM and empowerment, but also at the low level of GEDM, PARM and Empowerment.

It is observed that when the male alone controls the expenditure, they are highly distributed at the low level of GEDM, and hence they have the low level of empowerment. It is an interesting fact that when the expenditure is controlled by both male and female, the respondents are highly spread at the high level of GEDM, PARM and empowerment, and also at the low level of PARM and Empowerment. The income earner and the control over expenditure do not influence the levels of GEDM, PARM and empowerment.

Table 10
Distribution of the Respondents According to Levels of GEDM, PARM and Empowerment by Owner of Income and Expenditure

	Categories	N	Levels of GEDM			Levels of PARM			Levels of Empowerment		
			Low	*Medium*	*High*	*Low*	*Medium*	*High*	*Low*	*Medium*	*High*
Income Earner	MALE	96	58(41.7)	22(41.5)	16(33.3)	52(38.8)	20(40.8)	24(42.1)	43(41.4)	41(44.0)	12(27.9)
	FEMALE	12	10(7.2)	2(3.8)	-	1(0.7)	2(4.1)	9(15.8)	2(1.9)	2(2.2)	8(18.6)
	BOTH	132	71(51.1)	29(54.7)	32(66.7)	81(60.5)	27(55.1)	24(42.1)	59(56.7)	50(53.8)	23(53.5)
	N	240	139(100)	53(100)	48(100)	134(100)	49(100)	57(100)	104(100)	93(100)	43(100)
Control Over Expenditure	MALE	109	66(47.5)	25(47.2)	18(37.5)	62(46.3)	23(46.9)	24(42.1)	51(49.0)	46(49.5)	12(27.9)
	FEMALE	10	10(7.2)	-	-	1(0.7)	1(2.1)	8(14.0)	2(2.0)	1(1.0)	7(16.3)
	BOTH	121	63(45.3)	28(52.8)	30(62.5)	71(53.0)	25(51.0)	25(43.9)	51(49.0)	46(49.5)	24(55.8)
	N	240	139(100)	53(100)	48(100)	134(100)	49(100)	57(100)	104(100)	93(100)	43(100)

Source: Computed.
Figures in parentheses are percentage to column total.
N - Number of sample respondents, GEDM plus PARM equals Empowerment

Account Holder and Asset Holder

It is surprising to note that in Table 11, one-third of the respondents are at low level of GEDM, when the accounts are kept by the male alone, and thereby they are at the low levels of empowerment. Besides, when the accounts are kept by both male and female, two - thirds of the respondents are at high level of GEDM, and hence they are at the high level of empowerment. It is noted that even though the accounts are kept by both in the formal and informal institutions, one third of the respondents are at the low level of PARM. It is an interesting fact that when there is no account in the family, the respondents are in large numbers at the low level of empowerment. The respondents are highly spread at the high level of empowerment, when both have accounts in financial institutions [Private and public]. It is found that the respondents are highly distributed at the high level of GEDM, PARM and empowerment when the accounts are kept by both men and women in the financial institutions. When the saving accounts are kept by both male and female, GEDM in the family increases, and it leads to the raise of PARM and hence the empowerment of women will be achieved.

It is noted that when the asset holders are both male and female, the respondents are spread at the high levels and empowerment. The high level empowerment is due to high level of GEDM and PARM. When the assets are in the name of male alone, the respondents are highly distributed at the low level of empowerment. Since assets are in the name of male members the respondents have the low GEDM in the family and low PARM and hence the respondents are highly distributed at the low level of empowerment.

PERCEPTION ON EDUCATION, EMPLOYMENT AND EMPOWERMENT

When asked why education is needed, a vast majority of the respondents have opined that education is needed to get respect in the society. Very few respondents favour to bring equality irrespective of levels of GEDM, PARM and Empowerment. It is found (Table 12) that the majority of

Table 11

Distribution of the Respondents According to Levels of GEDM, PARM and Empowerment by Account Holder and Owner of Property

	Categories	N	Levels of GEDM			Levels of PARM			Levels of Empowerment		
			Low	*Medium*	*High*	*Low*	*Medium*	*High*	*Low*	*Medium*	*High*
Account Holder	NO ACCOUNT	40	35(25.2)	3(5.7)	2(4.1)	25(18.7)	7(14.3)	8(14.0)	27(26.0)	9(9.7)	4(9.3)
	MALE	59	43(30.9)	10(18.8)	6(12.5)	32(23.9)	13(26.5)	14(24.6)	29(27.9)	28(30.1)	2(4.7)
	FEMALE	57	31(22.3)	18(34.0)	8(16.7)	34(25.4)	11(22.5)	12(21.0)	23(22.1)	22(23.7)	12(27.9)
	BOTH	84	30(21.6)	22(41.5)	32(66.7)	43(32.0)	18(36.7)	23(40.4)	25(24.0)	34(36.5)	25(58.1)
	N	240	139(100)	53(100)	48(100)	134(100)	49(100)	57(100)	104(100)	93(100)	43(100)
Asset Holder	MALE	14	11(7.9)	3(5.7)	-	10(7.5)	3(6.1)	1(1.8)	9(8.7)	4(4.3)	1(2.3)
	FEMALE	57	34(24.5)	10(18.9)	13(27.1)	26(19.4)	12(24.5)	19(33.3)	18(17.3)	23(24.7)	16(37.2)
	BOTH	169	94(67.6)	40(75.4)	35(72.9)	98(73.1)	34(69.4)	37(64.9)	77(74.0)	66(71.0)	26(60.5)
	N	240	139(100)	53(100)	48(100)	134(100)	49(100)	57(100)	104(100)	93(100)	43(100)

Source: Computed.

Figures in parentheses are percentage to column total.

N - Number of sample respondents, GEDM plus PARM equals Empowerment

Table 12

Distribution of the Respondents According to Levels of GEDM, PARM and Empowerment by Views on Education and Employment

	Categories	N	Levels of GEDM			Levels of PARM			Levels of Empowerment		
			Low	Medium	High	Low	Medium	High	Low	Medium	High
Views on Education	To get respect	63	43(30.9)	10(18.9)	10(20.8)	31(23.1)	15(30.6)	17(29.8)	30(28.8)	22(23.7)	11(25.6)
	To get employment	44	25(18.0)	7(13.2)	12(25.0)	27(20.2)	8(16.3)	9(15.8)	21(20.2)	14(15.0)	9(20.9)
	To take decisions	33	20(14.4)	8(15.1)	5(10.4)	22(16.4)	4(8.2)	7(12.3)	17(16.4)	10(10.7)	6(13.9)
	To bring equality	49	27(19.4)	10(18.9)	12(25.0)	30(22.4)	12(24.5)	7(12.3)	20(19.2)	22(23.7)	7(16.3)
	To get knowledge	51	24(17.3)	18(33.9)	9(18.8)	24(17.9)	10(20.4)	17(29.8)	16(15.4)	25(26.9)	10(23.3)
	N	240	139(100)	53(100)	48(100)	134(100)	49(100)	57(100)	104(100)	93(100)	43(100)
Views on Employment	To support family	38	21(15.1)	9(17.0)	8(16.7)	21(15.7)	4(8.2)	13(22.8)	17(16.3)	11(11.8)	10(23.2)
	Financial Autonomy	69	44(31.7)	11(20.7)	14(29.2)	31(23.1)	19(38.8)	19(33.3)	29(27.9)	24(25.8)	16(37.2)
	To get respect	38	22(15.8)	11(20.7)	5(10.4)	24(17.9)	7(14.3)	7(12.3)	19(18.3)	16(17.2)	3(7.0)
	If necessary	75	40(28.8)	18(34.0)	17(35.4)	46(34.3)	16(32.6)	13(22.8)	29(27.9)	36(38.7)	10(23.3)

Source: Computed.

Figures in parentheses are percentage to column total.

N - Number of sample respondents, GEDM plus PARM equals Empowerment

respondents opine that employment is needed for financial autonomy. It is surprising to note that (Table 14) a vast majority of the respondents have stated that women empowerment has already been achieved but in the study only one sixth of the respondents are at the high level of Empowerment.

Reason for Not Employed, Not Educated and Lack Employment Status

When asked why they are employed (Table 15) a vast majority of the unemployed respondents have stated that they are not interested in taking employment irrespective of the level of GEDM, PARM and empowerment. At the high level of empowerment, the respondents do not have academic interest, and at the low level they have financial constraints. The reasons for employment are grouped as to support family, to save money, to kill leisure time and to earn livelihood (Table 13). When asked why they have opted for employment, half of the survey emphasize the importance of financial support for the family.

Criteria of Empowerment

While assessing (Table 14) the views on the criteria of empowerment with all levels of GEDM, PARM and Empowerment, their views are classified into three categories, (fully) namely 'fully', 'partially' and 'not at all'. If the respondents support all the criteria, they come under above 75 per cent categories. If they agree with more than half of the criteria (partially) they come under 50 to 75 per cent category, and if they do not agree with the criteria given (not at all) they come under below 50 per cent category. It is observed from Table 14 that three fourth of the respondents share the criteria of empowerment "partially" [The criteria of empowerment are T.V, magazine, education, employment property rights, marriage, type of family, etc.].

Home Violence

The reasons for home violence (Table 13) are grouped as drunkardness of men, insufficient money, ego problem,

Table 13

Distribution of the Respondents According to Levels of GEDM, PARM and Empowerment by the Reason For Home Violence and Employment

	Categories	*N*	*Levels of GEDM*			*Levels of PARM*			*Levels of Empowerment*		
			Low	*Medium*	*High*	*Low*	*Medium*	*High*	*Low*	*Medium*	*High*
Reason for Home Violence	Drunkard ness	33	19(13.7)	6(11.3)	8(16.7)	21(15.7)	5(10.2)	7(12.3)	15(14.4)	11(11.8)	7(16.3)
	Insufficient money	8	46(33.1)	21(39.6)	13(27.1)	48(35.8)	12(24.5)	20(35.1)	40(38.5)	29(31.2)	11(25.6)
	No violence	60	33(23.7)	13(24.5)	14(29.1)	28(20.9)	15(30.6)	17(29.8)	17(16.3)	28(30.1)	15(34.9)
	Ego	54	33(23.7)	12(22.7)	9(18.8)	28(20.9)	15(30.6)	11(19.3)	26(25.0)	20(21.5)	8(18.6)
	Dissatisfaction in household activities	13	8(5.8)	1(1.9)	4(8.3)	9(6.7)	2(4.1)	2(3.5)	6(5.8)	5(5.4)	2(4.6)
	N	240	139(100)	53(100)	48(100)	134(100)	49(100)	57(100)	104(100)	93(100)	43(100)
Reason for Employment	To support family	60	32(23.0)	15(28.3)	13(27.1)	36(26.9)	12(24.5)	12(21.1)	27(26.0)	22(23.7)	11(25.6)
	To kill leisure time	23	11(7.9)	4(7.6)	8(16.7)	11(8.2)	3(6.1)	9(15.8)	6(5.8)	8(8.6)	9(20.9)
	To save money	11	3(2.1)	4(7.6)	4(8.3)	5(3.7)	4(8.2)	2(3.5)	2(1.9)	7(7.5)	2(4.6)
	To earn livelihood	26	19(13.7)	3(5.6)	4(8.3)	15(11.2)	3(6.1)	8(14.0)	12(11.5)	7(7.5)	7(16.3)

Source: Computed.

Figures in parentheses are percentage to column total.

N - Number of sample respondents, GEDM plus PARM equals Empowerment

Table 14

Distribution of the Respondents According to Levels of GEDM, PARM and Empowerment by Levels of Awareness and Views on Empowerment

	Categories	N	Levels of GEDM			Levels of PARM			Levels of Empowerment		
			Low	Medium	High	Low	Medium	High	Low	Medium	High
Criteria of Empowerment	Below 50%	13	4(2.9)	5(9.4)	4(8.3)	5(3.7)	2(4.1)	6(10.5)	2(1.9)	7(7.5)	4(9.3)
	50 j 75 %	182	103(74.1)	43(81.2)	36(75.0)	97(72.4)	39(79.6)	46(80.7)	74(71.2)	74(79.6)	34(79.1)
	Above 75%	45	32(23.0)	5(9.4)	8(16.7)	32(23.9)	8(16.3)	5(8.8)	28(26.9)	12(12.9)	5(11.6)
	N	240	139(100)	53(100)	48(100)	134(100)	49(100)	57(100)	104(100)	93(100)	43(100)
Views on Employment	Yet to achieve more	46	27(19.4)	12(22.6)	7(14.6)	26(19.4)	9(18.4)	11(19.3)	22(21.2)	16(17.2)	8(18.6)
	Achieved already	58	31(22.3)	10(18.9)	17(35.4)	26(19.4)	10(20.4)	22(38.6)	18(17.3)	21(22.6)	19(44.2)
	No idea	41	25(18.0)	8(15.1)	8(16.7)	27(20.1)	6(12.2)	8(14.0)	20(19.2)	14(15.0)	7(16.3)
	If we get gender equality	46	26(18.7)	13(24.5)	7(14.6)	28(21.0)	11(22.5)	7(12.3)	21(20.2)	21(22.6)	4(9.3)
	Decision making	49	30(21.6)	10(18.9)	9(18.7)	27(20.1)	13(26.5)	9(15.8)	23(22.1)	21(22.6)	5(11.6)
	N	240	139(100)	53(100)	48(100)	134(100)	49(100)	57(100)	104(100)	93(100)	43(100)

Source: Computed.

Figures in parentheses are percentage to column total.

N - Number of sample respondents, GEDM plus PARM equals Empowerment

Table 15

Distribution of the Respondents According to Levels of GEDM, PARM and Empowerment by Reason for Unemployment and Non education

	Categories	N	Levels of GEDM			Levels of PARM			Levels of Empowerment		
			Low	Medium	High	Low	Medium	High	Low	Medium	High
Not Employed	Not interested	38	26(18.7)	4(7.6)	8(16.7)	22(16.4)	6(12.2)	10(17.5)	18(17.3)	13(14.0)	7(16.3)
	Problem of accessibility	36	23(16.5)	9(17.0)	4(8.3)	16(11.9)	13(26.5)	7(12.3)	15(14.4)	19(20.4)	2(4.7)
	situation not arrised	33	19(13.7)	9(17.0)	5(10.4)	21(15.7)	6(12.2)	6(10.5)	17(16.4)	12(12.9)	4(9.3)
	Not allowed	13	6(4.3)	5(9.4)	2(4.2)	8(6.0)	2(4.1)	3(5.3)	7(6.7)	5(5.4)	1(2.3)
	Employed	120	65(46.8)	26(49.0)	29(60.4)	67(50.0)	22(45.0)	31(54.4)	47(45.2)	44(47.3)	29(67.4)
	N	240	139(100)	53(100)	48(100)	134(100)	49(100)	57(100)	104(100)	93(100)	43(100)
Not Educated	Male preference	48	32(23.0)	8(15.1)	8(16.7)	27(20.2)	12(24.5)	9(15.8)	22(21.1)	21(22.6)	5(11.6)
	Financial constraint	71	46(33.1)	15(28.3)	10(20.8)	48(35.8)	11(22.5)	12(21.1)	34(32.7)	33(35.5)	4(9.3)
	Lack of interest	66	41(29.5)	15(28.3)	10(20.8)	43(32.1)	8(16.3)	15(26.3)	36(34.6)	19(20.4)	11(25.6)
	Lack of school facilities	15	7(5.0)	3(5.7)	5(10.4)	5(3.7)	5(10.2)	5(8.8)	4(3.9)	6(6.4)	5(11.6)
	Educated	40	13(9.4)	12(22.6)	15(31.3)	11(8.2)	13(26.5)	16(28.0)	8(7.7)	14(15.1)	18(41.9)
	N	240	139(100)	53(100)	48(100)	134(100)	49(100)	57(100)	104(100)	93(100)	43(100)

Source: Computed.

Figures in parentheses are percentage to column total.

N - Number of sample respondents, GEDM plus PARM equals Empowerment

dissatisfaction in household activities. Among the reasons, majority of the respondents at low levels of GEDM, PARM and empowerment opined that insufficient money in the family is the reason for home violence, whereas the majority of the respondents at the high levels of GEDM and empowerment respond to no violence in the family. Thus it is inferred that when there is insufficient money, there will be home violence and the respondents are at the low level. At the higher level, there is no home violence.

Summary of Chi-square Analysis

Chi-square is applied to verify whether there exists any association between GEDM and socio-economic variables, PARM and socio-economic variables, empowerment and socio-economic variables. The results of chi-square results (Table 16) are given in the following paragraphs:

Gender Equality in Decision Making (GEDM)

There is an association between female income and GEDM, Female expenditure and GEDM, female savings, total savings and GEDM, education and GEDM, total property control over of expenditure and GEDM and account holder and GEDM [The associations are significant].

There is no association between age and community and GEDM, type of household and GEDM, size of the household and GEDM, age difference and GEDM, the total income and GEDM, the total borrowings and GEDM, female borrowings and GEDM, total earners and GEDM, female earners and GEDM, total dependents and GEDM, female dependents and GEDM, occupation and GEDM, female property and GEDM, asset holder and GEDM, income earner and GEDM [The associations are not significant).

Power of Autonomy over Resources and Mobility (PARM)

There is an association between total income, female income and PARM, female expenditure and PARM, total saving and PARM, female saving and PARM, total borrowing and PARM,

Table 16
Summary of Chi-square Analysis

	GEDM			*PARM*			*Empowerment*		
Variables	*Chi square*	*P. Value*	*T* Cofficient*	*Chi square*	*P. Value*	*T Cofficient*	*Chi square*	*P. Value*	*T Cofficient*
Age	4.265	0.371	-	1.471	0.832	-	3.061	0.546	-
Community	9.085	0.169	-	4.581	0.591	-	5.921	0.432	-
Type of House Hold	0.150	0.928	-	0.693	0.707	-	0.499	0.779	-
Size of House Hold	2.889	0.577	-	1.826	0.768	-	1.303	0.861	-
Age difference	4.440	0.350	-	6.244	0.182	-	3.290	0.511	-
Total income	8.181	0.085	-	29.913	0.000	-	25.552	0.000	-
Female income	12.268	0.015	-	30.982	0.000	-	47.640	0.000	-
Total expenditure	8.062	0.089	-	12.326	0.015	-	14.650	0.005	-
Female expenditure	12.092	0.017	-	13.294	0.010	-	32.860	0.000	-
Total saving	22.812	0.000	0.22	9.269	0.055	-	29.976	0.000	0.12
Female saving	27.633	0.000	-	25.537	0.000	-	37.089	0.000	-
Total borrowing	9.508	0.147	0.13	15.651	0.016	0.16	16.774	0.010	0.17
Female borrowing	2.140	0.343	-	2.037	0.361	-	1.896	0.387	-
Total earners	1.569	0.456	-	2.752	0.253	-	1.474	0.478	-
Female earners	2.215	0.330	-	0.027	0.986	-	4.528	0.104	-
total dependents	1.542	0.463	0.07	0.955	0.620	0.05	0.075	0.963	-
Female dependents	3.690	0.450	0.10	6.612	0.158	0.14	1.944	0.746	-
Education	20,557	0.000	0.21	25:204	0.000	0.23	32.874	0.000	0.26
Occupation	2.885	0.261	-	0.949	0.622	-	6.463	0.039	-
Total Assets	13.391	0.037	0.15	11.337	0.079	0.14	14.584	0.024	0.16
Female Asset Structure	2.8116	0.589	0.08	3.576	0.466	0.09	2.605	0.626	0.07
Account holder	45.241	0.000	0.28	2.015	0.918	-	28.724	0.000	0.22
Asset holder	5.009	0.286	0.09	5.917	0.205	0.10	8.637	0.071	0.12
Income Earner	6.142	0.189	0.11	20.768	0.000	0.21	21.505	0.000	0.21
Control over expenditure	10.261	0.036	0.15	18.465	0.001	0.20	22.373	0.000	0.22

Source: Computed.
Figures in parentheses are percentage to column total.
N - Number of sample respondents, GEDM plus PARM equals Empowerment

education and PARM, income earner and PARM and control over of expenditure and PARM [The association is significant].

There is no association between age and PARM, Community and PARM, type of household, age difference and PARM, size of household and PARM, female borrowings and PARM, total earners and PARM, female earners and PARM, female dependents and PARM, occupation and PARM, total property and PARM, female property and PARM, account holder and PARM, asset holder and PARM [The associations are not significant].

Empowerment

There is an association between the total income and empowerment, female income and empowerment, total expenditure and empowerment, female expenditure and empowerment, total saving and empowerment, female saving and empowerment, total borrowing and empowerment, education, employment and empowerment, account holder and empowerment, income earner and empowerment, and total property control over of expenditure and empowerment [The associations are significant].

The insignificant chi-square result shows that there is no association between age and empowerment, community and empowerment, size of the household and empowerment, age difference and empowerment, female borrowings and empowerment, total earners and empowerment, female earners and empowerment, total dependents and empowerment, female dependents and empowerment, female property and empowerment.

Tschuprow's – Coefficient (T-coefficient)

The value of T-coefficient also shows that there exists association between the variables and the levels of GEDM, PARM and Empowerment. But it confirms that there exists a low association between the variables and the levels of GEDM, PARM and empowerment.

Key Findings

- Middle age population is more closely associated to high levels of empowerment.
- BC respondents are more empowered than other communities.
- Nuclear families have a positive influence on the levels of empowerment.
- Higher contribution of women to total family income and total family savings leads to higher levels of empowerment.
- The higher the levels of education, the higher the levels of empowerment.
- Employed women enjoy better status than unemployed women.
- When there is gender equality in keeping saving accounts in the formal and informal institution, there will be a high level of empowerment.
- When there is gender equality in acquisition of assets, there will be high level of empowerment.
- Education and employment are required in order to get respect in the society and reach financial autonomy.
- The views of unemployed respondents reflect mainly that they are not inclined to seek employment while the employed respondents take up employment in order to support their families.

The various findings listed above bring to light the complex nature of women empowerment, which is subject to various demographic, economic and social factors, besides the individual perception of the respondents. These empirical facts provide the rationale for promoting the study with a still greater precision. The researcher intends to accomplish this, in the succeeding three analytical chapters.

6

ANALYSIS OF GENDER EQUALITY IN DECISION MAKING

In setting the problem the introductory chapter observed the need for mainstreaming women, particularly the rural women, in view of various disadvantages they suffer from. Gender and gender relations in society define women's position and degree of empowerment. Unequal gender relations imply that men have and can exercise greater power than women in almost all spheres of functioning. They have culturally and often legally sanctioned power over women. Their greater control of and access to resources and information is facilitated by various societal institutions. Now this chapter analyses the issue of gender equality in decision-making relating the process to the levels of education and employment.

Decision-making is the process of empowering women. When a woman has Decision making power like her counter parts, then gender equality in the family is maintained. If gender equality in decision-making is established, she can gain power of autonomy over resources, leading her to achieve empowerment.

EDUCATION AND EMPLOYMENT-WISE ANALYSIS

Education and Employment are the means to achieve gender equality in decision making, as they increase the bargaining power of women. From common observation around one may be intrigued whether GEDM is absent among employed women. It is witnessed that often men accept the idea that their wives work, but they are not inclined to share housework, or childcare. However, more egalitarian relationships are perceived among stably married couples in which both members work and are better educated. These observations need empirical support to be validated. The precise question is to analyse whether GEDM varies with levels of Education and Employment Status and due to other various factors that influence the relationship.

Even at the outset, it is observed from Table 1 that GEDM varies at different levels of education and with employment status. However, it is surprising to note that employed respondents have more GEDM at lower levels of education than unemployed respondents; and lower GEDM at higher levels of education than unemployed respondents. The unemployed respondents have high degree of GEDM at higher levels of education and low level of GEDM at lower levels of education. But the level of GEDM varies at different levels of education of employed respondents. Precisely there exists positive relation between GEDM and education for unemployed respondents and this result does not sustain for employed respondents.

In spelling out the factors influencing GEDM, the researcher analyses her field data, in terms of age differences between spouses, community, type and size of family, income, saving and investment, besides asset structure. While each aspect is studied per se, conclusions emerge. Despite the fact that each result is important, they do not fully present the picture, as they host many interrelationships. Subsequently this necessitates a path analysis which follows next.

Age of the Respondents and Age Difference between Husband and Wife

Gender equality in decision-making differs according to the age of the respondents, educational levels and employment status and age difference between husband and wife. The higher the age of the respondents, the higher will be the GEDM. It is evident (Table 1) that among employed respondents, there exists high GEDM at lower levels of education. But among

Table 1
Score Values of GEDM According to Age, Levels of Education and Employment Status

Employment Status		*Unemployed (120)*				*Employed (120)*			
Age (Years)		*Below 25*	*25j 40*	*Above 40*	*Total*	*Below 25*	*25j 40*	*Above 40*	*Total*
Levels of Education									
Illiterates	N	11	2	7	20	1	11	8	20
	Min.	32	33	30	30	51	54	30	30
	Max.	51	54	51	54	45	66	64	66
	Mean	44.00	43.50	38.57	42.05	45.00	49.09	50.00	49.25
	C.V.	12.15	34.14	22.14	17.89	-	22.00	22.06	21.05
Primary	N	2	11	7	20	4	7	9	20
	Min.	45	26	41	26	40	28	44	28
	Max.	52	53	52	53	52	61	58	61
	Mean	48.50	41.55	48.29	44.60	47.25	48.29	50.91	49.65
	C.V.	10.21	21.46	7.91	17.33	10.84	23.91	8.35	15.36
Secondary	N	2	12	6	20	4	10	6	20
	Min.	45	30	41	30	25	41	44	25
	Max.	55	61	56	61	61	63	60	63
	Mean	50.00	47.75	46.5	47.60	48.50	51.10	51.83	50.80
	C.V.	14.14	17.77	11.44	15.26	33.69	11.54	10.87	16.29
High School	N	3	12	5	20	3	9	8	20
	Min.	30	43	58	30	36	44	39	36
	Max.	52	66	33	66	48	53	59	59
	Mean	42.67	49.92	51.8	49.30	42.33	48.50	50.91	48.90
	C.V.	26.65	13.25	8.89	14.66	14.24	6.74	14.01	13.35

Contd.

Higher Secondary	N	7	5	8	20	3	9	8	20
	Min.	41	43	38	38	38	37	35	35
	Max.	58	60	59	60	48	56	51	56
	Mean	49.86	50.20	48	49.20	42.67	47.44	42.13	44.60
	C.V.	11.55	12.71	14.90	12.68	11.80	14.61	14.44	14.79
Above Higher Secondary	N	4	6	10	20	2	11	7	20
	Min.	47	47	33	33	43	40	50	40
	Max.	58	67	60	67	52	63	61	63
	Mean	60.00	58.83	49	54.15	47.50	53.36	54.86	53.30
	C.V.	14.47	13.36	18.43	17.99	13.40	12.94	7.02	11.31

Source: Computed.

unemployed respondents higher age cohorts have obtained high GEDM at high school education. The unemployed respondents have obtained high GEDM when they belong to middle age group (25-40) at higher secondary level education. But younger age group and middle age group employed respondents have low GEDM. It is found that the employed respondents have GEDM at lower levels of education, when they fall under higher age group. But the unemployed respondents have high GEDM at higher levels of education irrespective of their age group.

Table 5 shows the relation between age difference and GEDM. Regarding the age difference between husband and wife, the unemployed respondents have high GEDM at the levels of high school and higher secondary education when they have lesser age difference with their spouses. When the age difference is high, the unemployed respondents have high GEDM at graduate level. Whereas the employed respondents have GEDM at the primary level, the age difference between husband and wife is below 5. When the age difference increases, they have high GEDM even if they are illiterates. With the higher age difference, the employed respondents have high GEDM at secondary education level. It is inferred that while there is higher age difference the unemployed respondents register a high GEDM at graduate level. When there is lower age difference, the employed respondents have high GEDM even at the primary level.

Community and GEDM

Higher caste people always have high level of GEDM and lower caste people have low level of GEDM. In the study, it is noted (Table 3) that the unemployed respondents belonging to OC have less GEDM and employed respondents belonging to OC have high GEDM at the primary level. It is surprising to note that the unemployed BC respondents have high GEDM at higher secondary education and employed BC respondents have high GEDM even if they are illiterates. On the contrary, the employed SC respondents have high GEDM at the graduate level and the unemployed SC respondents have high GEDM

Table 2

Score Values of GEDM According to Community, Levels of Education and Employment Status

Employment Status		*Unemployed (120)*					*Employed (120)*				
Community		*OC*	*BC*	*MBC*	*SC*	*Total*	*OC*	*BC*	*MBC*	*SC*	*Total*
Levels of Education											
Illiterates	N	3	5	8	4	20	6	6	7	1	20
	Min.	32	33	32	30	30	30	44	36	47	30
	Max.	51	49	51	54	54	66	64	59	47	66
	Mean	43	39.80	44.38	39.50	42.05	47.50	52.67	48.14	47.00	49.25
	C.V.	22.90	16.61	13.84	27.15	17.89	31.50	17.68	16.68	-	21.05
Primary	N	2	7	6	5	20	1	6	6	7	20
	Min.	49	26	38	41	26	54	28	44	40	28
	Max.	51	53	51	52	53	54	61	54	57	61
	Mean	50	41.43	45.00	46.40	44.60	54.00	48.83	48.50	50.71	49.65
	C.V	2.83	28.14	10.23	8.70	17.33	-	25.59	7.11	12.09	15.36
Secondary	N	1	6	8	5	20	3	6	8	3	20
	Min.	43	30	40	42	30	41	25	46	50	25
	Max.	43	55	56	61	61	49	63	61	58	63
	Mean	43	43.67	48.38	52.00	47.60	44.67	50.00	52.50	54.00	50.80
	C.V	-	21.56	9.94	12.97	15.26	9.05	26.17	10.43	7.41	16.29
High School	N	2	7	9	2	20	2	6	5	7	20
	Min.	46	43	30	52	30	44	39	42	36	36
	Max.	54	66	58	57	66	51	59	59	53	59
	Mean	50	50.71	46.89	54.50	49.30	47.50	51.83	49.40	46.43	48.90
	C.V	11.31	14.92	16.57	6.49	14.66	10.42	14.91	12.36	13.56	13.35

Contd.

Higher Secondary	N	4	9	6	1	20	2	5	7	6	20
	Min.	38	43	47	41	38	38	37	35	37	35
	Max.	59	60	56	41	60	51	51	56	56	56
	Mean	49.25	49.89	49.50	41.00	49.20	44.50	43.00	46.43	43.83	44.60
	C.V	17.57	13.68	7.53	-	12.68	20.66	14.43	14.33	17.16	14.79
Above Higher Secondary	N	5	8	3	4	20	3	4	12	1	20
	Min.	47	53	33	38	33	52	49	40	61	40
	Max.	67	67	60	47	67	61	63	60	61	63
	Mean	55.6	60.88	48.33	43.25	54.15	56.00	54.75	51.50	61.00	53.30
	C.V	13.91	8.44	28.69	8.93	17.99	8.18	11.39	17.75	-	11.31

Source: Computed.

Table 3
Score Values of GEDM According to Types of Family, Levels of Education and Employment Status

Employment Status		*Unemployed (120)*			*Employed (120)*		
Type of Family		*Joint*	*Nuclear*	*Total*	*Joint*	*Nuclear*	*Total*
Levels of Education							
Illiterates	N	6	14	20	5	15	20
	Min.	41	30	30	30	30	30
	Max.	54	49	54	64	66	66
	Mean	48.67	39.21	42.05	49.40	49.20	49.25
	C.V	9.43	17.24	17.89	25.59	20.34	21.05
Primary	N	1	19	20	7	13	20
	Min.	46	26	26	28	40	28
	Max.	46	53	53	58	61	61
	Mean	46.00	44.53	44.60	48.57	50.23	49.65
	C.V	-	7.82	17.33	22.49	11.15	15.36
Secondary	N	7	13	20	8	12	20
	Min.	30	38	30	25	41	25
	Max.	53	61	61	58	63	63
	Mean	44.86	49.08	47.60	48.63	52.25	50.80
	C.V	19.15	12.87	15.26	21.37	12.67	16.29
High School	N	5	15	20	7	13	20
	Min.	44	30	30	36	39	36
	Max.	66	58	66	54	59	59
	Mean	53.20	48.00	49.30	45.83	50.21	48.90
	C.V	19.14	13.59	14.66	11.55	12.79	13.35
Higher Secondary	N	5	15	20	3	17	20
	Min.	41	38	38	37	35	35
	Max.	51	60	60	56	56	56
	Mean	47.00	49.93	49.20	44.00	44.92	44.60
	C.V	7.96	13.66	12.68	15.02	15.22	14.79
Above Higher Secondary	N	5	15	20	3	17	20
	Min.	33	38	33	50	40	40
	Max.	67	67	67	61	63	63
	Mean	51.20	55.13	54.15	54.67	53.06	53.30
	C.V	26.15	15.54	17.99	10.40	11.72	11.31

Source: Computed.

at the high school level. It is inferred that the respondents belonging to SC and BC have high GEDM when compared with other communities irrespective of education and employment.

Type of Family and Size of Family and GEDM

Joint family system always affects GEDM in the family. Nuclear family will promote GEDM according to the bargaining power of women. Residence in non-nuclear families is likely to negatively affect women's ability to access resources directly and to exercise decision-making control (Dyson and Moore 1983; Dixon–Muller 1981). It is seen from the table that the respondents belonging to nuclear family have an opportunity to have higher GEDM than the respondents belonging to joint-family system. Table 4 reflects that the unemployed respondents from nuclear family have high GEDM at the higher education level whereas the employed respondents have high GEDM at the level of lower education. Another interesting fact is that the unemployed respondents who belong to joint family have a high GEDM at the high school level and the employed respondents from joint family have high GEDM even though they are illiterates.

Large size families affect gender equality and small sized families' favour gender equality. It is observed from Table 4 that the unemployed respondents belonging to small families have less GEDM and the employed respondents from large sized families have high GEDM at primary education when compared with the size of families. The unemployed respondents from small sized families have high GEDM at higher levels of education whereas the employed respondents have GEDM at lower levels with secondary school education. The employed respondents from medium sized families have high GEDM even at illiterate level and the unemployed respondents have low GEDM at high school and higher secondary education level. Compared to large sized families, small and medium sized families have high GEDM. It is noted that the unemployed respondents who belong to small and medium size families have high GEDM at higher levels of education, whereas the employed respondents have high GEDM at lower levels of education.

Income Status and GEDM

The total family income is one of the indicators of economic status of the family, which in turn decides the GEDM of women. Table 6 shows that when the total family income is low, the unemployed respondents have less GEDM, but employed illiterates have high GEDM. When the income increases, the GEDM also increases for unemployed

Table 4
Score Values of GEDM According to Size of Family, Levels of Education and Employment Status

Employment Status		*Unemployed (120)*				*Employed (120)*			
Size of Family		*Small*	*Medium*	*Large*	*Total*	*Small*	*Medium*	*Large*	*Total*
Levels of Education									
Illiterates	N	11	7	2	20	12	2	6	20
	Min.	30	49	33	30	30	56	30	30
	Max.	49	54	51	54	63	64	66	66
	Mean	39.82	45.57	42.00	42.05	49.25	60.00	45.67	49.25
	C.V.	16.69	16.27	30.30	17.89	18.65	9.43	27.23	21.05
Primary	N	11	4	5	20	9	9	2	20
	Min.	26	32	32	26	40	28	49	28
	Max.	51	53	52	53	55	61	58	61
	Mean	43.00	48.50	45.00	44.60	48.67	49.78	53.50	49.65
	C.V.	19.32	9.89	18.79	17.33	9.91	20.58	11.90	15.36
Secondary	N	9	7	4	20	10	5	5	20
	Min.	38	43	45	30	41	48	25	25
	Max.	61	55	53	61	63	56	58	63
	Mean	49.56	44.14	49.25	47.60	52.90	51.80	45.60	50.80
	C.V.	13.80	19.46	8.83	15.26	13.17	6.88	27.50	16.29
High School	N	9	5	6	20	7	6	7	20
	Min.	30	30	44	30	39	36	42	36
	Max.	58	66	54	66	59	59	54	59
	Mean	47.20	55.50	48.67	49.30	50.30	47.67	47.25	48.90
	C.V.	15.82	14.30	9.25	14.66	13.02	15.40	13.09	13.35

Contd.

Table 5

Score Values of GEDM According to Age Difference between Husband and Wife, Levels of Education, and Employment Status

Employment Status		*Unemployed (120)*				*Employed (120)*			
Age Difference (years)		*1-5*	*5-10*	*10-15*	*Total*	*1-5*	*5-10*	*10-15*	*Total*
Levels of Education									
Illiterates	N	1	10	9	20	5	6	9	20
	Min.	46	30	33	30	43	36	30	30
	Max.	46	49	54	54	55	64	66	66
	Mean	46.00	39.10	44.89	42.05	48.00	52.67	47.67	49.25
	C.V.	-	17.8	16.9	17.89	9.8	21.4	25.9	21.05
Primary	N	4	8	8	20	7	7	6	20
	Min.	38	32	26	26	48	40	28	28
	Max.	52	53	51	53	58	61	54	61
	Mean	47.00	45.75	42.25	44.60	52.57	50.29	45.50	49.65
	C.V.	14.1	15.1	21.8	17.33	8.1	16.1	20.5	15.36
Secondary	N	5	12	3	20	9	9	2	20
	Min.	30	41	38	30	25	41	61	25
	Max.	61	56	46	61	60	56	63	63
	Mean	49.00	48.58	41.33	47.60	49.56	49.56	62.00	50.80
	C.V.	23.7	10.6	10.1	15.26	20.7	9.6	2.3	16.29
High School	N	3	12	5	20	10	5	5	20
	Min.	30	44	43	30	36	39	42	36
	Max.	66	57	50	66	59	56	52	59
	Mean	51.33	49.67	47.20	49.30	49.70	49.20	47.00	48.90
	C.V.	36.80	8.8	5.9	14.66	15.6	13.0	9.3	13.35

Contd.

Higher Secondary	N	5	11	4	20	8	10	2	20
	Min.	44	38	47	38	37	35	46	35
	Max.	59	60	56	60	51	56	51	56
	Mean	52.20	47.36	50.50	49.20	45.25	43.30	48.50	44.60
	C.V.	12.3	13.9	8.0	12.68	10.9	18.7	7.3	14.79
Above Higher Secondary	N	8	10	2	20	6	8	6	20
	Min.	38	33	59	33	48	40	43	40
	Max.	67	67	64	67	61	63	60	63
	Mean	54.75	52.20	61.50	54.15	54.67	52.63	52.83	53.30
	C.V.	17.3	20.3	5.7	17.99	8.4	13.7	12.2	11.31

Source: Computed.

Table 6
Score Values of GEDM According to Total Income, Levels of Education and Employment Status

Employment Status		*Unemployed (120)*				*Employed (120)*			
Total Value of Income Levels (Rs.)		*Below 50000*	*50000 to 100000*	*Above 100000*	*Total*	*Below 50000*	*50000 to 100000*	*Above 100000*	*Total*
Levels of Education									
Illiterates	N	4	10	6	20	4	7	9	20
	Min.	32	32	30	30	30	43	30	30
	Max.	51	51	54	54	64	63	66	66
	Mean	39.75	43.10	41.83	42.05	50.50	48.57	49.22	49.25
	C.V.	22.63	15.25	21.67	17.89	29.75	14.31	23.45	21.05
Primary	N	5	9	6	20	4	9	7	20
	Min.	30	32	26	26	48	28	40	28
	Max.	49	52	53	53	54	58	61	61
	Mean	42.40	45.78	44.67	44.60	51.25	47.67	51.29	49.65
	C.V.	18.01	15.24	21.83	17.33	6.25	19.43	14.32	15.36
Secondary	N	3	12	5	20	11	1	8	20
	Min.	38	30	41	30	44	48	25	25
	Max.	53	61	53	61	61	48	63	63
	Mean	47.67	48.42	45.60	47.60	51.73	48.00	49.88	50.80
	C.V.	17.59	16.97	10.47	15.26	9.40	-	24.45	16.29
High School	N	6	9	5	20	6	8	6	20
	Min.	43	30	46	30	43	36	42	36
	Max.	66	54	57	66	59	53	59	59
	Mean	51.17	47.22	50.80	49.30	50.17	45.50	52.17	48.90
	C.V.	17.76	15.37	9.17	14.66	12.82	13.13	11.72	13.35

Contd.

Higher Secondary	N	4	11	5	20	5	8	7	20
	Min.	41	38	44	38	37	37	35	35
	Max.	51	60	59	60	56	56	51	56
	Mean	46.50	50.18	49.20	49.20	47.20	44.50	42.86	44.60
	C.V.	8.87	14.28	11.80	12.68	15.23	14.76	15.44	14.79
Above Higher Secondary	N	11	4	5	20	4	8	8	20
	Min.	33	43	45	33	43	40	51	40
	Max.	67	52	67	67	63	60	61	63
	Mean	55.64	47.25	56.40	54.15	54.00	50.88	55.38	53.30
	C.V.	19.45	7.80	16.61	17.99	17.76	12.00	5.71	11.31

Source: Computed.

respondents (higher secondary level) and not for employed respondents. When the total family income is high, the unemployed respondents have high GEDM at above higher secondary education level whereas the employed respondents have high GEDM at primary and high school level. Thus, it is seen that lower the total family income higher will be the GEDM for employed illiterates whereas higher the total income, higher will be the GEDM for unemployed respondents at above higher secondary education.

World Bank (1991) in its report observes that the increased participation of women in income earning activities would be the key to reducing gender inequality. It is interesting to note (Table 7.) that when female contribution to total income increases, the GEDM for unemployed respondents increases at higher education level. On the contrary when the level of income increases, the employed respondents have high GEDM up to high school education. It is clear that the higher the contribution, the higher will be GEDM among employed women. When there is nil earnings, GEDM is less among unemployed women.

It is also an interesting fact that (Table 8) when the male member of the family is the only earning member, GEDM is low among employed respondents, and it is high among unemployed respondents at high school level. Even though female is an income earner, they could not have high GEDM at all levels of education and employment status. When both male and female earn the income, the unemployed respondents have high GEDM at higher education level whereas the employed respondents have high GEDM at lower education level. Thus, it is inferred when income is earned by both male and female, there is high chance for GEDM in the family.

Level of Expenditure and GEDM

Total expenditure includes expenditure incurred by both male and female. From Table 9, it is noted that when the total expenditure in the family is below Rs.25, 000, the GEDM is less among unemployed respondents and high among employed respondents at secondary education level. When the

Table 7
Score Values of GEDM According to Female Income, Levels of Education and Employment Status

Employment Status		*Unemployed (120)*			*Employed (120)*		
Female Income (Rs.)		*No Earning*	*Upto 25,000*	*Total*	*Below 25,000*	*Above 25,000*	*Total*
Levels of Education							
Illiterates	N	6	14	20	5	15	20
	Min.	41	30	30	30	30	30
	Max.	54	49	54	64	66	66
	Mean	48.67	39.21	42.05	49.40	49.20	49.25
	C.V	9.43	17.24	17.89	25.59	20.34	21.05
Primary	N	1	19	20	7	13	20
	Min.	46	26	26	28	40	28
	Max.	46	53	53	58	61	61
	Mean	46.00	44.53	44.60	48.57	50.23	49.65
	C.V	-	7.82	17.33	22.49	11.15	15.36
Secondary	N	7	13	20	8	12	20
	Min.	30	38	30	25	41	25
	Max.	53	61	61	58	63	63
	Mean	44.86	49.08	47.60	48.63	52.25	50.80
	C.V	19.15	12.87	15.26	21.37	12.67	16.29
High School	N	5	15	20	7	13	20
	Min.	44	30	30	36	39	36
	Max.	66	58	66	54	59	59
	Mean	53.20	48.00	49.30	45.83	50.21	48.90
	C.V	19.14	13.59	14.66	11.55	12.79	13.35
Higher Secondary	N	5	15	20	3	17	20
	Min.	41	38	38	37	35	35
	Max.	51	60	60	56	56	56
	Mean	47.00	49.93	49.20	44.00	44.92	44.60
	C.V	7.96	13.66	12.68	15.02	15.22	14.79
Above Higher Secondary	N	5	15	20	3	17	20
	Min.	33	38	33	50	40	40
	Max.	67	67	67	61	63	63
	Mean	51.20	55.13	54.15	54.67	53.06	53.30
	C.V	26.15	15.54	17.99	10.40	11.72	11.31

Source: Computed.

level of expenditure increases, from Rs.25,000 to Rs.50,000, the unemployed respondents have high GEDM at higher secondary education, and employed respondents have less GEDM. When the level of expenditure is high (Above Rs.50,000), the unemployed respondents have high GEDM at higher levels of education, and the employed respondents at very low levels of education. The higher the level of expenditure, the higher will be GEDM among unemployed respondents at higher education level, and employed respondents at very low education level.

Table 8

Score Values of GEDM, According to Income Earner, Levels of Education and Employment Status

Employment Status		*Unemployed (120)**			*Employed (120)*			
Income Earner		*Male*	*Both*	*Total*	*Male*	*Female*	*Both*	*Total*
Levels of Education								
Illiterates	N	13	7	20	-	2	18	20
	Min.	32	30	30	-	43	30	30
	Max.	51	54	54	-	45	66	66
	Mean	42.38	41.43	42.05	-	44.00	49.83	49.25
	C.V.	17.59	19.80	17.89	-	3.21	21.65	21.05
Primary	N	15	5	20	-	3	17	20
	Min.	26	45	26	-	40	28	28
	Max.	53	52	53	-	54	61	61
	Mean	43.27	48.60	44.60	-	47.33	50.06	49.65
	C.V.	19.44	6.27	17.33	-	14.84	15.69	15.36
Secondary	N	15	5	20	1	3	16	20
	Min.	30	42	30	51	44	25	25
	Max.	56	61	61	51	51	63	63
	Mean	46.80	50.00	47.60	51.00	47.00	51.50	50.80
	C.V.	15.64	14.63	15.26	0.00	7.67	17.54	16.29
High School	N	15	5	20	-	2	18	20
	Min.	43	30	30	-	42	36	36
	Max.	66	54	66	-	49	59	59
	Mean	50.93	44.40	49.30	-	45.50	49.28	48.90
	C.V.	11.93	19.99	14.66	-	10.88	13.57	13.35

Contd.

Higher Secondary	N	19	1	20	-	1	19	20
	Min.	38	59	38	-	37	35	35
	Max.	60	59	60	-	37	56	56
	Mean	48.68	59.00	49.20	-	37.00	45.00	44.60
	C.V.	12.23	0.00	12.68	-	0.00	14.50	14.79
Above Higher Secondary	N	18	2	20	-	1	19	20
	Min.	33	53	33	-	43	40	40
	Max.	67	67	67	-	43	63	63
	Mean	53.50	60.00	54.15	-	43.00	53.84	53.30
	C.V.	18.29	16.50	17.99	-	0.00	10.53	11.31

Source: Computed.

Note: * In this category, women could not control over expenditure, since they are unemployed

Table 9

Score Values of GEDM, According to Total Expenditure of the Family, Levels of Education and Employment Status

Employment Status		*Unemployed (120)*				*Employed (120)*			
Total Expenditure (Rs.)		*Below 25,000*	*25,000 to 50,000*	*Above 50,000*	*Total*	*Below 25,000*	*25,000 to 50,000*	*Above 50,000*	*Total*
Levels of Education									
Illiterates	N	5	11	4	20	2	6	12	20
	Min.	32	30	33	30	30	44	30	30
	Max.	51	54	49	54	43	63	66	66
	Mean	38.60	43.55	42.25	42.05	36.50	49.50	51.25	49.25
	C.V.	21.25	17.41	16.55	17.89	25.18	14.38	21.46	21.05
Primary	N	4	9	7	20	3	13	4	20
	Min.	30	32	26	26	48	28	40	28
	Max.	48	52	53	53	57	58	61	61
	Mean	40.75	45.78	45.29	44.60	51.33	48.23	53.00	49.65
	C.V.	18.94	15.24	19.98	17.33	9.61	16.13	17.22	15.36
Secondary	N	4	14	2	20	6	4	10	20
	Min.	38	30	41	30	44	41	25	25
	Max.	53	61	45	61	61	58	63	63
	Mean	47.75	48.21	43.00	47.60	51.83	49.50	50.70	50.80
	C.V.	14.34	16.33	6.58	15.26	12.65	14.24	19.99	16.29
High School	N	3	9	8	20	6	9	5	20
	Min.	44	30	43	30	43	36	42	36
	Max.	50	57	66	66	59	59	56	59
	Mean	47.33	48.44	51.00	49.30	50.00	48.11	49.00	48.90
	C.V.	6.45	16.22	15.51	14.66	10.88	16.64	11.90	13.35

Contd.

Higher Secondary	N	2	10	8	20	4	9	7	20
	Min.	41	38	44	38	37	37	35	35
	Max.	52	60	59	60	51	56	56	56
	Mean	46.50	50.00	48.88	49.20	46.00	44.78	43.57	44.60
	C.V.	19.73	15.06	9.37	12.68	13.40	14.38	17.92	14.79
Above Higher Secondary	N	4	6	10	20	6	7	7	20
	Min.	33	43	38	33	43	40	51	40
	Max.	60	60	67	67	61	60	63	63
	Mean	48.25	52.67	57.40	54.15	51.17	51.57	56.86	53.30
	C.V.	23.77	13.03	17.56	17.99	12.45	12.51	7.21	11.31

Source: Computed.

Table 10 indicates the share of female income to the total expenditure. When the female share of female income to total expenditure increases, the GEDM increases at graduate level for the unemployed respondents and at secondary and high school level for the employed respondents. Even though female contribution to total expenditure is nil, the employed respondents have high GEDM at very low level of education. When the female contribution to the total expenditure is below Rs, 25000, the unemployed respondents have a high GEDM when compared with the employed respondents.

When male alone controls the expenditure, the employed respondents have high GEDM when compared with the unemployed respondents. When female alone controls the expenditure, the employed respondents have the high GEDM at the high school level education. It is interesting to note that (Table 11) when both male and female control the expenditure, the unemployed respondents have high GEDM at higher levels of education and employed respondents have high GEDM not only at the secondary level but also at the illiterate level.

Level of Savings and GEDM

It is observed from Table 14 that when the total savings of the family is low, the unemployed respondents have a high GEDM at higher secondary education levels. When the total saving is high, the unemployed respondents have high GEDM at higher level of education and employed respondents at lower levels of education. It is found (Table 15) that when the level of female saving is high the GEDM is also high at higher level of education for unemployed respondents and lower level of education for employed respondents.

It is surprising to note from Table 16 that when the account holders are male alone, the GEDM is less at all levels of education and employment status. When the female keeps the accounts, the unemployed respondents have a high GEDM at the higher secondary education. It is interesting to note that when the account is kept by both male and female, the unemployed respondents have a high GEDM at graduate level and employed respondents at the lower education level. Thus, it is found that when the accounts are kept by both, the GEDM

Table 10
Score Values of GEDM, According to Female Expenditure, Levels of Education and Employment Status

Employment Status		*Unemployed (120)*				*Employed (120)*			
Female Expenditure (Rs.)		*No Contribution*	*Below 25,000*	*Above 25,000*	*Total*	*No Contribution*	*Below 25,000*	*Above 25,000*	*Total*
Levels of Education									
Illiterates	N	14	6	-	20	4	12	4	20
	Min.	32	30	-	30	45	30	43	30
	Max.	51	54	-	54	60	66	64	66
	Mean	42.29	41.50	-	42.05	53.25	47.50	50.50	49.25
	CV	16.96	21.65	-	17.89	13.92	24.59	18.75	21.05
Primary	N	15	5	-	20	2	12	6	20
	Min.	26	45	-	26	50	40	28	28
	Max.	53	52	-	53	57	58	61	61
	Mean	43.27	48.60	-	44.60	53.50	50.25	47.17	49.65
	CV	19.44	6.27	-	17.33	9.25	10.87	24.74	15.36
Secondary	N	14	4	2	20	1	7	12	20
	Min.	30	42	48	30	49	25	49	25
	Max.	56	61	50	61	49	61	63	63
	Mean	46.57	50.50	49.00	47.60	49.00	46.14	53.67	50.80
	CV	16.19	16.53	2.89	15.26	-	25.69	8.04	16.29
High School	N	17	3	-	20	-	14	6	20
	Min.	43	30	-	30	-	36	49	36
	Max.	66	54	-	66	-	59	59	59
	Mean	50.24	44.00	-	49.30	-	46.50	54.50	48.90
	CV	12.00	28.39	-	14.66	-	13.01	6.64	13.35

Contd.

Higher Secondary	N	19	1	-	20	2	14	4	20
	Min.	38	59	-	38	51	35	37	35
	Max.	60	59	-	60	51	56	56	56
	Mean	48.68	59.00	-	49.20	51.00	43.14	46.50	44.60
	CV	12.23	-	-	12.68	-	14.08	18.46	14.79
Above Higher Secondary	N	19	-	1	20	1	12	7	20
	Min.	33	-	67	33	52	40	49	40
	Max.	67	-	67	67	52	61	63	63
	Mean	53.47	-	67.00	54.15	52.00	52.17	55.43	53.30
	CV	17.79	-	-	17.99	-	13.15	8.19	11.31

Source: Computed.

is promoted among unemployed respondents at graduate level and employed respondents, at the lower education level.

Level of Borrowing and GEDM

It is noted that (Table 12) when there is nil borrowing in the family, the employed respondents have high GEDM at above higher secondary education. When the borrowing is low, the unemployed respondents have high GEDM at the higher education level. When the total borrowing is high, the unemployed respondents have high GEDM at the high school level of education and employed respondents at the lower level of education. It is inferred that when the total borrowing is high, the unemployed respondents have a high GEDM at the middle school level and employed respondents at the lower education level (primary).

Regarding female borrowings, the converse exists (Table 16). When there is no borrowing, the unemployed respondents have high GEDM at the above higher secondary level, and the employed respondents at the very low level. When there are female borrowings, the employed respondents have a high GEDM at the middle school level, and unemployed respondents at the higher secondary level.

Asset Structure and GEDM

When the total asset structure in the family is low, the GEDM is low among the employed respondents and high among the unemployed respondents at the higher secondary education level. Table 17 presents the total asset structure of the family. When the level of property increases, the GEDM increases among the unemployed respondents at the high school level and above higher secondary level and not among employed respondents. When the total asset is high, the employed respondents have a high GEDM at the lower education level, and not among the unemployed respondents. It is an interesting fact that when the total asset is high, the employed respondents have a high GEDM at lower levels of education. When the asset is low, the unemployed respondents have a high GEDM at the higher secondary education level.

Table 11

Score Values of GEDM, According to Control Over Expenditure, Levels of Education and Employment Status

Employment Status		*Unemployed (120)*			*Employed (120)*			
Control over Expenditure		*Male*	*Both*	*Total*	*Male*	*Female*	*Both*	*Total*
Levels of Education								
Illiterates	N	14	6	20	4	2	14	20
	Min.	32	30	30	43	43	30	30
	Max.	51	54	54	60	45	66	66
	Mean	42.29	41.50	42.05	49.25	44.00	50.00	49.25
	CV	16.96	21.65	17.89	15.41	3.21	23.56	21.05
Primary	N	15	5	20	2	2	16	20
	Min.	26	45	26	50	40	28	28
	Max.	53	52	53	57	48	61	61
	Mean	43.27	48.60	44.60	53.50	44.00	49.88	49.65
	CV	19.44	6.27	17.33	9.25	12.86	15.99	15.36
Secondary	N	15	5	20	2	2	16	20
	Min.	30	42	30	49	44	25	25
	Max.	56	61	61	51	46	63	63
	Mean	46.80	50.00	47.60	50.00	45.00	51.63	50.80
	CV	15.64	14.63	15.26	2.83	3.14	17.45	16.29
High School	N	17	3	20	-	1	19	20
	Min.	43	30	30	-	49	36	36
	Max.	66	54	66	-	49	59	59
	Mean	50.24	44.00	49.30	-	49.00	48.89	48.90
	CV	12.00	28.39	14.66	-	-	13.72	13.35

Contd.

Higher Secondary	N	19	1	20	1	2	17	20
	Min.	38	59	38	51	37	35	35
	Max.	60	59	60	51	48	56	56
	Mean	48.68	59.00	49.20	51.00	42.50	44.47	44.60
	CV	12.23	-	12.68	-	18.30	15.05	14.79
Above Higher Secondary	N	19	1	20	1	1	18	20
	Min.	33	67	33	52	43	40	40
	Max.	67	67	67	52	43	63	63
	Mean	53.47	67.00	54.15	52.00	43.00	53.94	53.30
	CV	17.79	-	17.99	-	-	10.78	11.31

Source: Computed.

Note: * In this category, women could not control over expenditure, since they are unemployed

Higher Secondary	N	9	5	6	20	7	6	7	20
	Min.	43	48	44	38	37	35	37	35
	Max.	58	60	51	60	56	51	56	56
	Mean	50.00	50.00	47.33	49.20	43.00	44.17	46.57	44.60
	C.V.	11.62	20.25	5.12	12.68	16.77	13.39	15.02	14.79
Above Higher Secondary	N	12	4	4	20	12	5	3	20
	Min.	47	38	33	33	43	51	40	40
	Max.	67	67	64	67	60	61	63	63
	Mean	56.17	53.50	48.75	54.15	51.92	55.80	54.67	53.30
	C.V.	12.21	21.45	31.84	17.99	9.09	6.99	23.31	11.31

Source: Computed.

Table 12
Score Values of GEDM, According to Total Borrowing, Levels of Education and Employment Status

Employment Status		Unemployed (120)					Employed (120)				
Total Borrowing (Rs.)		No Borrowing	Below 10,000	10,000 to 50,000	Above 50,000	Total	No Borrowing	Below 10,000	10,000 to 50,000	Above 50,000	Total
Levels of Education											
Illiterates	N	3	8	6	3	20	9	3	6	2	20
	Min.	32	30	33	32	30	30	36	30	50	30
	Max.	51	49	54	51	54	66	50	63	64	66
	Mean	41.33	42.00	41.50	44.00	42.05	50.22	44.33	47.67	57.00	49.25
	CV	22.99	16.98	18.84	23.73	17.89	20.93	16.63	25.44	17.37	21.05
Primary	N	9	4	3	4	20	9	3	6	2	20
	Min.	26	43	41	45	26	40	40	28	52	28
	Max.	52	53	52	51	53	58	61	54	55	61
	Mean	40.89	48.25	48.00	46.75	44.60	50.00	51.50	45.20	53.67	49.65
	CV	23.76	8.52	12.67	6.14	17.33	12.42	18.25	22.20	2.85	15.36
Secondary	N	7	2	6	5	20	7	3	4	6	20
	Min.	41	48	30	38	30	25	-	41	49	25
	Max.	53	61	53	56	61	51	-	60	63	63
	Mean	47.14	54.50	45.67	47.80	47.60	44.86	-	52.25	54.78	50.80
	CV	11.05	16.87	18.46	17.53	15.26	20.33	-	16.57	8.65	16.29
High School	N	7	1	4	8	20	7	-	4	9	20
	Min.	43	52	30	44	30	39	43	36	44	36
	Max.	51	52	54	66	66	59	48	56	59	59
	Mean	47.43	52.00	46.50	52.00	49.30	49.50	46.33	48.00	50.67	48.90
	CV	6.31	0	23.92	15.35	14.66	13.84	6.23	17.76	15.07	13.35

Contd.

Higher Secondary	N	11	4	1	4	20	4	8	5	3	20
	Min.	41	56	48	38	38	37	37	35	38	35
	Max.	58	60	48	51	60	51	56	46	56	56
	Mean	47.18	58.25	48.00	46.00	49.20	46.50	45.88	40.60	45.33	44.60
	CV	9.98	2.93	0	12.17	12.68	14.21	14.80	11.37	20.85	14.79
Above Higher Secondary	N	10	1	5	4	20	9	5	5	1	20
	Min.	38	47	43	33	33	50	40	43	49	40
	Max.	65	47	67	67	67	63	61	56	49	63
	Mean	55.30	47.00	54.00	53.25	54.15	55.78	53.20	49.80	49.00	53.30
	CV	16.24	0	17.95	27.27	17.99	7.54	16.89	9.57	0	11.31

Source: Computed.

Table 13
Score Values of GEDM, According to Female Borrowing, Levels of Education and Employment Status

Employment Status		*Unemployed (120)*			*Employed (120)*		
Female Borrowing		*No Borrowing*	*Borrowing*	*Total*	*No Borrowing*	*Borrowing*	*Total*
Levels of Education							
Illiterates	N	15	5	20	15	5	20
	Min.	32	30	30	30	30	30
	Max.	54	47	54	66	60	66
	Mean	43.13	38.80	42.05	50.93	44.20	49.25
	CV	17.57	18.26	17.89	19.06	26.60	21.05
Primary	N	17	3	20	15	5	20
	Min.	26	41	26	40	28	28
	Max.	52	53	53	58	61	61
	Mean	43.94	48.33	44.60	50.13	48.20	49.65
	CV	18.02	13.30	17.33	11.13	26.54	15.36
Secondary	N	16	4	20	10	10	20
	Min.	30	46	30	25	41	25
	Max.	61	53	61	63	61	63
	Mean	47.19	49.25	47.60	48.60	53.00	50.80
	CV	16.98	6.06	15.26	20.28	11.43	16.29
High School	N	17	3	20	17	3	20
	Min.	43	30	30	36	49	36
	Max.	66	52	66	59	59	59
	Mean	50.12	44.67	49.30	47.88	54.67	48.90
	CV	12.16	28.44	14.66	13.21	9.39	13.35
Higher Secondary	N	17	3	20	13	7	20
	Min.	38	47	38	37	35	35
	Max.	60	59	60	56	56	56
	Mean	48.35	54.00	49.20	44.31	45.14	44.60
	CV	12.45	11.56	12.68	14.34	16.65	14.79
Above Highei Secondary	N	16	4	20	14	6	20
	Min.	33	47	33	48	40	40
	Max.	67	60	67	63	61	63
	Mean	54.75	51.75	54.15	54.71	50.00	53.30
	CV	19.21	11.95	17.99	8.37	16.10	11.31

Source: Computed.

Table 18 reveals that when the female asset is high, the employed respondents have a high GEDM at the very low level of education. When there is no female asset, the unemployed respondents have a high GEDM at the higher secondary education level. When the female asset increases, the unemployed respondents have a high GEDM at the above higher secondary education level and the employed respondents at the secondary level education level. Thus, it is found that the unemployed respondents have a high GEDM

Table 14

Score Values of GEDM, According to Total Saving, Levels of Education and Employment Status

Employment Status		Unemployed (120)				Employed (120)			
Total Savings (Rs.)		No Saving	Below 25,000	Above 25,000	Total	No Saving	Below 25,000	Above 25,000	Total
Levels of Education									
Illiterates	N	6	12	2	20	3	8	9	20
	Min.	32	30	43	30	30	30	43	30
	Max.	49	54	51	54	63	66	64	66
	Mean	39.00	42.75	47.00	42.05	46.67	47.13	52.00	49.25
	CV	20.38	17.51	12.04	17.89	35.36	23.83	15.05	21.05
Primary	N	3	10	7	20	3	9	8	20
	Min.	41	30	26	26	28	40	44	28
	Max.	48	53	52	53	48	57	61	61
	Mean	44.00	46.00	42.86	44.60	38.67	49.89	53.50	49.65
	CV	8.19	18.07	20.09	17.33	26.03	10.91	9.58	15.36
Secondary	N	3	15	2	20	3	9	8	20
	Min.	30	40	38	30	25	48	41	25
	Max.	55	61	47	61	46	58	63	63
	Mean	45.67	48.67	42.50	47.60	38.33	53.00	53.00	50.80
	CV	29.89	12.39	14.97	15.26	30.24	13.34	10.51	16.29
High School	N	2	10	8	20	3	2	15	20
	Min.	30	44	43	30	36	39	42	36
	Max.	52	57	66	66	46	54	59	59
	Mean	41.00	49.20	51.50	49.30	41.67	47.83	51.45	48.90
	CV	37.94	7.71	15.46	14.66	12.32	12.78	11.24	13.35

Contd.

Higher Secondary	N	3	13	4	20	7	7	6	20
	Min.	41	38	47	38	37	35	37	35
	Max.	60	59	49	60	49	56	56	56
	Mean	48.00	50.00	47.50	49.20	42.00	44.29	48.00	44.60
	CV	21.75	12.83	2.11	12.68	12.14	16.11	14.67	14.79
Above Higher Secondary	N	-	6	14	20	2	9	9	20
	Min.	-	43	33	33	43	40	49	40
	Max.	-	53	67	67	48	61	63	63
	Mean	-	48.83	56.43	54.15	45.50	54.56	53.78	53.30
	CV	-	7.82	18.96	17.99	7.77	12.67	8.25	11.31

Source: Computed.

Table 15

Score Values of GEDM, According to Female Savings, Levels of Education and Employment Status

Employment Status		*Unemployed (120)*				*Employed (120)*			
Female Savings (Rs.)		*No Saving*	*Below 25,000*	*Above 25,000*	*Total*	*No Saving*	*Below 25,000*	*Above 25,000*	*Total*
Levels of Education									
Illiterates	N	11	8	1	20	6	10	4	20
	Min.	32	30	51	30	30	44	43	30
	Max.	51	54	51	54	63	66	64	66
	Mean	39.45	44.50	51.00	42.05	42.67	53.00	49.75	49.25
	CV	18.39	15.80	-	17.89	30.58	13.98	19.92	21.05
Primary	N	11	8	1	20	5	14	1	20
	Min.	26	45	49	26	28	40	54	28
	Max.	51	53	49	53	57	61	54	61
	Mean	40.91	49.13	49.00	44.60	44.40	51.21	54.00	49.65
	CV	20.78	6.83	-	17.33	24.70	11.26	-	15.36
Secondary	N	9	9	2	20	5	3	12	20
	Min.	30	42	38	30	25	58	49	25
	Max.	56	61	45	61	48	63	61	63
	Mean	45.67	50.89	41.50	47.60	40.80	60.33	52.58	50.80
	CV	18.06	10.51	11.93	15.26	22.56	4.17	6.76	16.29
High School	N	9	8	3	20	5	9	6	20
	Min.	30	44	43	30	36	42	49	36
	Max.	58	57	66	66	46	59	59	59
	Mean	48.44	49.25	52.00	49.30	41.20	49.78	54.00	48.90
	CV	16.13	10.11	23.63	14.66	9.31	10.43	7.22	13.35

Contd.

Higher Secondary	N	15	4	1	20	9	7	4	20
	Min.	38	47	47	38	37	35	37	35
	Max.	60	59	47	60	49	56	51	56
	Mean	48.27	53.25	47.00	49.20	42.11	46.14	47.50	44.60
	CV	12.90	11.51	0.00	12.68	11.78	17.18	14.74	14.79
Above Higher Secondary	N	5	8	7	20	7	8	5	20
	Min.	43	38	33	33	40	48	49	40
	Max.	52	67	67	67	61	61	63	63
	Mean	47.60	56.00	56.71	54.15	50.00	54.88	55.40	53.30
	CV	8.08	17.86	19.78	17.99	14.70	8.00	9.60	11.31

Source: Computed.

Table 16
Score Values of GEDM, According to Account Holder, Levels of Education and Employment Status

Employment Status		Unemployed (120)					Employed (120)				
Account Holder		No Account	Male	Female	Both	Total	No Account	Male	Female	Both	Total
Levels of Education											
Illiterates	N	6	5	6	3	20	3	3	5	9	20
	Min.	32	33	41	30	30	30	30	43	43	30
	Max.	49	51	54	51	54	63	50	56	66	66
	Mean	39.00	40.00	47.17	41.33	42.05	46.67	38.67	48.60	54.00	49.25
	CV	20.38	18.03	9.04	25.64	17.89	35.36	26.54	10.35	16.36	21.05
Primary	N	4	8	3	5	20	3	2	5	10	20
	Min.	41	26	51	45	26	28	49	40	44	28
	Max.	48	51	53	52	53	48	57	49	61	61
	Mean	44.00	40.38	52.00	47.40	44.60	38.67	53.00	46.40	53.90	49.65
	CV	6.69	25.15	1.92	6.43	17.33	26.03	10.67	8.15	8.63	15.36
Secondary	N	3	7	6	4	20	3	2	6	9	20
	Min.	30	40	46	38	30	25	41	49	49	25
	Max.	55	56	61	53	61	46	48	58	63	63
	Mean	45.67	45.57	51.67	46.50	47.60	38.33	44..50	51.67	55.78	50.80
	CV	29.89	11.74	10.14	16.52	15.26	30.24	11.12	6.20	8.59	16.29
High School	N	2	7	6	5	20	4	2	7	7	20
	Min.	30	44	44	43	30	36	39	42	44	36
	Max.	52	58	54	66	66	48	42	59	59	59
	Mean	41.00	50.57	48.50	51.80	49.30	43.25	40.50	51.00	52.43	48.90
	CV	37.94	8.22	9.20	18.39	14.66	12.14	5.24	10.31	10.14	13.35

Contd.

Higher Secondary	N	3	11	2	4	20	7	2	6	5	20
	Min.	41	38	58	47	38	37	38	37	35	35
	Max.	60	56	59	58	60	49	47	56	56	56
	Mean	48.00	47.45	58.50	50.25	49.20	42.00	42.50	45.67	47.80	44.60
	CV	21.75	9.95	1.21	10.45	12.68	12.14	14.97	15.83	16.70	14.79
Above Higher Secondary	N	-	5	2	13	20	2	5	3	10	20
	Min.	-	43	47	33	33	43	40	53	48	40
	Max.	-	52	53	67	67	48	61	61	63	63
	Mean	-	47.60	50.00	57.31	54.15	45.50	51.80	56.00	54.80	53.30
	CV	-	8.08	8.49	18.49	17.99	7.77	15.41	7.78	8.76	11.31

Source: Computed.

Table 17

Score Values of GEDM, According to Total Asset Structure, Levels of Education and Employment Status

Employment Status		*Unemployed (120)*					*Employed (120)*				
Total Asset (Rs.)		*Below 50,000*	*50,000 to 200,000*	*200,000 to 400,000*	*Above 400,000*	*Total*	*Below 50,000*	*50,000 to 200,000*	*200,000 to 400,000*	*Above 400,000*	*Total*
Levels of Education											
Illiterates	N	4	3	7	6	20	9	1	-	10	20
	Min.	32	33	30	43	30	30	43	-	43	30
	Max.	46	47	51	54	54	56	43	-	66	66
	Mean	38.00	40.33	39.57	48.50	42.05	43.11	43.00	-	55.40	49.25
	CV	17.59	17.41	20.68	7.91	17.89	21.31	-	-	14.87	21.05
Primary	N	6	4	3	7	20	10	2	2	6	20
	Min.	30	38	44	26	26	28	49	44	52	28
	Max.	51	53	51	52	53	57	50	58	61	61
	Mean	40.83	45.75	48.67	45.43	44.60	46.20	49.50	51.00	55.00	49.65
	CV	20.63	13.40	8.30	19.89	17.33	18.59	1.43	19.41	5.63	15.36
Secondary	N	7	2	2	9	20	2	3	2	13	20
	Min.	30	48	42	38	30	25	50	46	41	25
	Max.	61	53	47	56	61	44	58	48	63	63
	Mean	48.71	50.50	44.50	46.78	47.60	34.50	53.00	47.00	53.38	50.80
	CV	19.68	7.00	7.95	14.65	15.26	38.94	8.22	3.01	11.07	16.29
High School	N	3	4	3	10	20	5	5	1	9	20
	Min.	51	44	48	30	30	36	46	42	39	36
	Max.	52	54	57	66	66	59	53	42	59	59
	Mean	51.67	49.25	53.00	47.50	49.30	46.20	48.80	42.00	51.22	48.90
	CV	1.12	8.35	8.65	19.95	14.66	19.32	5.30	-	12.57	13.35

Contd.

Higher Secondary	N	7	3	5	5	20	14	-	3	3	20
	Min.	41	43	38	44	38	35	-	42	46	35
	Max.	60	59	51	48	60	56	-	51	56	56
	Mean	52.00	51.33	46.80	46.40	49.20	42.71	-	47.00	51.00	44.60
	CV	14.94	15.62	10.83	3.27	12.68	15.16	-	9.75	9.80	14.79
Above Higher Secondary	N	-	3	3	14	20	7	4	3	6	20
	Min.	-	43	47	33	33	40	48	51	49	40
	Max.	-	51	64	67	67	61	61	56	63	63
	Mean	-	47.00	57.00	55.07	54.15	52.00	53.50	54.00	54.33	53.30
	CV	-	8.51	15.59	19.00	17.99	15.70	12.26	4.90	9.29	11.31

Source: Computed.

Table 18

Score Values of GEDM, According to Female Asset Structure, Levels of Education and Employment Status

Employment Status		*Unemployed (120)*				*Employed (120)*			
Female Asset (Rs.)		*No Property*	*50,000 to 100000*	*Above 100000*	*Total*	*No Property*	*50,000 to 100000*	*Above 100000*	*Total*
Levels of Education									
Illiterates	N	2	5	13	20	4	6	10	20
	Min.	32	32	30	30	30	30	44	30
	Max.	34	51	54	54	63	64	66	66
	Mean	33.00	41.00	43.85	42.05	44.75	45.83	53.10	49.25
	C.V.	4.29	21.47	15.46	17.89	33.01	24.19	13.65	21.05
Primary	N	-	9	11	20	-	7	13	20
	Min.	-	26	30	26	-	28	40	28
	Max.	-	52	53	53	-	55	61	61
	Mean	-	45.22	44.09	44.60	-	46.71	51.23	49.65
	C.V.	-	17.89	17.64	17.33	-	19.37	12.85	15.36
Secondary	N	-	7	13	20	4	6	10	20
	Min.	-	42	30	30	25	49	44	25
	Max.	-	56	61	61	51	60	63	63
	Mean	-	50.00	46.31	47.60	40.75	54.17	52.80	50.80
	C.V.	-	10.26	17.44	15.26	27.65	7.14	11.53	16.29
High School	N	-	5	15	20	1	6	13	20
	Min.	-	43	30	30	42	42	36	36
	Max.	-	57	66	66	42	57	59	59
	Mean	-	48.60	49.53	49.30	42.00	48.50	49.62	48.90
	C.V.	-	12.05	15.75	14.66	-	12.00	14.07	13.35

Contd.

Higher Secondary	N	1	7	12	20	3	4	13	20
	Min.	52	41	38	38	37	37	35	35
	Max.	52	60	59	60	49	48	56	56
	Mean	52.00	49.57	48.75	49.20	41.33	41.00	46.46	44.60
	C.V.	-	14.59	12.59	12.68	16.11	12.11	14.37	14.79
Above Higher Secondary	N	3	6	11	20	-	8	12	20
	Min.	47	53	33	33	-	43	40	40
	Max.	64	65	67	67	-	61	63	63
	Mean	58.33	58.67	50.55	54.15	-	54.63	52.42	53.30
	C.V.	16.83	7.60	21.61	17.99	-	10.85	11.80	11.31

Source: Computed.

even though the female asset is nil, and when the female asset is high, the employed respondents have a high GEDM at various levels of education.

It is observed from Table 19 that when the total assets are in the name of male alone, the unemployed respondents have a high GEDM at the higher secondary education level, and when the assets are in the name of female alone, the unemployed respondents have high GEDM at the high school and higher secondary level of education. On the contrary when the assets are kept by both male and female together, the employed respondents have a high GEDM up to the high school education level. Thus, it is found that when the assets are kept by both male and female jointly, employed respondents will get high GEDM up to the high school education level.

INTEGRATED APPROACH TO GENDER EQUALITY IN DECISION - MAKING: PATH ANALYSIS

The foregoing results have brought to focus the relationship between some variables taken independently and GEDM. Despite the direction they show, to assess and understand the relationship, one can gain integrated view, only when the analysis is extended to the next level. However, the gender equality in decision-making in terms of various independent variables is analyzed using the model of stepwise regression. It indicates that out of eighteen independent variables, only six variables are found to be statistically significant in determining factors on gender equality in decision-making.

The six significant variables in determining the gender equality in decision making are *total years of schooling in the family, age difference between husband and wife, account holder, levels of education, employment status and proportion of asset structure.* The co-efficient of adjusted multiple determination ($\overline{R}^2$), through regression analysis, indicates 0.28. It means that out of 100 per cent variation in the gender equality in the decision making of the respondents, about 28 per cent of variation is explained by the specified six independent

Table 19
Score Values of GEDM, According to Asset Holder, Levels of Education and Employment Status

Employment Status		*Unemployed (120)**				*Employed (120)*			
Asset Holder		*Male*	*Female*	*Both*	*Total*	*Male*	*Female*	*Both*	*Total*
Levels of Education									
Illiterates	N	3	1	16	20	3	6	11	20
	Min.	32	49	30	30	30	30	43	30
	Max.	51	49	54	54	50	63	66	66
	Mean	39.00	49.00	42.19	42.05	38.67	47.83	52.91	49.25
	CV	26.77	-	17.10	17.89	26.54	24.82	15.01	21.05
Primary	N	-	8	12	20	-	7	13	20
	Min.	-	32	26	26	-	28	40	28
	Max.	-	52	53	53	-	57	61	61
	Mean	-	43.38	45.42	44.60	-	46.43	51.38	49.65
	CV	-	14.89	19.04	17.33	-	21.78	10.94	15.36
Secondary	N	-	5	15	20	3	4	13	20
	Min.	-	46	30	30	25	44	48	25
	Max.	-	53	61	61	51	51	63	63
	Mean	-	50.00	46.80	47.60	39.00	47.75	54.46	50.80
	CV	-	6.48	17.34	15.26	33.63	6.92	9.11	16.29
High School	N	-	2	18	20	4	5	11	20
	Min.	-	52	30	30	-	36	39	36
	Max.	-	52	66	66	-	59	59	59
	Mean	-	52.00	49.00	49.30	-	46.67	49.86	48.90
	CV	-	-	15.46	14.66	-	17.29	11.69	13.35

Contd.

Higher Secondary	N	1	4	15	20	-	5	15	20
	Min.	52	41	38	38	37	37	35	35
	Max.	52	60	59	60	49	56	56	56
	Mean	52.00	51.25	48.47	49.20	40.50	45.80	45.55	44.60
	CV	-	17.98	11.72	12.68	14.04	16.73	14.07	14.79
Above Higher Secondary	N	-	4	16	20	-	5	15	20
	Min.	-	47	33	33	-	43	40	40
	Max.	-	64[	67	67	-	61	63	63
	Mean	-	55.75	53.75	54.15	-	54.00	53.07	53.30
	CV	-	13.77	19.29	17.99	-	15.04	10.36	11.31

Source: Computed.

variables. The balance 72 per cent is attributed to "other factors" which are not included in the given analysis. The 'F' test based on $\overline{R}^2$ indicates 15.91, which is found to be statistically significant at 5 per cent level with 6,233 degrees of freedom. It implies that all the selected six independent variables are statistically significant to justify the selection of this model and suitable to verify the parameters of the general population.

Table 6.a
Stepwise Regression Analysis of Explanatory Variables with Gender Equality in Decision-Making Index as Dependent Variable

Explanatory Variables	*Regression Co-efficient* ($\hat{B}$)	*'t' value*	*p value*
Total years of schooling in the family	0.15	2.57*	0.011
Age difference between husband and wife	-0.09	-1.77*	0.078
Account holder	0.42	7.35*	0.000
Levels of Education	0.27	2.29*	0.023
Employment Status	-0.23	-1.95*	0.052
Proportion of female asset	0.05	2.04*	0.042
($\overline{R}^2$) = 0.28; df = 6.233;	'F' value = 15.91		0.000

df – degrees of freedom.
Source: Computed.

It is observed from the results of regression co-efficient and 't' values based on standardized regression co-efficient, the factors like total years of schooling in the family, age difference between husband and wife, account holder, levels of education, employment status and proportion of female asset structure, are found to be statistically significant in deciding about GEDM.

Four out of six explanatory variables, namely total years of schooling in the family, account holder, levels of education and proportion of female asset structure, have positive influence on GEDM, and have direct relationship with the GEDM. In other words, when the total family literacy increases, the effect of GEDM also increases, since the coefficient of effect is given as 0.15. This could be argued as the total family literacy rises; obviously one could see that there exists gender equality at the household level. Similarly, the factor account holder has positive direct effect on GEDM which indicates that when both men and women maintain the accounts, GEDM is assured. If the value of account holder is negative, it reflects that GEDM is not prevailing in the family. It is reasoned out that when the accounts are maintained by both, irrespective of gender, they will have financial autonomy which enhances their decision making power without discrimination.

Education also has significant positive effect on GEDM. This indicates that the levels of education of the respondents and gender equality in the decision–making move together. When the level of education increases, the bargaining power of women also increases which leads to decision-making power of women equally with their counterparts. The variable, namely the proportion of the female asset, has a significant positive direct effect on GEDM. It is obvious that when the contribution of female assets in the family increases, they will have control over resources and it enhances their decision-making power, and it brings the gender equality. When women command assets, their status and bargaining position is improved, and financial assets being new, they are not bound by the convention which often restrict the major real assets, land and lives of male ownership (Agarwal 2001).

It is an interesting fact that the factor age difference between husband and wife has a significant inverse direct effect on GEDM. The high age and educational difference between the husband and wife can put the wife at a relative disadvantage with regard to her ability to exercise power within the marriage. (Kishore and Gupta 2004). When the difference between husband and wife is higher, the gender equality in the decision-making at the household level decreases and is skewed for men. The employment status has a significantly negative direct effect on GEDM to the tune of 0.23. It means that if the level of female employment increases, the GEDM at the household level decreases. The evidences from the present study show that the patriarchy system prevails in the society, the employed women are engaged in informal sector and their contribution to the family income is very low. This makes an indirect relation between employment status and the GEDM.

It is observed from the path analysis (Fig.1 & Table 6.b) that the employment status of women has positive indirect effect (0.33) as against negative direct effect (-0.23) caused by levels of education (0.24), proportion of female assets (0.03), and account holder (0.06) and the indirect effect is low by proportion of female assets (0.04) as against positive direct effect (0.05). The employment status of women has negative influence on all the factors such as total years of schooling in the family, age difference between husband and wife, account holder, levels of education and proportion of female assets.

On the whole, the effect of explanatory factors on GEDM, the independent factor namely the account holder exerts a higher contribution to the tune of 0.42, followed by the levels of education (0.27), total years of schooling (0.15), proportion of female asset structure(0.05),age difference between husband and wife(-0.09) and employment status(-0.25). The direct and indirect effects and their relationships in terms of positive and negative are illustrated through path diagram Fig. 1.

A few key findings emerge from this chapter, and they may be summed up as follows:

- Lower age employed women have a high GEDM at the lower levels of education; and the higher age unemployed women have a high GEDM at the higher levels of education.
- Caste hierarchies influence GEDM in the family. The schedule caste women have a high GEDM at higher levels of education irrespective of their employment status.
- The rural employed women of joint families have a high GEDM even without education.
- The unemployed women have a high GEDM even at a higher age difference with their spouse, and at higher levels of education.
- The higher the contribution of female income to the total income of the family, the higher will be GEDM

Table 6.b

Path Analysis of Explanatory Variables with Gender Equality in Decision Making as Dependent Variable

Explanatory Variables	*Regression Co-efficient*				*Correlation with lYm*
	Direct Effect	*Total Indirect Effect*	*Substantial indirect effect channeled through other variables*		
Total Years of Schooling	0.15	0.13	0.10	Account Holder	0.28*
			0.02	Levels of Education	
			-0.01	Employment Status	
Age Difference between Husband and Wife	-0.09	-0.04	0.03	Employment Status	-0.13*
			-0.01	Account Holder	
			-0.05	Levels of Education	
Account Holder	0.42	0.05	0.04	Total Years of Schooling	0.47*
			0.04	Levels of Education	
			-0.03	Employment Status	
Levels of Education	0.27	- 0.09	0.06	Account Holder	0.18*
			0.03	Proportion of Female Assets	
			-0.21	Employment Status	
Employment Status	-0.23	0.33	0.24	Levels of Education	0.10
			0.03	Proportion of Female Assets	
			-0.06	Account Holder	
Proportion of Female Assets	0.05	0.04	0.13	Levels of Education	0.09
			0.02	Account Holder	
			-0.12	Employment Status	

Source: Computed

* - Significant at 5% level

in the family at the lower levels of education for the employed women.

- The higher the share of female income to the total expenditure of the family, the higher will be GEDM in the family for the employed women at the higher levels of education.

Fig. 1. Direct and Indirect Effect of Significant Erogenous Variables on GEDM

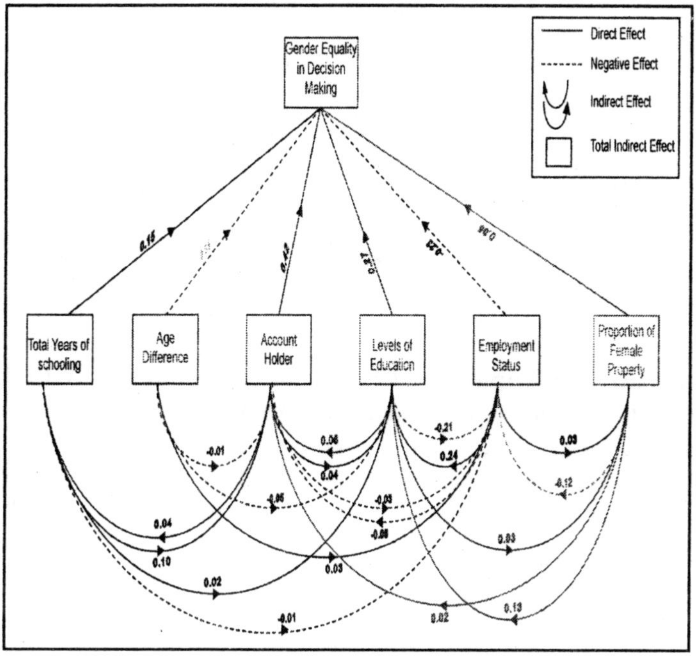

- The unemployed women have a high GEDM at the higher level of education, even though the female contribution to the total saving is low.
- When there is female's indebtedness in the family, the rural women with a higher education have a high GEDM irrespective of the employment status.
- The rural employed women with a lower education have high GEDM at the higher level of female asset structure in the family.

- The rural unemployed women with a higher level of education have a high GEDM when the asset structure of the family is titled by the female alone.
- GEDM is high among the rural employed women at higher education level, while the expenditure of the family is controlled by both men and women.
- The factors such as total years of schooling, age difference between husband and wife, being an account holder, levels of education, employment status and proportion of female income are important in deciding the extent of GEDM.
- Among all factors, the fact that women are account holders is a predominant one in deciding GEDM in the family.

The above findings bring to focus that gender equality in decision-making is high among the higher educated women even if they are unemployed. It is the level of education of women that influences their decision making power much more than their employment status. But the analysis of GEDM alone is not sufficient to determine the extent of empowerment of rural women. Another important analysis, that is, analysis on PARM is also required in order to obtain a precise idea on empowerment of rural women. The succeeding chapter intends to analyse the rationale of PARM as a major influence on empowerment.

7

ANALYSIS OF POWER OF AUTONOMY OVER RESOURCES AND MOBILITY

The empowerment acknowledges the importance of the increase of the power of women. However, it seeks to identify power less in terms of domination over others, and more in terms of the capacity of women to increase their own self-reliance and internal strength. This is identified as the right to determine choices in life and to influence the direction of change, through the ability to gain control over crucial material and non-material resources. One may say, if a woman is employed, she will have more PARM when compared with the unemployed women. Obviously this has reference to women's control over their resources, which is expected to enhance their bargaining capacity and ensure greater participation in family decision-making. This chapter centers on PARM, which facilitates empowerment of women. As done earlier, it is analysed with reference to education and employment. Analysis of gender equality in decision making, brought to light certain empirical facts on empowerment of women, as related to the educational and employment status. Now the next fold of analysis is Power of Autonomy over Resources (PARM).

EDUCATION AND EMPOWERMENTWISE ANALYSIS

It is observed that the employed respondents have a greater power of autonomy over resources and mobility than the unemployed respondents at various levels of education excluding the higher secondary education. Positive relation between education and PARM is observed among the unemployed women excluding the secondary education, whereas in the case of employed women, the positive relation is observed up to secondary education and beyond that the converse exists.

Age of the Respondents and Age Difference Between Husband and Wife and PARM

In deciding the power of autonomy over resources and mobility, the social and demographic variables play a significant role. Regarding age, the respondents are grouped into three: The respondents who belong to the lower age are below 25 and the cohorts who belong to 25 to 40 are middle age, and the cohorts who belong to above 40 are the higher age. It is an interesting factor that the unemployed illiterates are not empowered when compared with the employed illiterates. Similarly the unemployed graduates are also not empowered when compared with employed graduates. The employed cohorts belonging to the higher age group are empowered at the high school level, whereas the unemployed cohorts are empowered at the primary and higher secondary level. It is found from Table 1 that at the lower age, the employed illiterates and employed graduates have PARM, and the middle aged employed respondents have more PARM at the middle school level. At the higher age, the employed respondents are at the high school levels and unemployed respondents are not only at higher secondary level but also at the primary level. Lower age groups have less PARM when they are employed at all levels of education. On the contrary the higher age group cohorts have PARM, when they are employed at the lower and the higher education level.

The unemployed respondents have more PARM than employed respondents even at the low (primary) level of

Table 1
Score Values of PARM According to Age, Levels of Education and Employment Status

Employment Status		*Unemployed (120)*				*Employed (120)*			
Age		*Below 25*	*25 j 40*	*Above 40*	*Total*	*Below 25*	*25 j 40*	*Above 40*	*Total*
Levels of Education									
Illiterates	N	11	2	7	20	1	11	8	20
	Min.	42	38	42	38	55	34	41	34
	Max.	55	45	68	68	55	81	59	81
	Mean	49.36	41.50	49.14	48.50	55.00	53.36	48.63	51.55
	C.V.	8.70	11.93	18.74	13.60	-	26.96	11.53	21.83
Primary	N	2	11	7	20	4	7	9	20
	Min.	42	37	44	37	52	39	43	39
	Max.	59	69	63	69	78	56	58	78
	Mean	50.50	51.09	54.57	52.25	67.50	48.57	50.56	53.25
	C.V.	23.80	17.54	10.30	15.18	16.34	12.40	10.33	18.44
Secondary	N	2	12	6	20	4	10	6	20
	Min.	49	37	43	37	52	44	53	44
	Max.	60	61	67	67	60	81	77	81
	Mean	54.50	49.50	53.33	51.15	55.25	63.20	60.83	60.90
	C.V.	14.27	16.33	18.17	16.37	7.14	20.82	14.08	17.47
High School	N	3	12	5	20	3	6	11	20
	Min.	52	43	48	43	50	44	45	44
	Max.	60	69	69	69	53	77	81	81
	Mean	55.33	55.17	54.60	55.05	51.33	56.33	57.91	56.45
	C.V.	7.52	12.84	15.57	12.34	2.98	20.42	18.59	17.84

Contd.

Higher Secondary	N	7	5	8	20	3	9	8	20
	Min.	51	43	50	43	45	31	47	31
	Max.	63	58	67	67	53	68	81	81
	Mean	55.00	51.60	57.13	55.00	49.67	49.33	56.63	52.30
	C.V.	7.50	11.27	10.14	9.92	8.38	20.40	20.70	19.89
Above Higher Secondary	N	4	6	10	20	2	11	7	20
	Min.	50	53	49	49	58	50	49	49
	Max.	64	81	81	81	77	78	77	78
	Mean	57.50	62.67	59.00	59.80	67.50	57.91	58.57	59.10
	C.V.	9.99	16.33	15.33	14.53	19.90	14.25	15.39	15.07

Source: Computed.

education, when the age difference between husband and wife is less (below 5). The employed respondents have more PARM at the high school level when the age difference between husband and wife is low. When the age difference is high, the unemployed respondents have less PARM when compared with the employed respondents; but the employed respondents have more PARM at various levels of education. It is observed from Table 5 that the age difference between husband and wife affect the PARM of the unemployed respondents at all levels of education excluding primary education, whereas it does not affects the PARM of the employed respondents at various levels of education.

Community and PARM

It is noted from Table 2 that the PARM is high among unemployed OC respondents at the higher secondary level and the employed respondents at the high school level. The unemployed MBC respondents have more PARM at graduates level. But the employed MBC respondents have more PARM at illiterates and secondary level. SC employed respondents have a high PARM at the primary education level. BC respondents have a less PARM when compared with other communities.

Type of Family and Size of Family

Table 3 shows the relation between the type of family and PARM. It is observed that the size of family influences at the higher levels of education for the unemployed respondents, and the employed respondents at the lower levels of education.

It is seen that when the family size is large, the employed respondents' PARM is affected; and when the family size is small and medium, the unemployed respondents acquire more PARM at a higher education level; and the employed respondents at lower education level. The Medium size of family influences the unemployed respondents at the higher secondary level, but it influences the employed respondents to have more PARM even though the respondents are illiterates. In a large sized family, the unemployed respondents

Table 2
Score Values of PARM According to Community, Levels of Education and Employment Status

Employment Status		*Unemployed (120)*					*Employed (120)*				
Community		*OC*	*BC*	*MBC*	*SC*	*Total*	*OC*	*BC*	*MBC*	*SC*	*Total*
Levels of Education											
Illiterates	N	3	5	8	4	20	6	6	7	7	20
	Min.	43	42	44	38	38	41	42	34	51	34
	Max.	54	51	68	52	68	54	59	81	51	81
	Mean	50.33	46.00	51.50	44.25	48.50	47.83	50.67	55.57	51.00	51.55
	C.V.	12.62	7.37	14.86	13.35	13.60	10.61	11.55	32.07	-	21.83
Primary	N	2	7	6	5	20	1	6	6	7	20
	Min.	56	37	42	44	37	56	39	43	47	39
	Max.	56	56	69	60	69	56	71	55	78	78
	Mean	56.00	49.43	53.50	53.20	52.25	56.00	52.67	48.33	57.57	53.25
	C.V.	-	16.05	19.16	13.12	15.18	-	21.70	8.65	20.13	18.44
Secondary	N	1	6	8	5	20	3	6	8	3	20
	Min.	44	39	37	52	37	53	44	53	52	44
	Max.	44	63	67	56	67	77	81	78	59	81
	Mean	44.00	53.17	48.50	54.40	51.15	62.67	60.67	62.88	54.33	60.90
	C.V.	-	18.06	20.23	3.34	16.37	20.21	26.06	11.70	7.44	17.47
High School	N	2	7	9	2	20	2	6	5	7	20
	Min.	48	51	43	48	43	50	45	51	44	44
	Max.	58	62	69	69	69	77	68	81	60	81
	Mean	53.00	57.00	53.22	58.50	55.05	63.50	58.33	59.20	50.86	56.45
	C.V.	13.34	8.35	12.98	25.38	12.34	30.07	15.20	21.51	9.59	17.84

Contd.

Higher Secondary	N	4	9	6	1	20	2	5	7	6	20
	Min.	53	43	50	55	43	45	31	49	47	31
	Max.	67	62	58	55	67	67	53	68	81	81
	Mean	60.75	53.33	53.67	55.00	55.00	56.00	44.40	53.00	56.83	52.30
	C.V.	9.73	10.14	6.42	-	9.92	27.78	20.06	12.70	21.68	19.89
Above Higher Secondary	N	5	8	3	4	20	3	4	12	1	20
	Min.	53	49	57	50	49	53	50	49	56	49
	Max.	81	67	81	58	81	61	78	77	56	78
	Mean	62.60	58.13	66.67	54.50	59.80	57.33	62.25	58.75	56.00	59.10
	C.V.	17.15	11.20	18.99	6.78	14.53	7.05	18.66	16.31		15.07

Source: Computed.

Table 3
Score Values of PARM According to Type of Family, Levels of Education and Employment Status

Employment Status		*Unemployed (120)*			*Employed (120)*		
Type of Family		*Joint*	*Nuclear*	*Total*	*Joint*	*Nuclear*	*Total*
Levels of Education							
Illiterates	N	6	14	20	5	15	20
	Min.	38	42	38	43	34	34
	Max.	68	55	68	59	81	81
	Mean	51.17	47.36	48.50	51.40	51.60	51.55
	C.V.	19.25	9.82	13.60	12.35	24.54	21.83
Primary	N	1	19	20	7	13	20
	Min.	56	37	37	39	43	39
	Max.	56	69	69	78	71	78
	Mean	56.00	52.05	52.25	54.29	52.69	53.25
	C.V.	-	15.56	15.18	22.43	16.71	18.44
Secondary	N	7	13	20	8	12	20
	Min.	37	43	37	44	47	44
	Max.	63	67	67	78	81	81
	Mean	48.00	52.85	51.15	57.88	62.92	60.90
	C.V.	20.34	13.97	16.37	17.36	17.43	17.47

Contd.

High School	N	5	15	20	7	13	20
	Min.	48	43	43	50	44	44
	Max.	61	69	69	60	81	81
	Mean	54.20	55.33	55.05	53.33	57.79	56.45
	C.V.	10.87	13.08	12.34	7.28	20.18	17.84
Higher Secondary	N	5	15	20	7	13	20
	Min.	50	43	43	31	40	31
	Max.	63	67	67	68	81	81
	Mean	55.20	54.93	55.00	50.86	53.08	52.30
	C.V.	8.73	10.58	9.92	21.22	19.87	19.89
Above Higher Secondary	N	5	15	20	7	13	20
	Min.	49	50	49	56	49	49
	Max.	61	81	81	77	78	78
	Mean	54.00	61.73	59.80	64.00	58.24	59.10
	C.V.	9.26	14.43	14.53	17.75	14.65	15.07

Source: Computed.

have more PARM at the high school level whereas it influences to have less PARM for the employed respondents.

From Table 4, it is found that the unemployed cohorts who belong to the joint families have more PARM at the primary and higher secondary level. The employed cohorts who belong to the joint families have more PARM at above higher secondary level, whereas the employed cohorts who belong to nuclear families have more PARM even though they are illiterates, and they have more PARM at secondary and high school level. It is observed that the unemployed cohorts who belong to nuclear families have less PARM when compared with employed cohorts. The employed respondents who belong to nuclear families have more PARM up to high school only.

Income Status and PARM

When the income of the total family is low, the unemployed respondents have less PARM when compared with the employed respondents. It is observed from Table 6 that the total income of the family affects the PARM of the unemployed respondents at all levels of education. The employed respondents have PARM event at the lower levels of income. At the middle and higher levels of income, both the employed and unemployed respondents do not have PARM at all levels of education, whereas the converse exists in the case of female contribution to total income when the female contribution to total income is higher, the level of PARM is also higher among employed respondents. It is clear from Table 7 that the unemployed respondents have PARM at the higher secondary level of education when their contribution to total income is low. Moreover, when the female alone earns the income, the level of PARM is high among the employed respondents at all level of education (Table 8). The economic independence makes them have more power of autonomy than unemployed respondents.

Level of Expenditure and PARM

Table 9 presents the level of expenditure and PARM. It is observed that when the level of total expenditure is low, the

Table 4

Score Values of PARM According to Size of Family, Levels of Education and Employment Status

Employment Status		*Unemployed (120)*				*Employed (120)*			
Size of Family		*Small (1-4)*	*Medium (5 & 6)*	*Large (7 & Above)*	*Total*	*Small*	*Medium*	*Large*	*Total*
Levels of Education									
Illiterates	N	11	7	2	20	12	2	6	20
	Min.	42	38	45	38	41	56	34	34
	Max.	68	53	54	68	81	59	55	81
	Mean	49.00	47.43	49.50	48.50	51.92	57.50	48.83	51.55
	C.V.	15.91	11.08	12.86	13.60	25.91	3.69	15.72	21.83
Primary	N	11	4	5	20	9	9	2	20
	Min.	39	50	37	37	43	39	47	39
	Max.	69	59	56	69	78	58	52	78
	Mean	51.55	54.75	51.80	52.25	56.89	50.44	49.50	53.25
	C.V.	17.85	6.89	16.00	15.18	22.26	12.50	7.14	18.44
Secondary	N	9	7	4	20	10	5	5	20
	Min.	43	39	37	37	47	44	52	44
	Max.	61	63	67	67	81	78	77	81
	Mean	51.44	51.43	50.00	51.15	61.60	59.40	61.00	60.90
	C.V.	12.60	18.13	24.98	16.37	17.67	20.60	17.77	17.47

Contd.

High School	N	9	5	6	20	7	6	7	20
	Min.	43	48	49	43	44	50	49	44
	Max.	62	61	69	69	81	68	77	81
	Mean	53.10	55.00	58.33	55.05	56.40	56.00	57.25	56.45
	C.V.	9.66	11.78	15.55	12.34	20.06	12.53	23.10	17.84
Higher Secondary	N	9	5	6	20	7	6	7	20
	Min.	49	43	50	43	45	40	31	31
	Max.	57	67	63	67	81	53	68	81
	Mean	53.44	56.60	56.00	55.00	55.14	48.83	52.43	52.30
	C.V.	5.13	15.53	9.97	9.92	21.95	9.29	23.95	19.89
Above Higher Secondary	N	12	4	4	20	12	5	3	20
	Min.	49	50	57	49	50	49	53	49
	Max.	81	61	63	81	78	77	64	78
	Mean	62.00	54.25	58.75	59.80	59.83	57.40	59.00	59.10
	C.V.	16.55	8.69	4.89	14.53	15.18	19.81	9.44	15.07

Source: Computed.

Table 5
Score Values of PARM According to Age Difference between Husband and Wife, Levels of Education and Employment Status

Employment Status		*Unemployed (120)*				*Employed (120)*			
Age Difference		*1-5*	*5-10*	*10-15*	*Total*	*1-5*	*5-10*	*10-15*	*Total*
Levels of Education									
Illiterates	N	1	10	9	20	5	6	9	20
	Min.	50	42	38	38	41	34	41	34
	Max.	50	68	54	68	51	78	81	81
	Mean	50.00	50.70	45.89	48.50	46.40	52.67	53.67	51.55
	C.V.	-	15.39	9.95	13.60	9.95	28.05	21.35	21.83
Primary	N	4	8	8	20	7	7	6	20
	Min.	48	37	39	37	47	43	39	39
	Max.	69	63	56	69	69	78	71	78
	Mean	57.75	52.75	49.00	52.25	53.43	53.86	52.33	53.25
	C.V.	15.19	15.36	13.32	15.18	14.65	21.88	21.34	18.44
Secondary	N	5	12	3	20	9	9	2	20
	Min.	37	43	40	37	52	44	47	44
	Max.	56	63	67	67	67	81	60	81
	Mean	47.40	51.50	56.00	51.15	58.89	64.56	53.50	60.90
	C.V.	19.14	12.54	25.32	16.37	8.21	22.00	17.18	17.47
High School	N	3	12	5	20	10	5	5	20
	Min.	54	43	48	43	50	44	49	44
	Max.	60	69	62	69	77	81	60	81
	Mean	56.33	55.50	53.20	55.05	57.90	57.20	52.80	56.45
	C.V.	5.71	14.59	9.89	12.34	15.75	27.49	9.41	17.84

Higher Secondary	N	5	11	4	20	8	10	2	20
	Min.	53	43	51	43	31	45	50	31
	Max.	60	67	63	67	57	81	67	81
	Mean	56.60	53.73	56.50	55.00	47.13	55.20	58.50	52.30
	C.V.	4.77	12.09	8.85	9.92	17.33	19.75	20.55	19.89
Above Higher Secondary	N	8	10	2	20	6	8	6	20
	Min.	49	50	50	49	49	56	50	49
	Max.	81	81	61	81	61	78	77	78
	Mean	61.25	59.50	55.50	59.80	53.33	64.25	58.00	59.10
	C.V.	15.77	14.46	14.01	14.53	8.44	13.20	16.96	15.07

Source: Computed.

Table 6

Score Values of PARM According to Total Income, Levels of Education and Employment Status

Employment Status		*Unemployed (120)*				*Employed (120)*			
Total Income		*Below 50000*	*50000 to 100000*	*Above 100000*	*Total*	*Below 50000*	*50000 to 100000*	*Above 100000*	*Total*
Levels of Education									
Illiterates	N	4	10	6	20	4	7	9	20
	Min.	42	43	38	38	41	42	34	34
	Max.	50	68	54	68	78	81	56	81
	Mean	45.50	51.00	46.33	48.50	55.25	53.43	48.44	51.55
	C.V.	7.29	14.17	13.56	13.60	31.08	23.94	14.12	21.83
Primary	N	5	9	6	20	4	9	7	20
	Min.	44	37	39	37	55	39	43	39
	Max.	63	69	59	69	69	78	71	78
	Mean	52.60	53.78	49.67	52.25	59.50	51.89	51.43	53.25
	C.V.	13.48	16.26	16.14	15.18	10.85	20.79	19.11	18.44
Secondary	N	3	12	5	20	11	1	8	20
	Min.	55	39	37	37	44	61	47	44
	Max.	61	67	63	67	79	61	81	81
	Mean	57.33	50.08	50.00	51.15	61.73	61.00	59.75	60.90
	C.V.	5.61	17.29	18.76	16.37	16.28	-	21.20	17.47
High School	N	6	9	5	2	6	8	6	20
	Min.	43	51	48	43	50	44	51	44
	Max.	69	69	53	69	77	56	81	81
	Mean	56.83	56.56	50.20	55.05	62.17	49.38	60.17	56.45
	C.V.	15.79	10.65	5.16	12.34	16.07	7.57	18.96	17.84

Contd.

Higher Secondary	N	4	11	5	20	5	8	7	20
	Min.	50	43	51	43	40	45	31	31
	Max.	63	67	62	67	81	57	53	81
	Mean	55.75	54.00	56.60	55.00	62.00	50.25	47.71	52.30
	C.V.	9.65	11.23	8.15	9.92	25.12	7.04	15.95	19.89
Above Higher Secondary	N	11	4	5	20	4	8	8	20
	Min.	50	50	49	49	56	49	50	49
	Max.	81	81	64	81	78	77	61	78
	Mean	60.55	62.75	55.80	59.80	67.75	57.25	56.63	59.10
	C.V.	13.30	20.96	10.86	14.53	16.80	16.67	6.87	15.07

Source: Computed.

Table 7
Score Values of PARM According to Female Income, Levels of Education and Employment Status

Employment Status		Unemployed (120)			Employed (120)		
Female Income		No Earning	Below 25000	Total	Below 25000	Above 50000	Total
Levels of Education							
Illiterates	N	13	7	20	15	5	20
	Min.	42	38	38	34	48	34
	Max.	68	54	68	56	81	81
	Mean	49.46	46.71	48.50	47.33	64.20	51.55
	C.V.	14.41	11.84	13.60	12.54	22.66	21.83
Primary	N	15	5	20	16	4	20
	Min.	37	53	37	39	56	39
	Max.	69	60	69	69	78	78
	Mean	50.73	56.80	52.25	50.13	65.75	53.25
	C.V.	16.88	4.89	15.18	13.80	16.02	18.44
Secondary	N	15	5	20	7	13	20
	Min.	37	47	37	47	44	44
	Max.	63	67	67	77	81	81
	Mean	50.07	54.40	51.15	58.57	62.15	60.90
	C.V.	17.01	14.45	16.37	16.72	18.09	17.47
High School	N	15	5	20	13	7	20
	Min.	43	48	43	44	52	44
	Max.	69	58	69	60	81	81
	Mean	55.93	52.40	55.05	50.92	66.71	56.45
	C.V.	13.28	7.22	12.34	8.19	14.78	17.84

Contd.

Higher Secondary	N	19	1	20	16	4	20
	Min.	43	60	43	40	31	31
	Max.	67	60	67	81	68	81
	Mean	54.74	60.00	55.00	51.69	54.75	52.30
	C.V.	10.00	0.00	9.92	16.82	31.51	19.89
Above Higher Secondary	N	18	2	20	16	4	20
	Min.	49	55	49	49	50	49
	Max.	81	59	81	77	78	78
	Mean	60.11	57.00	59.80	58.63	61.00	59.10
	C.V.	15.15	4.96	14.53	14.30	19.76	15.07

Source: Computed.

Table 8

Score Values of PARM According to Income earner, Levels of Education and Employment Status

Employment Status		*Unemployed (120)**			*Employed (120)*			
Income Earner		*Male*	*Both*	*Total*	*Male*	*Female*	*Both*	*Total*
Levels of Education								
Illiterates	N	13	7	20	-	2	18	20
	Min.	42	38	38	-	55	34	34
	Max.	68	54	68	-	81	78	81
	Mean	49.46	46.71	48.50	-	68.00	49.72	51.55
	C.V.	14.41	11.84	13.60	-	27.04	18.69	21.83
Primary	N	15	5	20	-	3	17	20
	Min.	37	53	37	-	58	39	39
	Max.	69	60	69	-	78	71	78
	Mean	50.73	56.80	52.25	-	68.33	50.59	53.25
	C.V.	16.88	4.89	15.18	-	14.66	14.22	18.44
Secondary	N	15	5	20	1	3	16	20
	Min.	37	47	37	67	63	44	44
	Max.	63	67	67	67.00	78	81	81
	Mean	50.07	54.40	51.15	67	72.67	58.31	60.90
	C.V.	17.01	14.45	16.37	-	11.54	16.87	17.47

Contd.

High School	N	15	5	20	-	2	18	20
	Min.	43	48	43	-	51	44	44
	Max.	69	58	69	-	81	77	81
	Mean	55.93	52.40	55.05	-	66.00	55.39	56.45
	C.V.	13.28	7.22	12.34	-	32.14	15.63	17.84
Higher Secondary	N	19	1	20	-	1	19	20
	Min.	43	60	43	-	81	31	31
	Max.	67	60	67	-	81	68	81
	Mean	54.74	60.00	55.00	-	81.00	50.79	52.30
	C.V.	10.00	-	9.92	-	-	16.00	19.89
Above Higher Secondary	N	18	2	20	-	1	19	20
	Min.	49	55	49	-	77	49	49
	Max.	81	59	81	-	77	78	78
	Mean	60.11	57.00	59.80	-	77.00	58.16	59.10
	C.V.	14.74	-	14.53	-	-	14.27	15.07

Source: Computed.

Note: * In this category, women could not control over expenditure, since they are unemployed

Table 9

Score Values of PARM According to Total Expenditure, Levels of Education and Employment Status

Employment Status		*Unemployed (120)*				*Employed (120)*			
Total Expenditure		*Below 25000 (Rs.)*	*25000 to 50000 (Rs.)*	*Above 50000 (Rs.)*	*Total*	*Below 25000 (Rs.)*	*25000 to 50000 (Rs.)*	*Above 50000 (Rs.)*	*Total*
Levels of Education									
Illiterates	N	5	11	4	20	2	6	12	20
	Min.	42	38	44	38	43	42	34	34
	Max.	50	55	68	68	81	55	78	81
	Mean	45.60	48.09	53.25	48.50	62.00	48.83	51.17	51.55
	C.V.	6.32	11.71	20.07	13.60	43.34	8.92	21.46	21.83
Primary	N	4	9	7	20	3	13	4	20
	Min.	44	37	39	37	55	39	45	39
	Max.	55	69	63	69	69	78	56	78
	Mean	50.00	53.78	51.57	52.25	60.00	52.38	51.00	53.25
	C.V.	9.38	16.26	17.23	15.18	13.02	20.92	11.43	18.44
Secondary	N	4	14	2	20	6	4	10	20
	Min.	49	37	49	37	44	52	47	44
	Max.	61	67	63	67	77	81	79	81
	Mean	55.25	49.29	56.00	51.15	58.83	61.75	61.80	60.90
	C.V.	8.91	17.79	17.68	16.37	18.79	21.78	16.73	17.47

Contd.

High School	N	3	9	8	20	6	9	5	20
	Min.	43	48	49	43	44	45	50	44
	Max.	51	69	69	69	81	64	77	81
	Mean	48.33	55.89	56.63	55.05	59.50	52.11	60.60	56.45
	C.V.	9.56	12.18	11.60	12.34	22.42	10.35	18.32	17.84
Higher Secondary	N	2	10	8	20	4	9	7	20
	Min.	55	43	50	43	40	45	31	31
	Max.	58	67	63	67	81	57	68	81
	Mean	56.50	53.60	56.38	55.00	59.75	50.33	50.57	52.30
	C.V.	3.75	11.64	8.79	9.92	30.11	7.23	21.38	19.89
Above Higher Secondary	N	4	6	10	20	6	7	7	20
	Min.	57	49	50	49	50	49	53	49
	Max.	81	81	64	81	78	77	61	78
	Mean	65.00	61.17	56.90	59.80	62.83	57.14	57.86	59.10
	C.V.	16.85	19.49	7.43	14.53	18.71	18.00	5.50	15.07

Source: Computed.

unemployed respondents have more PARM at above higher secondary education level, whereas at higher levels of incomes they could not get PARM. The employed respondents have more PARM even at the lower levels of education when the total expenditure is low. They also have a high PARM at the higher secondary education, when the level of expenditure is high. The employed respondents have PARM at secondary and high school education level. Thus, it is inferred that when the total expenditure is high, the employed respondents have PARM at middle level of education and the unemployed respondents have more PARM at graduate level when the total expenditure is low.

The female share in the total expenditure decides the power of autonomy over resources and mobility. It is noted from Table 10 that when the female share in the total expenditure increases, the PARM also increases up to the high school for the employed respondents. It is surprising to note that the unemployed respondents have more PARM even if there is no contribution by females at the above higher secondary education level. Moreover, they also have more PARM when the share in total expenditure is low at the higher secondary education. Table 11 reflects that when the female members alone control the income, the employed respondents have more PARM when compared with unemployed respondents at all levels of education. Since the female members are employed, they could get financial independence, and hence, they obtain the PARM.

Level of Savings and PARM

It is clear from Table 12 that when there is no saving, the unemployed respondent's PARM is less when compared with the employed respondent's PARM at the level of primary, secondary, and above higher secondary education. The employed respondents are the earning members in the family. The access to resources to the families also leads them to have control over resources and thereby their PARM is high. It is interesting to note that the employed respondents could not get PARM when the level of saving is low (below Rs.25000) at

Table 10

Score Values of PARM According to Female Expenditure,, Levels of Education and Employment Status

Employment Status		*Unemployed (120)*				*Employed (120)*			
Female Expenditure		*No Contri-bution*	*Below 25000 (Rs.)*	*Above 25000 (Rs.)*	*Total*	*No Contri-bution*	*Below 25000 (Rs.)*	*Above 25000 (Rs.)*	*Total*
Levels of Education									
Illiterates	N	14	6	-	20	4	12	4	20
	Min.	42	38	-	38	41	34	48	34
	Max.	68	54	-	68	78	56	81	81
	Mean	49.29	46.67	-	48.50	53.00	48.00	60.75	51.55
	C.V.	13.95	12.98	-	13.60	32.57	12.66	23.45	21.83
Primary	N	15	5	-	20	2	12	6	20
	Min.	37	53	-	37	43	45	39	39
	Max.	69	60	-	69	47	58	78	78
	Mean	50.73	56.80	-	52.25	45.00	51.42	59.67	53.25
	C.V.	16.88	4.89	-	15.18	6.29	8.14	26.04	18.44
Secondary	N	14	4	2	20	1	7	12	20
	Min.	37	47	49	37	58	52	44	44
	Max.	63	67	58	67	58	77	81	81
	Mean	49.50	55.75	53.50	51.15	58.00	60.43	61.42	60.90
	C.V.	17.25	15.03	11.90	16.37	-	13.84	20.35	17.47

Contd.

High School	N	17	3	-	20	-	14	6	20
	Min.	43	51	-	43	-	44	52	44
	Max.	69	58	-	69	-	77	81	81
	Mean	55.18	54.33	-	55.05	-	52.79	65.00	56.45
	C.V.	13.21	6.46	-	12.34	-	15.23	14.76	17.84
Higher Secondary	N	19	1	-	20	2	14	4	20
	Min.	43	60	-	43	48	40	31	31
	Max.	67	60	-	67	67	81	68	81
	Mean	54.74	60.00	-	55.00	57.50	52.07	50.50	52.30
	C.V.	10.00	-	-	9.92	23.37	17.78	30.10	19.89
Above Higher Secondary	N	19	-	1	20	1	12	7	20
	Min.	49	-	55	49	58	51	49	49
	Max.	81	-	55	81	58	77	78	78
	Mean	60.05	-	55.00	59.80	58.00	60.00	57.71	59.10
	C.V.	14.74	-	-	14.53	-	14.72	17.69	15.07

Source: Computed.

Table 11

Score Values of PARM According to control over Expenditure, Levels of Education and Employment Status

Employment Status		*Unemployed (120)**			*Employed (120)*			
Control over Expenditure		*Male*	*Both*	*Total*	*Male*	*Female*	*Both*	*Total*
Levels of Education								
Illiterates	N	14	6	20	4	2	14	20
	Min.	42	38	38	41	55	34	34
	Max.	68	54	68	51	81	78	81
	e	49.29	46.67	48.50	43.75	68.00	51.43	51.55
	C.V.	13.95	12.98	13.60	11.10	27.04	18.79	21.83
Primary	N	15	5	20	2	2	16	20
	Min.	37	53	37	43	69	39	39
	Max.	69	60	69	47	78	71	78
	Mean	50.73	56.80	52.25	45.00	73.50	51.75	53.25
	C.V.	16.88	4.89	15.18	6.29	8.66	14.03	18.44
Secondary	N	15	5	20	2	2	16	20
	Min.	37	47	37	58	63	44	44
	Max.	63	67	67	67	77	81	81
	Mean	50.07	54.40	51.15	62.50	70.00	59.56	60.90
	C.V.	17.01	14.45	16.37	10.18	14.14	18.46	17.47

Contd.

High School	N	17	3	20	-	1	19	20
	Min.	43	51	43	-	81	44	44
	Max.	69	58	69	-	81	77	81
	Mean	55.18	54.33	55.05	-	81.00	55.16	56.45
	C.V.	13.21	6.46	12.34	-	-	15.36	17.84
Higher Secondary	N	19	1	20	1	2	17	20
	Min.	43	60	43	48	40	31	31
	Max.	67	60	67	48	81	68	81
	Mean	54.74	60.00	55.00	48.00	60.50	51.59	52.30
	C.V.	10.00	-	9.92	-	47.92	15.73	19.89
Above Higher Secondary	N	19	1	20	1	1	18	20
	Min.	49	55	49	58	77	49	49
	Max.	81	55	81	58	77	78	78
	Mean	60.05	55.00	59.80	58.00	77.00	58.17	59.10
	C.V.	14.74	-	14.53	-	-	14.27	15.07

Source: Computed.
Note: * In this category, women could not control over expenditure, since they are unemployed

Table 12

Score Values of PARM According to Total Borrowings, Levels of Education and Employment Status

Employment Status		*Unemployed (120)*					*Employed (120)*				
Total Borrowings		*No Borrowing*	*Below 10,000*	*10,000 to 50,000*	*Above 50,000*	*Total*	*No Borrowing*	*Below 10,000*	*10,000 to 50,000*	*Above 50,000*	*Total*
Levels ofEducation											
Illiterates	N	3	8	6	3	20	9	3	6	2	20
	Min.	45	42	38	43	38	41	34	41	48	34
	Max.	54	54	55	68	68	81	51	55	59	81
	Mean	50.33	47.25	46.67	53.67	48.50	56.67	44.00	47.00	53.50	51.55
	C.V.	9.39	10.23	12.25	24.03	13.60	24.04	20.20	12.26	14.54	21.83
Primary	N	9	4	3	4	20	8	4	5	3	20
	Min.	37	44	53	42	37	43	45	39	53	39
	Max.	69	56	59	60	69	78	56	55	71	78
	Mean	51.11	51.00	55.67	53.50	52.25	54.88	51.25	48.20	60.00	53.25
	C.V.	20.13	10.38	5.49	14.76	15.18	23.00	10.97	12.04	16.07	18.44
Secondary	N	7	2	6	5	20	7	-	4	9	20
	Min.	44	49	37	40	37	57	-	52	44	44
	Max.	63	56	67	61	67	81	-	58	79	81
	Mean	51.71	52.50	49.00	52.40	51.15	66.29	-	53.75	59.89	60.90
	C.V.	12.11	9.43	22.84	19.21	16.37	14.12	-	5.34	20.32	17.47

Contd.

High School	N	7	1	4	8	20	10	3	4	3	20
	Min.	51	60	43	48	43	44	51	50	50	44
	Max.	62	60	69	69	69	64	60	77	81	81
	Mean	54.71	60.00	56.00	54.25	55.05	52.30	54.67	60.75	66.33	56.45
	C.V.	8.62	-	19.18	13.28	12.34	12.03	8.64	21.10	23.47	17.84
Higher Secondary	N	11	4	1	4	20	4	8	5	3	20
	Min.	49	43	52	50	43	48	40	31	45	31
	Max.	62	60	52	67	67	81	57	54	68	81
	Mean	54.91	53.25	52.00	57.75	55.00	61.50	50.00	46.80	55.33	52.30
	C.V.	6.59	13.92	-	14.79	9.92	25.28	9.91	19.31	21.10	19.89
Above Higher Secondary	N	10	1	5	4	20	9	5	5	1	20
	Min.	49	58	50	55	49	50	51	49	78	49
	Max.	81	58	81	61	81	77	64	77	78	78
	Mean	60.10	58.00	61.20	57.75	59.80	59.22	56.60	57.60	78.00	59.10
	C.V.	15.62	-	19.89	4.33	14.53	12.74	8.34	20.60	-	15.07

Source: Computed.

all levels of education excluding higher secondary education. When the total saving exceeds Rs.25000, the unemployed respondents' PARM is low. The employed respondents have obtained PARM, not only at the primary level, but also at the illiterate level.

Regarding female savings, it is surprising to note from Table 13 that the unemployed respondents are benefited at the higher secondary education level even if there is no female savings. When the female saving exceeds Rs.25000, the benefits go to the employed respondents at the secondary and high school level and even at illiterate level. It is observed from Table 14 that when the accounts are kept by male alone, the employed respondents, PARM is low when compared with unemployed respondents at all levels of education excluding higher secondary education. When the female alone keep the accounts, the employed respondents obtain PARM at lower levels of education, whereas the unemployed respondents obtain PARM not only at higher levels of education but also at illiterate level. Gender influences the PARM regarding the account holder.

Level of borrowings and PARM

It is obvious from Table 15 that the unemployed respondents could not obtain PARM in respect of all levels of education, or with reference to all levels of borrowings. It is noted that when the borrowing is nil, the employed respondents obtain PARM at the higher secondary education level and at the illiterate level. When the total borrowing is high, the employed respondents have PARM at primary, secondary and at graduate level. Thus, it is inferred that the level of borrowing influences the PARM of the employed respondents at all levels of education, whereas it is not so in the case of the unemployed respondents.

It is interesting to note (Table 16) that the unemployed illiterates have obtained PARM when there is no borrowing. When there is female borrowing, it affects PARM of the unemployed respondents at the higher levels of education, whereas the female borrowings affect PARM of the employed respondents at middle level of education.

Table 13

Score Values of PARM According to Female Borrowings, Levels of Education and Employment Status

Employment Status		*Unemployed (120)*			*Employed (120)*		
Female Borrowings		*No Borrowing*	*Borrowing*	*Total*	*No Borrowing*	*Borrowing*	*Total*
Levels of Education							
Illiterates	N	15	5	20	15	5	20
	Min.	38	42	38	41	34	34
	Max.	68	53	68	81	55	81
	Mean	49.40	45.80	48.50	53.40	46.00	51.55
	C.V.	14.27	9.93	13.60	22.05	17.53	21.83
Primary	N	17	3	20	15	5	20
	Min.	37	53	37	43	39	39
	Max.	69	55	69	78	56	78
	Mean	51.94	54.00	52.25	54.73	48.80	53.25
	C.V.	16.55	1.85	15.18	18.90	14.52	18.44
Secondary	N	16	4	20	10	10	20
	Min.	37	49	37	47	44	44
	Max.	63	67	67	81	79	81
	Mean	49.56	57.50	51.15	63.00	58.80	60.90
	C.V.	16.19	12.90	16.37	15.93	19.29	17.47

Contd.

High School	N	17	3	20	17	3	20
	Min.	43	54	43	44	65	44
	Max.	69	69	69	77	81	81
	Mean	54.00	61.00	55.05	53.82	71.33	56.45
	C.V.	11.69	12.38	12.34	14.69	11.92	17.84
Higher Secondary	N	17	3	20	13	7	20
	Min.	43	50	43	31	49	31
	Max.	67	60	67	81	57	81
	Mean	54.88	55.67	55.00	52.85	51.29	52.30
	C.V.	10.30	9.22	9.92	24.42	5.48	19.89
Above Higher Secondary	N	16	4	20	14	6	20
	Min.	49	58	49	49	55	49
	Max.	81	81	81	78	77	78
	Mean	58.44	65.25	59.80	58.00	61.67	59.10
	C.V.	13.56	16.43	14.53	15.95	13.36	15.07

Source: Computed.

Table 14
Score Values of PARM According to Total Savings, Levels of Education and Employment Statu

Employment Status		*Unemployed (120)*				*Employed (120)*			
Total Savings Levels		*No Savings*	*Below 25000 (Rs.)*	*Above 25000 (Rs.)*	*Total*	*No Savings*	*Below 25000 (Rs.)*	*Above 25000 (Rs.)*	*Total*
Levels of Education									
Illiterates	N	6	12	2	20	3	8	9	20
	Min.	43	38	42	38	43	34	41	34
	Max.	51	68	50	68	51	56	81	81
	Mean	45.83	50.25	46.00	48.50	48.00	49.50	54.56	51.55
	C.V.	6.24	15.44	12.30	13.60	9.08	14.20	28.03	21.83
Primary	N	3	10	7	20	3	9	7	20
	Min.	44	37	39	37	39	47	43	39
	Max.	55	60	69	69	69	78	71	78
	Mean	49.67	53.10	52.14	52.25	54.67	53.67	52.25	53.25
	C.V.	11.09	12.47	20.90	15.18	27.52	17.99	17.98	18.44
Secondary	N	8	15	2	20	3	2	15	20
	Min.	39	37	48	37	57	52	44	44
	Max.	60	67	61	67	77	61	81	81
	Mean	51.33	50.67	54.50	51.15	65.67	56.50	60.53	60.90
	C.V.	21.37	16.52	16.87	16.37	15.63	11.26	18.69	17.47

Contd.

High School	N	2	10	8	20	3	6	11	20
	Min.	54	43	49	43	50	44	50	44
	Max.	60	69	69	69	56	60	81	81
	Mean	57.00	52.90	57.25	55.05	53.00	49.83	61.00	56.45
	C.V.	7.44	13.79	11.19	12.34	5.66	11.59	18.08	17.84
Higher Secondary	N	3	13	4	20	7	7	6	20
	Min.	43	51	50	43	31	47	48	31
	Max.	55	67	55	67	81	53	68	81
	Mean	49.00	57.23	52.25	55.00	51.14	50.00	56.33	52.30
	C.V.	12.24	8.38	4.24	9.92	30.95	3.65	15.66	19.89
Above Higher Secondary	N	-	6	14	20	2	9	9	20
	Min.	-	50	49	49	51	50	49	49
	Max.	-	81	81	81	77	77	78	78
	Mean	-	61.67	59.00	59.80	64.00	58.00	59.11	59.10
	C.V.	-	16.75	13.88	14.53	28.73	14.30	14.17	15.07

Source: Computed.

Table 15
Score Values of PARM According to Female Savings, Levels of Education and Employment Status

Employment Status		*Unemployed (120)*				*Employed (120)*			
Female Savings		*No Savings*	*Below 25000 (Rs.)*	*Above 25000 (Rs.)*	*Total*	*No Savings*	*Below 25000 (Rs.)*	*Above 25000 (Rs.)*	*Total*
Levels of Education									
Illiterates	N	11	8	1	20	6	10	4	20
	Min.	43	38	50	38	34	42	41	34
	Max.	55	68	50	68	51	78	81	81
	Mean	47.82	49.25	50.00	48.50	46.67	52.90	55.50	51.55
	C.V.	9.11	19.19	-	13.60	14.89	18.47	34.23	21.83
Primary	N	11	8	1	20	6	10	4	20
	Min.	37	42	63	37	39	43	58	39
	Max.	69	60	63	69	69	78	58	78
	Mean	49.73	54.38	63.00	52.25	53.60	52.79	58.00	53.25
	C.V.	17.53	10.17	-	15.18	20.72	19.03	-	18.44
Secondary	N	9	9	2	20	5	3	12	20
	Min.	39	37	49	37	53	47	44	44
	Max.	63	67	61	67	77	58	81	81
	Mean	48.67	52.78	55.00	51.15	62.20	52.33	62.50	60.90
	C.V.	17.85	15.68	15.43	16.37	14.66	10.52	18.68	17.47

Contd.

High School	N	9	8	3	20	5	9	6	20
	Min.	43	48	53	43	45	44	60	44
	Max.	69	58	62	69	56	60	81	81
	Mean	57.33	51.25	58.33	55.05	51.00	51.00	69.17	56.45
	C.V.	14.62	6.41	8.10	12.34	7.96	8.32	11.76	17.84
Higher Secondary	N	15	4	1	20	9	7	4	20
	Min.	43	50	55	43	31	47	48	31
	Max.	67	60	55	67	81	68	67	81
	Mean	55.33	53.75	55.00	55.00	51.22	52.57	54.25	52.30
	C.V.	10.81	8.09	-	9.92	26.80	13.40	15.95	19.89
Above Higher Secondary	N	5	8	7	20	7	8	5	20
	Min.	50	49	50	49	51	49	50	49
	Max.	62	81	81	81	77	77	78	78
	Mean	56.60	61.00	60.71	59.80	60.43	57.13	60.40	59.10
	C.V.	8.80	16.18	16.27	14.53	13.97	16.00	17.43	15.07

Source: Computed.

Table 16

Score Values of PARM According to Account Holder, Levels of Education and Employment Status

Employment Status		*Unemployed (120)*					*Employed (120)*				
Account Holder		*No A/C*	*Male*	*Female*	*Both*	*Total*	*No A/C*	*Male*	*Female*	*Both*	*Total*
Levels ofEducation											
Illiterates	N	6	5	6	3	20	3	3	5	9	20
	Min.	43	44	38	42	38	43	34	41	41	34
	Max.	51	55	68	50	68	51	51	81	78	81
	Mean	45.83	50.20	51.67	44.67	48.50	48.00	45.33	56.00	52.33	51.55
	C.V.	6.24	9.80	19.07	10.34	13.60	9.08	21.65	27.26	21.21	21.83
Primary	N	4	8	3	5	20	3	2	5	10	20
	Min.	44	37	53	42	37	39	48	48	43	39
	Max.	55	69	59	60	69	69	56	78	71	78
	Mean	49.50	51.50	55.33	53.80	52.25	54.67	52.00	56.40	51.50	53.25
	C.V.	9.11	21.40	5.81	12.77	15.18	27.52	10.88	21.95	16.43	18.44
Secondary	N	3	7	6	4	20	3	2	6	9	20
	Min.	39	40	49	37	37	57	53	52	44	44
	Max.	60	63	67	61	67	77	61	81	63	81
	Mean	51.33	47.57	56.33	49.50	51.15	65.67	57.00	69.17	54.67	60.90
	C.V.	21.37	15.68	10.92	20.44	16.37	15.63	9.92	17.57	11.42	17.47

Contd.

High School	N	2	7	6	5	20	4	2	7	7	20
	Min.	54	43	48	48	43	50	45	44	50	44
	Max.	60	69	58	62	69	60	51	81	77	81
	Mean	57.00	57.43	51.67	55.00	55.05	54.75	48.00	54.14	62.14	56.45
	C.V.	7.44	16.58	6.89	10.60	12.34	7.80	8.84	22.53	15.31	17.84
Higher Secondary	N	3	11	2	4	20	7	2	6	5	20
	Min.	43	51	52	50	43	31	50	47	48	31
	Max.	55	67	60	55	67	81	53	53	68	81
	Mean	49.00	57.27	56.00	52.75	55.00	51.14	51.50	50.50	56.40	52.30
	C.V.	12.24	8.94	10.10	3.91	9.92	30.95	4.12	4.11	18.02	19.89
Above Higher Secondary	N	-	5	2	13	20	2	5	3	10	20
	Min.	-	50	59	49	49	51	55	53	49	49
	Max.	-	62	81	81	81	77	64	77	78	78
	Mean	-	56.60	70.00	59.46	59.80	64.00	59.00	63.00	57.00	59.10
	C.V.	-	8.80	22.22	14.01	14.53	28.73	6.23	19.83	15.09	15.07

Source: Computed.

Asset Structure and PARM

Asset structure shows the economic status of the family. When the total asset of the respondents is low, the unemployed respondents have PARM at the middle level of education, and the employed respondents at the secondary level of education. Table 17 represents that when the level of total asset increases from Rs.50,000 to Rs.2,00,000, the unemployed respondents have PARM at the primary level of education. When the total asset is high, the unemployed respondents have a less PARM, whereas employed respondents have a high PARM. It is inferred that when the asset is high, the PARM is also high at the higher secondary school education for the employed respondents; and when the asset is low, the PARM is high at the secondary education level for the employed respondents.

It is interesting to note that though the respondents are not employed, they have a high PARM at the higher secondary school education level. It is also interesting to note from Table 18 that the unemployed respondents have PARM at the high levels of education when the female asset in the family is low. The employed respondents have PARM at lower levels of education when the asset is high.

In the rural areas, the females are restricted to get inheritance of the asset, as the parents believe that the sons not their daughters could give security to them when they are old. Women's Asset Rights are insisted by government by passing acts to enable them to inherit assets. However, in the rural areas, women could not get asset. In the study, it is observed (Table 19) that when the asset holders are females, their PARM increases at all levels of education excluding the higher secondary education. The unemployed women have more PARM at the high school and above higher secondary education level and even at the level of illiteracy. The employed respondents have obtained PARM at lower levels of education. It is found that when the asset is in the name of women, the employed respondents have PARM at the lower levels of education, and the unemployed respondents at all levels of education.

Table 17

Score Values of PARM According to Total Asset Structure,, Levels of Education and Employment Status

Employment Status		*Unemployed (120)*					*Employed (120)*				
Total Assets		*Below 50,000 (Rs.)*	*50000 to 200000 (Rs.)*	*200000 to 400000 (Rs.)*	*Above 400000 (Rs.)*	*Total*	*Below 50,000 (Rs.)*	*50000 to 200000 (Rs.)*	*200000 to 400000 (Rs.)*	*Above 400000 (Rs.)*	*Total*
Levels ofEducation											
Illiterates	N	4	3	7	6	20	9	1	-	10	20
	Min.	43	44	42	38	38	34	81	-	41	34
	Max.	55	53	54	68	68	56	81	-	78	81
	Mean	49.25	49.67	47.43	48.67	48.5	48.44	81	-	51.4	51.55
	C.V.	12.45	9.93	8.33	21.69	13.6	13.85	-	-	21.43	21.83
Primary	N	6	4	3	7	20	10	2	2	6	20
	Min.	37	48	49	39	37	39	43	45	45	39
	Max.	55	69	56	63	69	78	55	47	71	78
	Mean	47.67	56.75	52.67	53.43	52.25	54.2	49	46	55.5	53.25
	C.V.	13.44	15.59	6.67	17.32	15.18	21.16	17.32	3.07	15.98	18.44
Secondary	N	7	2	2	9	20	2	3	2	13	20
	Min.	39	47	46	37	37	57	52	61	44	44
	Max.	67	49	53	63	67	77	78	63	81	81
	Mean	53.29	48	49.5	50.56	51.15	67	60.67	62	59.85	60.9
	C.V.	16.06	2.95	10	19.86	16.37	21.11	24.74	2.28	18.1	17.47

Contd.

High School	N	3	4	3	10	20	5	5	1	9	20
	Min.	60	43	48	48	43	49	44	51	45	44
	Max.	69	52	58	69	69	53	60	51	81	81
	Mean	63.33	48.75	52.33	55.9	55.05	50.8	52.4	51	62.44	56.45
	C.V.	7.79	8.27	9.81	10.88	12.34	4.03	11.5	-	19.37	17.84
Higher Secondary	N	2	3	5	5	20	14	-	3	3	20
	Min.	43	49	52	50	43	31	-	48	50	31
	Max.	57	60	67	62	67	81	-	53	68	81
	Mean	52.57	55.67	58	55	55	50.64	-	50.67	61.67	52.3
	C.V.	9.18	10.53	11.44	8.81	9.92	21.42	-	4.97	16.4	19.89
Above Higher Secondary	N	-	3	3	14	20	7	4	3	6	20
	Min.	-	50	58	49	49	51	50	50	49	49
	Max.	-	60	81	67	81	77	57	61	78	78
	Mean	-	56	73.33	57.71	59.8	62.29	53.5	57.33	60	59.1
	C.V.	-	9.45	18.11	9.28	14.53	17.51	6.56	11.08	16.09	15.07

Source: Computed.

Table 18

Score Values of PARM According to Female Asset Structure,, Levels of Education and Employment Status

Employment Status		*Unemployed (120)*				*Employed (120)*			
Female Asset		*No Property*	*50000 to 100000 (Rs.)*	*Above 100000 (Rs.)*	*Total*	*No Property*	*50000 to 100000 (Rs.)*	*Above 100000 (Rs.)*	*Total*
Levels of Education									
Illiterates	N	2	5	13	20	4	6	10	20
	Min.	43	45	38	38	34	41	41	34
	Max.	46	68	55	68	51	81	78	81
	Mean	44.5	52.6	47.54	48.5	46.5	54.5	51.8	51.55
	C.V.	4.77	17.97	11.15	13.6	17.95	26.96	19.98	21.83
Primary	N	-	9	11	20	-	7	13	20
	Min.	-	39	37	37	-	39	43	39
	Max.	-	60	69	69	-	69	78	78
	Mean	-	51.78	52.64	52.25	-	51.71	54.08	53.25
	C.V.	-	13.85	16.78	15.18	-	18.33	19	18.44
Secondary	N	-	7	13	20	4	6	10	20
	Min.	-	43	37	37	53	44	47	44
	Max.	-	67	63	67	67	78	81	81
	Mean	-	54	49.62	51.15	60	58.67	62.6	60.9
	C.V.	-	14.5	17.23	16.37	10.36	19.39	19.39	17.47

Contd.

High School	N	-	5	15	20	1	6	13	20
	Min	-	48	43	43	51	49	44	44
	Max.	-	69	69	69	51	77	81	81
	Mean	-	58.4	53.93	55.05	51	59.83	55.31	56.45
	C.V.	-	13.94	11.48	12.34	-	16.56	18.97	17.84
Higher Secondary	N	1	7	12	20	3	4	13	20
	Min.	58	43	50	43	31	40	47	31
	Max.	58	63	67	67	57	81	68	81
	Mean	58	53	55.92	55	47	54	53	52.3
	C.V.	-	11.93	9.01	9.92	29.79	34.18	12.66	19.89
Above Higher Secondary	N	3	6	11	20	-	8	12	20
	Min.	50	49	50	49	-	50	49	49
	Max.	81	81	62	81	-	77	78	78
	Mean	63	63.83	56.73	59.8	-	58.88	59.25	59.1
	C.V.	25.55	16.41	6.51	14.53	-	13.81	16.44	15.07

Source: Computed.

Table 19

Score Values of PARM According to Asset holder, Levels of Education and Employment Status

Employment Status		*Unemployed (120)*				*Employed (120)*			
Asset Holder		*Male*	*Female*	*Both*	*Total*	*Male*	*Female*	*Both*	*Total*
Levels of Education									
Illiterates	N	3	1	16	20	3	6	11	20
	Min.	43	68	38	38	34	43	41	34
	Max.	54	68	55	68	51	81	59	81
	Mean	47.67	68.00	47.44	48.50	45.33	59.67	48.82	51.55
	C.V.	11.93	-	10.35	13.60	21.65	26.60	12.32	21.83
Primary	N	-	8	12	20	-	7	13	20
	Min.	-	37	39	37	53	39	43	39
	Max.	-	69	63	69	-	78	71	78
	Mean	-	52.38	52.17	52.25	-	55.71	51.92	53.25
	C.V.	-	18.59	13.33	15.18	-	24.16	14.49	18.44
Secondary	N	-	5	15	20	-	6	14	20
	Min.	-	48	37	37	-	63	44	44
	Max.	-	67	63	67	67	79	81	81
	Mean	-	55.60	49.67	51.15	59.00	74.25	57.23	60.90
	C.V.	-	12.76	17.01	16.37	12.22	10.16	15.78	17.47
High School	N	-	2	18	20	-	6	14	20
	Min.	-	60	43	43	-	49	44	44
	Max.	-	69	69	69	-	81	77	81
	Mean	-	64.50	54.00	55.05	-	55.83	56.71	56.45
	C.V.	-	9.87	11.34	12.34	-	22.32	16.56	17.84

Contd.

Higher Secondary	N	1	4	15	20	4	5	11	20
	Min.	58	43	49	43	31	50	40	31
	Max.	58	57	67	67	57	81	68	81
	Mean	58.00	51.75	55.67	55.00	46.50	57.00	52.27	52.30
	C.V.	-	11.95	9.52	9.92	24.68	23.73	15.82	19.89
Above Higher Secondary	N	-	4	16	20	-	5	15	20
	Min.	-	58	49	49	-	50	49	49
	Max.	-	81	67	81	-	77	78	78
	Mean	-	70.50	57.13	59.80	-	58.60	59.27	59.10
	C.V.	-	17.35	9.19	14.53	-	18.16	14.63	15.07

Source: Computed.

INTEGRATED ANALYSIS FOR POWER OF AUTONOMY OVER RESOURCES AND MOBILITY: PATH ANALYSIS

Economic contribution by itself is not enough for women to have an equal status. They must have control over the means of production and should have opportunities for equal participation in family and community decision-making. Empowerment is an abstract concept. It requires an analysis of power. While empowerment literally means "to invest with power" in the context of women's empowerment, the term has come to denote women's increased control over their own lives, bodies, and environment. The results of relationship between dependent variables (Power of Autonomy over Resources and Mobility) and the independent variables such as age of the respondents, community, type of households, size of households, total literacy of family members, age difference between husband and wife, income earner, controller of expenditure, account holder, asset holder, proportion of female income, proportion of expenditure, proportion of savings, proportion of borrowings, proportion of asset structure, education level, sex ratio, and employment status. Stepwise regression analysis indicate that out of eighteen variables, only eight variables are found to be statistically significant in determining the factors on PARM.

The eight significant variables in determining PARM are *proportion of female income, employment status, Income earner, levels of education, proportion of female borrowings, control over expenditure, proportion of female asset structure and account holder.*

The co-efficient of multiple determination $(\overline{R})^2$, through regression analysis, indicates 0.24. It means that out of 100 per cent variations in PARM of the respondents, about 24per cent of variation is explained by the specified eight independent variables. The balance 76per cent is attributed to "other factors" or variables, which are not included in the given analysis. The 'F' test based on $(\overline{R})^2$ indicates 10.52, which is found to be statistically significant at 5 per cent level with 8.231 degrees of freedom. It implies that all the selected eight independent variables are significant to justify the selection of this model and suitability to verify the parameters of the general population.

It is seen from the results of the step wise regression analysis that the level of education affects PARM which occupies the top most position, with 't' value of (4.87). It has been followed by proportion of female income (4.81), proportion of female asset structure (2.82), account holder (2.55), proportion of female borrowing (2.41) and control over expenditure (1.96). These factors have positive influence on PARM. On the other hand, employment status (-2.15) and income earner (-3.53) have inverse relation with PARM.

Table 7.a
Stepwise Regression Analysis of Explanatory Variables with PARM Index as Dependent Variable

Explanatory Variables	*Regression Co-efficient* $(\hat{B})$	*'t' value*	*'p' value*
Levels of Education	0.42	4.87	0.000
Employment Status	-0.32	-2.15	0.032
Proportion of female income	0.33	4.81	0.000
Proportion of female borrowings	0.14	2.41	0.017
Account holder	0.15	2.55	0.011
Proportion of female assets	0.17	2.82	0.005
Income Earner	-0.47	-3.53	0.001
Control over expenditure	0.24	1.96	0.051
$\overline{R}^2$ = 0.27; df = 8.231;		F = 10.52	000

df = degrees of freedom
Source: Computed

The final result of the stepwise regression analysis given in Table 7.a. reveals that eight out of eighteen factors have significant effect on PARM. Among them, the regression coefficients are positive for six factors namely levels of education, proportion of female income, proportion of female borrowings, account holder, proportion of female assets and control over expenditure; and negative for two factors for namely employment status and income earner, indicating direct and inverse relationship respectively with the PARM.

The above indicated eight variables alone are sufficient to make significant influence in determining PARM. The path analysis of explanatory variables with PARM as dependent variable is given in Table 21. The variables levels of education (0.42), the proportion of female income (0.33), the proportion of female borrowings (0.14), the account holder (0.15), the proportion of female asset (0.17) and the control over expenditure (0.24) have positively direct effect on PARM. The most significant variable is the level of education. It is argued that as education enhances the bargaining power of women, PARM of women also increases. (Sen 1991) When girls are educated, they have economic opportunities. Their families have more of a stake in their survival and their success, and are able to take part in house hold decision and hence, their power of autonomy over resources and mobility (PARM) increases. Two variables, employment (-0.32), and income earner (-0.47), have negative effect on PARM.

It is observed from Table 7.b that the factor income earner has positive indirect effect (0.44) as against negative direct effect (0.47) by the levels of education, control over expenditure and employment status. It is followed by employment status which has positive indirect effect (0.22) as against negative direct effect (-0.32) caused by proportion of female income (0.17) levels of education (0.37) and income earner (-0.36).

In contrast, the indirect effect of the levels of education is negative (-0.22) as against positive direct effect (0.42) caused by proportion of female income (0.14), employment status (-0.28) and income earner (-0.30). An interesting fact is that the factor proportion of female assets has positive direct and indirect effects caused by proportion of female income, levels of education and employment status.

The level of education positively influences the employment status, proportion of female income, proportion of female borrowings, account holder, income earner and control over expenditure which implies that education plays a significant role in determining the PARM of rural women through the above specified factors. On the contrary, the factor income earner negatively influences the employment status,

Table 7.b

Path Analysis of Explanatory Variables with Power of Autonomy Over Resources and Mobility as Dependent Variable

Explanatory Variables	*Regression Co-efficient*				*Correlation with IYm*
	Direct Effect	*Total Indirect Effect*	*Substantial Indirect Effect Channeled through Significant Variables*		
Levels of Education	0.42	-0.22	0.14	*Proportion of Female Income*	0.20*
			-0.28	Employment Status	
			-0.30	Income earner	
Employment Status	-0.32	0.4 2	0.17	Proportion of Female Income	0.10
			0.37	Levels of Education	
			-0.36	Earner of Income	
Proportion of Female Income	0.33	-0.02	0.18	Levels of Education	0.31*
			-0.16	Employment Status	
			-0.21	Income Earner	
Proportion of Female Borrowings	0.14	0.06	0.06	Levels of Education	0.20*
			0.03	Account holder	
			-0.04	Employment Status	
Account Holder	0.15	-0.04	0.06	Levels of Education	0.11
			-0.04	Employment Status	
			-0.10	Income Earner	
Proportion of Female Assets	0.17	0.09	0.08	Proportion of Income	0.26*
			0.06	Levels of Education	
			-0.05	Employment Status	
Income Earner	-0.47	0.44	0.26	Levels of Education	-0.03
			0.21	Control over Expenditure	
			-0.24	Employment Status	
Control over Expenditure	0.24	-0.19	0.25	Levels of Education	0.05
			-0.22	Employment Status	
			-0.41	Income Earner	

Source: Computed

* - Significant at 5% level

proportion of female income, account holder and control over expenditure. Since women are located in different households, castes, communities, and regions, and are bound by distinct rituals, practices and structures of power, they rarely view themselves as a group with similar demands and needs. They are often governed by decision that others take on their behalf. Case studies based on qualitative surveys have shown that even when women work and earn their own incomes, they have little or no control over expenditure (Batliwala *et al.* 1998; Visaria 1993). In addition, education, employment, proportion of female income, account holder and control over expenditure have inverse indirect impact on PARM though income earner, education, employment and proportion female assets have positive direct impact through proportion of female income. Control over expenditure has positive indirect effect only on income earner and not on any other variables. It reflects that when female contribution to the total income increases, the controlling power of expenditure also increases.

The effect of explanatory variables on PARM, the independent variables viz, proportion of female income, exerts higher contribution to the tune of 0.31, followed by proportion of female asset structure (0.26), proportion of female borrowings and levels of education (0.20), account holder (0.11) employment (0.10), control over expenditure (0.05) and income earner (-0.03).

It is inferred from the above findings that the respondents who contribute more to the total family income have power over resources and mobility. On the contrary, half of the respondents could not have power of autonomy over resources and mobility because they are unemployed.

In other words, when the level of education increases, the effect on PARM also increases, and its direct effect is indicated as 0.42. When the level of education increases, women will equally participate in decision-making of the family and PARM also increases. Likewise, proportion of female income has a direct effect on PARM, because, when the proportion of female income increases, their financial autonomy also increases. The other factor is the proportion of female borrowings. When women possess financial autonomy, they are likely to borrow more. The account holder also has a positive effect on PARM. When both male and female keep the saving accounts, gender equality is neither skewed for men nor for women. Both will have PARM and thereby the variable account holder has positive effect. Likewise, the proportion of female asset structure and the control over expenditure also have a positive effect on PARM as these factors provide financial autonomy to women. The female asset structure in the family determines PARM. Higher the asset structure, higher will be the PARM. Moreover, PARM and control over expenditure are inter related. When there is control over expenditure by females, there will be a high PARM and hence, this variable has a positive effect on PARM.

Fig. 1. Direct and Indirect Effect of Significant Exogenous Variables on PARM

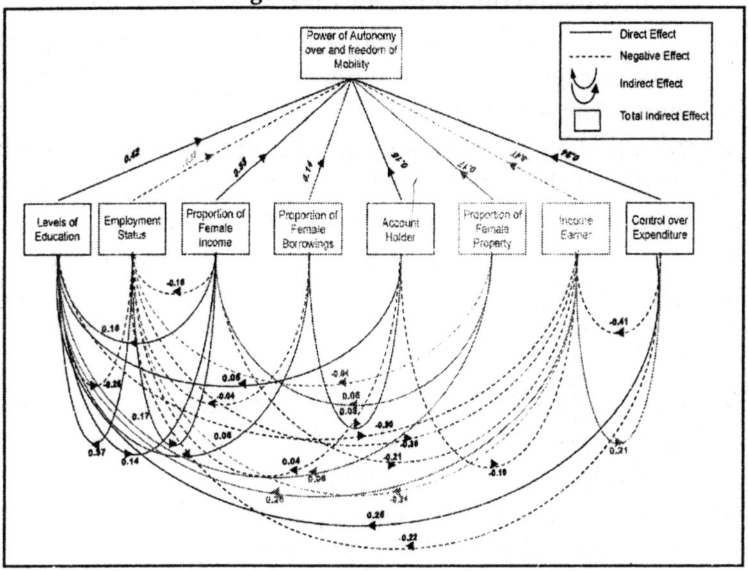

It is noted that the employment status and the income earner have negative direct effects on PARM. Most women have come to consider the paid employment as part of their domestic role. They work for the household and not for their own self-esteem or personal autonomy, and thereby employment has a negative effect. To the researchers who consider women's access to income earning work as a vehicle to gain control over resources and attain a level of autonomy in making their 'life choices', the evidences seem to throw challenges, says Lingam (2006).

On the whole, it is interesting to note that the contribution of indirect effect on PARM is the maximum for four factors, namely income earner, employment, education and control over expenditure. Thus, direct and indirect effects and their relationships in terms of positive and negative are illustrated through path diagram Fig. 2.

KEY FINDINGS

- Lower age employed women have a high PARM not only at the higher level of education. Some are entitled to PARM even without education.
- The rural women who belong to OC have a high PARM only at higher levels of education, irrespective of their employment status.
- The employed rural women from joint families have a high PARM at the higher levels of education and those from nuclear families at the lower levels of education.
- The employed rural women from small families have a high PARM at the lower level of education, and unemployed women have a high PARM at the higher levels of education.
- The employed women with higher age difference have PARM not only at the higher education level but also have PARM even without education.
- Higher contribution of employed women to total income leads to a higher PARM at all levels of education.
- Higher share of employed women's income to the total expenditure of the family leads to high PARM at lower levels of education.

- Higher contribution of employed women to total savings of the family leads to a high PARM at the lower levels of education.
- When female indebtedness is high in the total indebtedness of the family, the unemployed women have a high PARM at higher levels of education.
- The employed rural women have a high PARM at the lower levels of education when the female asset structure in the family is high.
- When the savings accounts are kept by the employed women alone, they have a high PARM at the lower levels of education.
- The employed women have high a PARM at the lower levels of education when the female alone titles the asset structure.
- The factors which determine the level of PARM are the proportion of female income, employment status, proportion of female borrowings, levels of education, income earner, control over expenditure, proportion of female property and account holder.
- Among the factors, the level of education plays an important role in influencing PARM of rural women.

The research has analysed GEDM and PARM of rural women in the previous chapters. The results show that generally GEDM moves along with PARM in the same direction to attain empowerment. The succeeding chapter will attempts to present an overall empowerment profile of rural women blending the observations on GEDM and PARM of the rural women together.

8

ANALYSIS OF EMPOWERMENT

By women's empowerment, one could refer to the expansion in women's ability and freedom to make strategic life choices, a process that occurs over time and involves women as agents who have the ability to formulate choices, control resources, or enact decisions that affect important life outcomes (Malhotra and Schuler *et al.* 2002). There are several cogent and pressing reasons for evaluating, promoting and monitoring the level of women's empowerment in India. Their empowerment is necessary to ensure not just their own welfare, but also the well being of the entire household. The empowerment of women is also critical for the very development of India, since it will enhance both the quality and the quantity of human resource available for development. Further, the success of development efforts depends on the fruits of development reaching men and women, boys and girls. The extent to which this happens, however, depends critically on gender relations within the society that set the worth of sex relation to the other (Kishor and Gupta 2004).

EDUCATION AND EMPLOYMENT WISE ANALYSIS

It is obvious that the employed respondents are highly empowered as compared to unemployed respondents at all levels of education excluding above higher secondary education.

Age of the Respondents and Age Difference between Husband and Wife

It is an interesting fact that the employed illiterates belonging to the age group of 25–40 years are empowered more than unemployed illiterates (Tables 1 and 5). It is noted that lower age group respondents are not empowered at all levels of education among unemployed respondents. At the primary level of education, the employed respondents are highly empowered as compared to unemployed respondents when the respondents belong to the age group of below 25 years. At the middle age, the unemployed respondents are empowered more than the employed respondents at above higher secondary education level. At the secondary level of education the employed respondents are highly empowered when the cohorts belong to 25–40 years. At the high school level, the employed respondents are empowered more than their counter parts when their age is above 40 years. It is surprising to note that the unemployed respondents are highly empowered at the higher secondary education level when the respondents belong to above 40 years.

It is noted that the employed illiterates are empowered as compared to the unemployed illiterates when the age difference between husband and wife is between 5 and 10 years. At the highest level of education, the employed respondents are empowered as compared to unemployed respondents who belong to the age group of 5 to 10 years. When the age difference is 1 to 5 years, the respondents are empowered at the high school education level irrespective of employment status. It is found that the majority of the respondents who belong to a lesser age difference with their spouse have been empowered at various levels of education and employment status.

Community

Table 2 reveals that the employed respondents belonging to MBC are more empowered than the unemployed respondents at the lower level of education (upto secondary). The unemployed SC respondents are empowered at the high school

Table 1

Score Values of Empowerment According to Age, Levels of Education and Employment Status

Employment Status		*Unemployed (120)*				*Employed (120)*			
Age (year)		*Before 25*	*25-40*	*Above 40*	*Total*	*Below 25*	*25-40*	*Above All*	*Total*
Levels of Education									
Illiterates	N	11	2	7	20	1	11	8	20
	Min.	77	78	72	72	100	70	81	70
	Max.	101	92	117	117	100	137	123	137
	Mean	93.36	85	87.71	90.55	100.00	102.45	98.62	100.80
	C.V.	7.66	11.64	19.41	12.80	-	20.57	14.36	17.50
Primary	N	2	11	7	20	4	7	9	20
	Min.	87	65	92	65	101	67	89	67
	Max.	111	107	112	117	123	113	112	123
	Mean	99	92.63	102.85	96.85	114.75	96.85	102.33	102.9
	C.V.	17.14	15.99	6.69	13.45	8.31	15.14	7.74	11.97
Secondary	N	2	12	6	20	4	10	6	20
	Min.	94	69	93	69	82	94	102	82
	Max.	115	117	113	117	121	132	121	132
	Mean	104.5	97.25	99.83	98.75	103.75	114.3	112.66	111.7
	C.V.	14.20	14.03	7.56	11.96	15.86	11.11	6.46	10.97

Contd.

High School	N	3	12	5	20	3	6	11	20
	Min.	84	93	94	84	86	94	84	84
	Max.	112	126	121	126	99	128	130	130
	Mean	98	105.08	106.4	104.35	93.67	104.83	108.81	105.35
	C.V.	14.28	8.89	9.98	9.71	7.27	11.73	14.13	13.35
Higher Secondary	N	7	5	8	20	3	9	8	20
	Min.	96	92	97	92	83	68	84	68
	Max.	114	110	119	119	99	124	118	124
	Mean	104.85	101.8	105.12	104.20	92.33	96.77	98.75	96.9
	C.V.	7.06	6.30	6.75	6.55	9.02	15.45	13.83	13.65
Above Higher Secondary	N	4	6	10	20	2	11	7	20
	Min.	105	112	90	90	110	99	100	99
	Max.	129	128	141	141	120	127	130	130
	Mean	117.5	121.5	108	113.95	115.00	111.27	113.42	112.4
	C.V.	8.80	4.76	14.53	11.83	6.15	7.57	7.91	7.29

Source: Computed.

Table 2
Score Values of Empowerment According to Community, Levels of Education and Employment Status

Employment Status		*Unemployed (120)*					*Employed (120)*				
Community		*OC*	*BC*	*MBC*	*SC*	*Total*	*OC*	*BC*	*MBC*	*SC*	*Total*
Levels of Education											
Illiterates	N	3	5	8	4	20	6	6	7	1	20
	Min.	75	77	77	72	72	73	87	70	98	70
	Max.	105	96	117	93	117	120	123	137	98	137
	Mean	93.33	85.8	95.87	83.75	90.55	95.33	103.33	103.71	98.00	100.80
	C.V.	17.22	9.08	11.7	12.42	12.80	18.70	18.82	22.10	-	17.50
Primary	N	2	7	6	5	20	1	6	6	7	20
	Min.	105	65	87	92	65	110	67	89	97	67
	Max.	107	107	112	111	112	110	123	104	118	123
	Mean	106.00	90.85	98.50	99.60	96.85	110.00	101.50	96.83	108.28	102.90
	C.V.	1.33	20.30	9.60	8.11	13.45	-	18.82	6.24	7.45	11.97
Secondary	N	1	6	8	5	20	3	6	8	3	20
	Min.	87	69	80	95	69	94	82	102	102	82
	Max.	87	115	113	117	117	121	132	129	113	132
	Mean	87.00	96.83	96.87	106.4	98.75	107.33	110.66	115.37	108.33	111.70
	C.V.	-	15.85	10.60	7.50	11.96	12.58	16.79	7.28	5.24	10.97

Contd.

High School	N	1	6	8	5	20	3	6	8	3	20
	Min.	4	95	84	105	84	94	84	93	86	84
	Max.	112	126	113	121	126	128	127	130	112	130
	Mean	103	107.7	100.11	113.00	104.35	111.00	110.16	108.60	97.28	105.35
	C.V.	12.35	9.34	9.07	10.01	9.71	21.65	14.56	12.91	8.34	13.35
Higher Secondary	N	4	9	6	1	20	2	5	7	6	20
	Min.	102	92	97	96	92	83	68	84	87	68
	Max.	119	111	113	96	119	118	99	124	118	124
	Mean	110.00	103.2	103.16	96.00	104.20	100.50	87.40	99.42	100.66	96.90
	C.V.	7.15	5.47	6.52	-	6.55	24.62	13.25	12.19	8.34	13.65
Above Higher Secondary	N	5	8	3	4	20	3	4	12	1	20
	Min.	111	103	90	93	90	110	106	99	117	99
	Max.	128	129	141	105	141	116	127	130	117	130
	Mean	118.20	119.00	115.00	97.75	113.95	113.33	117.00	110.25	117	112.4
	C.V.	18.70	7.29	22.18	5.37	11.83	2.69	8.28	7.80	-	7.29

Source: Computed.

education level. It is an interesting fact that the employed respondents who belong to OC are empowered at a very low level of education, whereas the unemployed respondents belonging to the same community are empowered at higher level of education. The unemployed respondents of BC are empowered at the above higher secondary education.

Type of Family and Size of Family

It is noted from Table 3 that the employed illiterates are highly empowered as compared to the unemployed illiterates irrespective of type of families. Moreover, it is noted that the employed respondents belonging to nuclear families are highly empowered as compared to the unemployed respondents at the lower level of education, when the unemployed respondents who belong to nuclear families are empowered at higher level of education.

It is observed from Table 4 that the employed respondents belonging to smaller families are empowered at the low level of education. On the contrary, the unemployed respondents belonging to smaller families are empowered at the highest level of education. Likewise the employed respondents belonging to medium sized families are empowered even though they are illiterate. The unemployed respondents belonging to medium sized families are empowered at the higher level of education. It is inferred that small and medium sized family's respondents are more empowered than the large sized families.

Level of Income and Empowerment

From Table 6, it is surprising to note that the employed respondents are empowered at all levels of education when the total income is low. The higher earnings of female income raise the level of empowerment. It is observed that when the females earn above Rs.25,000, the level of empowerment is high at all levels of education excluding higher secondary education. They also obtain the maximum score at the higher level of income. When the female income is nil, the mpowerment is low at all levels of education.

Table 3
Score Values of Empowerment According to Types of Family and Employment Status

Employment Status		*Unemployed (120)*			*Employed (120)*		
Type of Household		*Joint*	*Nuclear*	*Total*	*Joint*	*Nuclear*	*Total*
Levels of Education							
Illiterates	N	6	14	20	5	15	20
	Min.	88	72	72	73	70	70
	Max.	117	100	117	123	137	137
	Mean	99.83	86.57	90.55	100.80	100.80	100.80
	C.V.	10.39	11.45	12.80	18.60	17.80	17.50
Primary	N	1	19	20	7	13	20
	Min.	102	65	65	67	89	67
	Max.	102	112	112	118	123	123
	Mean	102.00	96.57	96.85	102.85	102.92	102.90
	C.V.	-	13.80	13.45	16.41	9.61	11.97
Secondary	N	7	13	20	8	12	20
	Min.	69	87	69	82	94	82
	Max.	109	117	117	129	132	132
	Mean	92.85	101.92	98.75	106.50	115.16	111.70
	C.V.	15.56	9.07	11.96	12.36	9.37	10.97

Contd.

High School	N	5	15	20	6	14	20
	Min.	95	84	84	86	84	84
	Max.	126	121	126	108	130	130
	Mean	107.4	103.33	104.35	99.16	108	105.35
	C.V.	11.37	9.30	9.71	8.37	14.26	13.35
Higher Secondary	N	5	15	20	7	13	20
	Min.	96	92	92	68	83	68
	Max.	114	119	119	124	118	124
	Mean	102.20	104.86	104.20	94.85	98.00	96.90
	C.V.	7.00	6.51	6.55	17.31	6.79	13.65
Above Higher Secondary	N	5	15	20	3	17	20
	Min.	90	95	90	109	99	99
	Max.	120	141	141	130	127	130
	Mean	105.20	116.86	113.95	118.66	111.29	112.40
	C.V.	13.63	10.52	11.83	8.93	6.79	7.29

Source: Computed.

Table 4

Score Values of Empowerment According to Size of family, Levels of Education and Employment

Employment Status		*Unemployed (120)*				*Employed (120)*			
Size of Household		*Small*	*Medium*	*Large*	*Total*	*Small*	*Medium*	*Large*	*Total*
Levels of Education									
Illiterates	N	11	7	2	20	12	2	6	20
	Min.	72	75	78	72	73	112	70	70
	Max.	117	101	105	117	137	123	120	137
	Mean	88.81	93.00	91.5	90.55	101.16	117.50	94.50	100.80
	C.V.	14.47	9.41	20.86	12.80	17.81	6.61	18.25	17.50
Primary	N	11	4	5	20	9	9	2	20
	Min.	65	93	69	65	89	67	101	67
	Max.	112	111	107	112	123	113	105	123
	Mean	94.54	103.25	96.80	96.85	105.55	100.22	103.00	102.90
	C.V.	8.95	7.51	16.72	13.45	11.75	13.74	2.74	11.97
Secondary	N	9	7	4	20	10	5	5	20
	Min.	87	69	90	69	94	100	82	82
	Max.	117	115	113	117	132	129	121	132
	Mean	101.00	95.57	99.25	98.75	114.50	111.20	106.60	111.70
	C.V.	8.95	16.97	10.12	11.96	10.11	9.69	14.64	10.97

Contd.

High School	N	10	4	6	20	10	6	4	20
	Min.	84	99	95	84	84	86	91	84
	Max.	113	126	121	126	130	127	128	130
	Mean	100.30	110.50	107.00	104.35	106.70	103.66	104.50	105.35
	C.V.	8.74	10.51	9.32	9.71	13.75	13.03	16.28	13.35
Higher Secondary	N	9	5	6	20	7	6	7	20
	Min.	92	96	97	92	83	84	68	68
	Max.	113	119	114	119	118	101	124	124
	Mean	103.44	106.60	103.33	104.20	98.14	93.00	99.00	96.90
	C.V.	6.50	8.03	5.98	6.55	12.85	7.03	18.55	13.65
Above Higher Secondary	N	12	4	4	20	12	5	3	20
	Min.	103	93	90	90	99	100	104	99
	Max.	141	120	123	141	127	130	123	130
	Mean	118.16	107.75	107.50	113.95	111.75	113.20	113.66	112.40
	C.V.	9.52	13.26	16.22	11.83	6.46	9.98	8.36	7.29

Source: Computed.

Table 5

Score Values of Empowerment According to Age Difference, Levels of Education and Employment

Employment Status		*Unemployed (120)*				*Employed (120)*			
Age Difference (year)		*1-5*	*5-10*	*10-15*	*Total*	*1-5*	*5-10*	*10-15*	*Total*
Levels of Education									
Illiterates	N	1	10	9	20	5	6	9	20
	Min.	96	72	78	72	84	72	73	70
	Max.	96	117	105	117	105	137	124	137
	Mean	96.00	89.80	90.77	90.55	94.40	105.30	101.33	100.80
	C.V.	-	16.01	9.98	12.80	9.19	16.01	17.14	17.50
Primary	N	4	8	8	20	7	7	6	20
	Min.	94	69	65	65	96	93	67	67
	Max.	111	112	105	112	117	118	123	123
	Mean	104.75	98.00	91.25	96.85	106.00	104.14	97.83	102.90
	C.V.	7.07	13.70	14.72	13.45	7.42	13.70	19.82	11.97
Secondary	N	5	12	3	20	9	9	2	20
	Min.	69	87	80	69	82	94	110	82
	Max.	117	115	113	117	118	132	121	132
	Mean	96.40	100.08	97.33	98.75	108.44	114.11	115.50	111.70
	C.V.	19.23	7.82	17.01	11.96	10.42	7.82	6.73	10.97

Contd.

High School	N	3	12	5	20	10	5	5	20
	Min.	84	93	94	84	86	84	91	84
	Max.	126	121	105	126	128	130	112	130
	Mean	107.66	105.16	100.40	104.35	107.60	106.40	99.8	105.35
	C.V.	19.97	8.29	4.20	9.71	13.44	8.29	8.15	13.35
Higher Secondary	N	5	11	4	20	8	10	2	20
	Min.	101	92	99	92	68	83	96	68
	Max.	119	110	114	119	106	124	118	124
	Mean	108.8	101.09	107	104.20	92.37	98.50	107	96.90
	C.V.	6.57	5.07	7.11	6.55	12.57	5.07	14.53	13.65
Above Higher Secondary	N	8	10	2	20	6	8	6	20
	Min.	95	90	114	90	99	104	105	99
	Max.	129	141	120	141	116	130	120	130
	Mean	116.00	111.70	117.00	113.95	108.00	116.87	110.83	112.40
	C.V.	10.86	14.06	3.62	11.83	6.85	14.06	4.68	7.29

Source: Computed

Table 6
Score Values of Empowerment According to Total Income, Levels of Education and Employment

Employment Status		*Unemployed (120)*				*Employed (120)*			
Total Income		*Below 50000*	*50000 to 100000*	*Above 100000*	*Total*	*Below 50000*	*50000 to 100000*	*Above 100000*	*Total*
Levels of Education									
Illiterates	N	4	10	6	20	4	7	9	20
	Min.	77	75	72	72	73	87	70	70
	Max.	101	117	100	117	137	124	120	137
	Mean	85.25	94.10	88.17	90.55	105.75	102.00	97.67	100.80
	C.V.	13.01	12.44	13.24	12.80	27.81	12.40	16.85	17.50
Primary	N	5	9	6	20	4	9	7	20
	Min.	82	69	65	65	104	67	89	67
	Max.	112	107	111	112	117	118	123	123
	Mean	95.00	99.55	94.33	96.85	110.75	99.56	102.71	102.90
	C.V.	11.43	12.42	17.81	13.45	4.86	14.52	11.10	11.97
Secondary	N	3	12	5	20	11	1	8	20
	Min.	99	69	90	69	100	109	82	82
	Max.	109	117	104	117	129	109	132	132
	Mean	105.00	98.50	95.60	98.75	113.45	109	109.63	111.70
	C.V.	5.04	14.76	5.36	11.96	7.73	-	15.46	10.97

Contd.

High School	N	6	9	5	20	6	8	6	20
	Min.	93	84	94	84	94	84	93	84
	Max.	126	121	105	126	128	102	130	130
	Mean	108.00	103.78	101.00	104.35	112.33	94.88	112.33	105.35
	C.V.	11.02	10.94	4.26	9.71	13.54	7.31	11.27	13.35
Higher. Secondary	N	4	11	5	20	5	8	7	20
	Min.	96	92	99	92	88	83	68	68
	Max.	114	113	119	119	124	106	101	124
	Mean	102.25	104.18	105.80	104.20	109.20	94.75	90.57	96.90
	C.V.	8.08	6.14	7.36	6.55	14.10	9.11	12.60	13.65
Above Higher Secondary.	N	11	4	5	20	4	8	8	20
	Min.	90	93	98	90	117	99	106	99
	Max.	141	128	129	141	127	130	116	130
	Mean	116.18	110.00	112.20	113.95	121.75	108.12	112.00	112.40
	C.V.	9.80	3.47	10.11	11.83	6.38	4.46	8.68	7.29.

Source: Computed

Table 7

Score Values of Empowerment According to Female Income, Levels of Education and Employment

Employment Status		*Unemployed (120)*			*Employed (120)*		
Female Income		*No Earning*	*Below 25000*	*Total*	*No Earning*	*Below 25000*	*Total*
Levels of Education							
Illiterates	N	13	7	20	15	5	20
	Min.	75	72	72	70	98	70
	Max.	117	100	117	120	137	137
	Mean	91.85	88.14	90.55	95.60	116.40	100.80
	C.V.	13.71	11.24	12.80	15.72	14.46	17.50
Primary	N	15	5	20	16	4	20
	Min.	65	102	65	67	110	67
	Max.	112	111	112	117	123	123
	Mean	94.00	105.40	96.85	99.69	115.75	102.90
	C.V.	14.76	3.19	13.45	11.45	5.10	11.97
Secondary	N	15	5	20	7	13	20
	Min.	69	95	69	82	100	82
	Max.	115	117	117	121	132	132
	Mean	96.87	104.40	98.75	105.00	115.31	111.70
	C.V.	12.48	9.52	11.9	8.12	9.32	10.97

Contd.

High School	N	15	5	20	13	7	20
	Min.	93	84	84	84	106	84
	Max.	126	112	126	112	130	130
	Mean	106.87	96.80	104.35	97.08	120.71	105.35
	C.V.	8.52	10.47	9.71	8.12	7.34	13.35
Higher Secondary	N	19	1	20	16	4	20
	Min.	92	119	92	83	68	68
	Max.	114	119	119	118	124	124
	Mean	103.42	119	104.20	95.81	101.25	96.90
	C.V.	5.83	-	6.55	9.67	25.13	13.65
Above Higher Secondary.	N	18	2	20	16	4	20
	Min.	90	112	90	99	107	99
	Max.	141	122	141	130	137	130
	Mean	113.61	117.00	113.95	111.13	117.50	112.40
	C.V.	13.35	6.04	11.83	6.96	11.49	7.29

Source: Computed.

It is found from the above discussion that (Table 7) the higher female income leads to the higher empowerment for the employed respondents at all levels of education (except higher secondary). The skilled and educated work force might well increase household productivity, since it has extended entitlements (Dreze and Sen, 1991). Moreover, increased importance of women's contribution to the household economy enables women to challenge the myth of male bread-winner and male authority to a certain extent.

The female earnings determine the level of empowerment. It is observed that when the female is also an income earner in the family, the level of empowerment is high in the family. Table 8 shows that the employed respondents are highly empowered, when the female alone at all levels of education, excluding higher secondary education, earns an income. At the higher secondary levels of education, the unemployed respondents are empowered when the income earners are both males and females. It is an interesting fact that only the minimum score value is obtained by the employed primary educated people, when the male alone earns the income. Thus, it is found that when income earners are the female, the level of empowerment is high among the employed respondents.

Level of Expenditure and Empowerment

Regarding the total expenditure of the family, it is observed from Table 9 that higher the level of expenditure, the higher the level of empowerment among the employed respondents. Since women are employed, they contribute more to the total expenditure, and thereby the employed respondents are empowered more than the unemployed respondents, and the higher score value is also obtained by the employed respondents. When the expenditure is below Rs.25,000, the employed respondents are at primary level of education and higher secondary level of education.

Table 10 represents that when the level of female expenditure is high (above Rs.25,000), the employed illiterates are empowered. The employed respondents are empowered upto the high school education when the school education is

Table 8
Score Values of Empowerment According to Income Earner, Levels of Education and Employm

Employment Status		*Unemployed (120)**			*Employed (120)*			
Income Earner		*Male*	*Both*	*Total*	*Male*	*Female*	*Both*	*Total*
Levels of Education								
Illiterates	N	13	7	20	-	2	18	20
	Min.	75	72	72	-	100	70	70
	Max.	117	100	117	-	124	137	137
	Mean	91.85	88.14	90.55	-	112.00	99.56	100.80
	C.V.	13.71	11.24	12.80	-	15.15	17.82	17.50
Primary	N	15	5	20	-	3	17	20
	Min.	65	102	65	-	112	67	67
	Max.	112	11	112	-	118	123	123
	Mean	94.00	105.40	96.85	-	115.67	100.65	102.90
	C.V.	14.76	3.19	13.45	-	2.78	11.89	11.97
Secondary	N	15	5	20	1	3	16	20
	Min.	69	95	69	118	109	82	82
	Max.	115	117	117	118	129	132	132
	Mean	96.87	104.40	98.75	118.00	119.67	109.81	111.70
	C.V.	12.48	9.52	11.96	-	8.41	11.44	10.97

Contd.

High School	N	19	1	20	-	2	18	20
	Min.	93	84	84	-	93	84	84
	Max.	126	112	126	-	130	128	130
	Mean	106.87	96.80	104.35	-	111.50	104.67	105.35
	C.V.	8.52	10.47	9.71	-	23.46	12.67	13.35
Higher Secondary	N	19	1	20	-	1	19	20
	Min.	92	119	92	-	118	68	68
	Max.	114	119	119	-	118	124	124
	Mean	103.42	119.00	104.20	-	118.00	95.79	96.90
	C.V.	5.83	-	6.55	-	-	13.15	13.65
Above Higher. Secondary.	N	18	2	20	-	1	19	20
	Min.	90	112	90	-	120	99	99
	Max.	141	122	141	-	120	130	130
	Mean	113.61	117.00	113.95	-	120.00	112.00	112.40
	C.V.	12.42	6.04	11.83	-	-	7.34	7.29

Source: Computed.
Note: * In this category, women could Not control over expenditure, since they are unemployed

Table 9

Score Value of Empowerment According to Total Expenditure, Levels of Education and Employment

Employment Status		*Unemployed (120)*				*Employed (120)*			
Total Expenditure		*Below 25000*	*25000 to 50000*	*Above 50000*	*Total*	*Below 25000*	*25000 to 50000*	*Above 50000*	*Total*
Levels of Education									
Illiterates	N	5	11	4	20	2	6	12	20
	Min.	77	72	77	72	73	87	70	70
	Max.	101	105	117	117	124	113	137	137
	Mean	84.20	91.63	95.50	90.55	98.50	98.33	102.41	100.80
	C.V.	11.74	10.75	17.94	12.80	36.61	9.04	18.95	17.50
Primary	N	4	9	7	20	3	13	420	20
	Min.	82	69	65	65	104	67	96	67
	Max.	96	107	112	112	117	123	110	123
	Mean	90.75	99.55	96.85	96.85	111.33	100.61	104.00	102.90
	C.V.	6.70	12.42	17.27	13.45	5.98	14.08	5.66	11.97
Secondary	N	4	14	2	20	6	4	10	20
	Min.	97	69	94	69	100	94	82	82
	Max.	109	117	104	117	121	132	129	132
	Mean	103.00	97.50	99.00	98.75	110.66	111.25	112.50	111.70
	C.V.	5.12	13.95	7.14	11.96	8.14	14.07	12.23	10.97

Contd.

High School	N	3	9	8	20	6	9	5	20
	Min.	93	84	98	84	96	84	93	84
	Max.	99	121	126	126	130	121	128	130
	Mean	95.66	104.33	107.62	104.35	109.50	100.22	109.60	105.35
	C.V.	3.19	10.85	8.57	9.71	14.01	12.00	14.38	13.35
Higher Secondary	N	2	10	8	20	4	9	7	20
	Min.	96	92	97	92	88	83	68	68
	Max.	110	113	119	119	118	106	124	124
	Mean	103.00	103.60	105.25	104.20	105.75	95.11	94.14	96.90
	C.V.	9.61	6.21	7.18	6.55	14.03	8.56	18.08	13.65
Above Higher Secondary	N	4	6	10	20	6	7	7	20
	Min.	90	93	95	90	105	99	112	99
	Max.	128	141	129	141	127	130	123	130
	Mean	113.25	113.33	114.30	113.95	114.00	108.71	114.71	112.40
	C.V.	14.90	15.42	9.47	11.83	7.69	9.61	3.40	7.29

Source: Computed.

Table 10

Score Values of Empowerment According to Female Expenditure, Levels of Education and Employment

Employment Status		*Unemployed (120)*				*Employed (120)*			
Female Expenditure		*No Contribution*	*Below 25000*	*Above 25000*	*Total*	*No Contribution*	*Below 25000*	*Above 25000*	*Total*
Levels of Education									
Illiterates	N	14	6	-	20	4	12	4	20
	Min.	75	72	-	72	87	70	98	70
	Max.	117	100	-	117	137	120	124	137
	Mean	91.57	88.16	-	90.55	106.25	95.50	111.25	100.80
	C.V.	13.26	12.30	-	12.80	21.75	16.76	12.74	17.50
Primary	N	15	5	-	20	2	12	6	20
	Min.	65	102	-	65	93	89	67	67
	Max.	112	111	-	112	104	113	123	123
	Mean	94.00	105.40	-	96.85	98.50	101.66	106.83	102.90
	C.V.	14.75	3.18	-	13.45	7.89	7.19	19.12	11.97
Secondary	N	14	4	2	20	1	7	12	20
	Min.	69	95	97	69	107	82	100	82
	Max.	115	117	108	117	107	121	132	132
	Mean	96.07	106.25	102.5	98.75	107.00	106.57	115.08	111.70
	C.V.	12.62	9.82	7.58	11.96	-	13.27	9.48	10.97

Contd.

High School	N	17	3	-	20	-	14	6	20
	Min.	93	84	-	84	-	84	106	84
	Max.	126	112	-	126	-	128	130	130
	Mean	105.41	98.33	-	104.5	-	99.28	119.5	105.35
	C.V.	8.97	14.24	-	9.71	-	11.28	7.57	13.35
Higher Secondary	N	19	1	-	20	2	14	4	20
	Min.	92	119	-	92	65	83	68	68
	Max.	114	119	-	119	141	118	124	124
	Mean	103.42	119.00	-	104.20	101.91	95.21	97.00	96.90
	C.V.	5.83	-	-	6.55	13.36	10.28	23.73	13.65
Above Higher Secondary	N	19	-	1	20	1	12	7	20
	Min.	90	-	122	90	110	99	100	99
	Max.	141	-	122	141	110	130	127	130
	Mean	113.52	-	122	113.95	110.00	112.16	113.14	112.40
	C.V.	12.07	-	-	11.83	-	7.16	8.52	7.29

Source: Computed.

high. It is interesting to note that when the level of expenditure is high, the unemployed respondents are empowered at the higher level of education. When the expenditure is low (below Rs. 25,000), the unemployed respondents are empowered at higher level of education. The household expenditure depends on women's earnings, on the ground that women are likely to have greater access and control over resources if they are the primary earners in the household (Kishore and Gupta 2004). Thus, it is inferred when the female expenditure is high, the empowerment is also high for unemployed respondents at the highest level of education, and for the employed respondents up to high school education.

From Table 11 it is seen that the employed respondents are empowered upto high school education, when the female alone controls the expenditure. The unemployed respondents are empowered when their expenditure is controlled by both male and female at the higher level of education. When male controls the level of expenditure, the empowerment is low. Thus, it is inferred that when expenditure is controlled by both men and women, the empowerment is high among the unemployed respondents than among the employed respondents at the higher level of education.

Level of Savings and Empowerment

When the total saving is high, the employed respondents are empowered up to the high school education and the unemployed respondents are empowered at the above higher secondary education. When the saving is low, the unemployed respondents are empowered at the higher secondary education. When there is no saving, the empowerment is low at all levels of education and employment status. It is inferred from Table 14 that only at high level of savings, the employed respondents are empowered up to the high school level and the unemployed education.

It is interesting to note that (Table 15) when the female saving is high, the employed respondents are highly empowered up to high school education; when the female saving is low, the employed respondents are empowered at

Table 11

Score Values of Empowerment According to Owner of Expenditure, Levels of Education and Employment

Employment Status		*Unemployed (120)**			*Employed (120)*			
Control over Expenditure		*Male*	*Both*	*Total*	*Male*	*Female*	*Both*	*Total*
Levels of Education								
Illiterates	N	14	6	20	4	2	14	20
	Min.	75	72	72	84	100	70	70
	Max.	117	100	117	111	124	137	137
	Mean	91.57	88.17	90.55	93.00	112.00	101.43	100.80
	C.V.	13.26	12.31	12.80	13.17	15.15	18.71	17.50
Primary	N	15	5	20	2	2	16	20
	Min.	65	102	65	93	117	67	67
	Max.	122	111	112	104	118	123	123
	Mean	94.00	105.40	96.85	98.50	117.50	101.63	102.90
	C.V.	12.48	3.19	13.45	7.90	0.60	12.27	11.97
Secondary	N	15	5	20	2	2	16	20
	Min.	69	95	69	107	109	82	82
	Max.	115	117	117	118	121	132	132
	Mean	96.87	104.40	98.75	112.50	115.00	111.19	111.70
	C.V.	12.48	9.52	11.96	6.91	7.38	12.06	10.97
High School	N	17	3	20	-	1	19	20
	Min.	93	84	84	-	130	84	84
	Max.	126	112	126	-	130	128	130
	Mean	105.41	98.33	104.35	-	130.00	104.05	105.35
	C.V.	8.98	14.25	9.71	-	-	12.65	13.35

Contd.

Higher Secondary	N	19	1	20	1	2	17	20
	Min.	92	119	92	99	88	68	68
	Max.	114	119	119	99	118	124	124
	Mean	103.42	119.00	104.20	99.00	103.00	96.06	96.90
	C.V.	5.83	-	6.55	-	20.60	13.73	13.65
Above Higher Secondary	N	19	1	20	1	1	18	20
	Min.	90	122	90	110	120	99	99
	Max.	141	122	141	110	120	130	130
	Mean	113.53	122.00	113.95	110.00	120.00	112.11	112.40
	C.V.	12.08	-	11.83	-	-	7.54	7.29

Note: * In this category, women could Not control over expenditure, since they are unemployed
Source: Computed.

Table 12

Score Values of Empowerment According to Total Borrowing, Levels of Education and Employment

Employment Status		*Unemployed (120)*					*Employed (120)*				
Total Borrowings		*No Borrowing*	*Below 10,000*	*10,000 to 50,000*	*Above 50,000*	*Total*	*No Borrowing*	*Below 10,000*	*10,000 to 50,000*	*Above 50,000*	*Total*
Levels ofEducation											
Illiterates	N	3	8	6	3	20	9	3	6	2	20
	Min.	77	72	77	75	72	81	70	73	98	70
	Max.	105	100	96	117	117	137	98	113	123	137
	Mean	91.67	89.25	88.17	97.66	90.55	106.89	88.33	94.67	110.50	100.80
	C.V.	15.32	11.44	9.20	21.70	12.80	76.91	17.98	16.86	16.00	17.50
Primary	N	9	4	3	4	20	8	4	5	3	20
	Min.	65	92	96	87	65	89	96	67	108	67
	Max.	112	107	111	107	112	118	113	104	123	123
	Mean	92.00	99.25	103.67	100.25	96.85	104.88	102.75	93.40	113.67	102.90
	C.V.	18.28	7.91	7.24	9.05	13.45	10.06	8.08	16.39	7.17	11.97
Secondary	N	7	2	6	5	20	7	-	4	9	20
	Min.	87	97	69	80	69	82	-	94	100	82
	Max.	107	117	113	115	117	132	-	118	129	132
	Mean	98.86	107.00	94.67	100.20	98.75	111.14	-	106.00	114.67	111.70
	C.V.	7.04	13.22	16.54	13.12	11.96	14.01	-	9.74	9.09	10.97
High School	N	7	1	4	8	20	10	3	4	3	20
	Min.	95	112	84	94	84	84	96	86	94	84
	Max.	112	112	121	126	126	121	108	128	130	130
	Mean	102.14	112.00	102.50	106.25	104.35	101.80	101.00	108.75	117.00	105.35
	C.V.	5.25	-	16.57	9.93	9.71	11.01	6.18	17.73	17.07	13.35

Contd.

Higher Secondary	N	11	4	1	4	20	4	8	5	3	20
	Min.	92	103	100	97	92	97	87	68	83	68
	Max.	110	119	100	114	119	118	106	98	124	124
	Mean	102.09	111.50	100.00	103.75	104.20	108.00	95.87	87.40	100.67	96.90
	C.V.	5.36	5.93	-	7.36	6.55	10.72	8.39	13.86	20.94	13.65
Above Higher Secondary	N	10	1	5	4	20	9	5	5	1	20
	Min.	95	105	93	90	90	107	104	99	127	99
	Max.	141	105	128	122	141	130	117	120	127	130
	Mean	115.40	105.00	115.20	111.00	113.95	115.00	109.80	107.40	127.00	112.40
	C.V.	12.64	-	11.89	13.20	11.83	6.33	4.88	8.16	-	7.29

Source: Computed.

Table 13

Score Values of Empowerment According to Female Borrowing, Levels of Education and Employment

Employment Status		*Unemployed (120)*			*Employed (120)*		
Female Borrowings		*No Borrowing*	*Borrowing*	*Total*	*No Borrowing*	*Borrowing*	*Total*
Levels of Education							
Illiterates	N	15	5	20	15	5	20
	Min.	75	72	72	81	70	70
	Max.	117	100	117	137	111	137
	Mean	92.53	84.60	90.55	104.33	90.20	100.80
	C.V.	12.48	12.55	12.80	15.98	19.82	17.50
Primary	N	17	3	20	15	15	20
	Min.	65	96	65	89	67	67
	Max.	112	107	112	123	113	123
	Mean	95.88	102.33	96.85	104.87	97.00	102.90
	C.V.	14.41	5.56	13.45	9.41	18.51	11.97
Secondary	N	16	4	20	10	10	20
	Min.	69	97	69	82	94	82
	Max.	117	113	117	132	129	132
	Mean	96.75	106.75	98.75	111.60	111.80	111.70
	C.V.	12.50	6.42	11.96	11.52	11.03	10.97

Contd.

High School	N	17	3	20	17	3	20
	Min.	93	84	84	84	121	84
	Max.	126	121	126	128	130	130
	Mean	104.12	105.67	104.35	101.71	126.00	105.35
	C.V.	8.32	18.26	9.71	11.56	3.64	13.35
Higher Secondary	N	17	3	20	13	7	20
	Min.	92	97	92	68	84	68
	Max.	114	119	119	124	106	124
	Mean	103.24	109.67	104.20	97.15	96.43	96.90
	C.V.	5.53	10.73	6.55	16.02	8.65	13.65
Above Higher Secondary	N	16	4	20	14	6	20
	Min.	90	105	90	99	104	99
	Max.	141	128	141	130	120	130
	Mean	113.19	117.00	113.95	112.71	111.67	112.40
	C.V.	12.66	8.91	11.83	8.06	5.68	7.29

Source: Computed.

Table 14

Score Values of Empowerment According to Value of Total Savings, Levels of Education and Employment

Employment Status		*Unemployed (120)*				*Employed (120)*			
Total Savings		*No Saving*	*Below 25000*	*Above 50000*	*Total*	*No Savings*	*Below 25000*	*Above 50000*	*Total*
Levels of Education									
Illiterates	N	6	12	2	20	3	8	9	20
	Min.	75	72	85	72	73	70	84	70
	Max.	96	117	101	117	113	120	137	137
	Mean	84.83	93.00	93.00	90.55	94.67	96.63	106.56	100.80
	C.V.	10.79	13.48	12.17	12.80	21.35	16.54	17.44	17.50
Primary	N	3	10	7	20	3	9	8	20
	Min.	92	69	65	65	67	95	89	67
	Max.	96	111	112	112	117	118	123	123
	Mean	93.67	99.10	95.00	96.85	93.33	103.56	105.75	102.90
	C.V.	2.22	13.31	16.90	13.45	26.90	7.47	10.13	11.97
Secondary	N	3	15	2	20	3	2	12	20
	Min.	69	80	95	69	82	109	94	82
	Max.	115	117	99	117	121	110	132	132
	Mean	97.00	99.33	97.00	98.75	104.00	109.50	113.53	111.70
	C.V.	25.34	10.13	2.92	11.96	19.21	0.65	10.04	10.97

Contd.

High School	N	2	10	8	20	3	6	11	20
	Min.	84	93	98	84	86	84	93	84
	Max.	112	121	126	126	102	108	130	130
	Mean	98.00	102.10	108.75	104.35	94.67	97.67	112.45	105.35
	C.V.	20.20	8.58	8.40	9.71	8.54	9.31	12.46	13.35
Higher Secondary	N	3	13	4	20	7	7	6	20
	Min.	92	99	97	92	68	84	89	68
	Max.	103	119	102	119	118	106	124	124
	Mean	97.00	107.23	99.75	104.20	93.14	97.67	104.33	96.90
	C.V.	5.74	5.70	2.64	6.55	17.38	7.98	13.11	13.65
Above HigherSecondary.	N	-	6	14	20	2	9	920	
	Min.	-	93	90	90	99	104	100	99
	Max.	-	128	141	141	120	130	127	130
	Mean	-	110.50	115.43	113.95	109.50	112.56	112.89	112.40
	C.V.	-	10.38	12.47	11.83	1356	6.95	7.34	7.29

Source: Computed.

Table 15
Score Value of Empowerment According to Female Savings, Levels of Education and Employment

Employment Status		*Unemployed (120)*				*Employed (120)*			
Female Savings		*No Saving*	*Below 25000*	*Above 50000*	*Total*	*No Savings*	*Below 25000*	*Above 50000*	*Total*
Levels of Education									
Illiterates	N	11	8	1	20	6	10	4	20
	Min.	75	72	85	72	73	70	84	70
	Max.	96	117	101	117	113	120	137	137
	Mean	84.83	93.00	93.00	90.55	94.66	96.62	106.55	100.80
	C.V.	10.79	13.48	12.17	12.80	21.35	16.54	17.44	17.50
Primary	N	11	8	1	20	5	14	1	20
	Min.	92	69	65	65	67	95	89	67
	Max.	96	111	112	112	117	118	123	123
	Mean	93.66	99.10	95.00	96.85	93.33	103.55	105.75	102.90
	C.V.	2.22	13.31	16.90	13.45	26.90	7.47	10.13	11.97
Secondary	N	9	9	2	20	5	3	12	20
	Min.	69	99	95	69	82	109	94	82
	Max.	115	119	99	117	121	110	132	132
	Mean	97.00	107.23	96.50	98.75	104.00	109.50	113.53	111.70
	C.V.	25.34	10.13	2.92	11.96	19.21	0.65	10.04	10.97

Contd.

High School	N	9	8	3	20	5	9	6	20
	Min.	84	93	98	84	86	84	93	84
	Max.	112	121	126	126	102	108	130	130
	Mean	98.00	102.10	108.75	104.35	94.60	97.66	112.45	105.35
	C.V.	20.20	8.58	8.40	9.71	8.54	9.31	12.46	13.35
Higher Secondary	N	15	4	1	20	9	7	4	20
	Min.	92	93	97	92	68	84	89	68
	Max.	103	128	102	119	118	106	124	124
	Mean	97.00	110.50	99.75	104.20	93.33	94.28	104.33	96.90
	C.V.	5.74	5.70	2.64	6.55	17.38	7.98	13.11	13.65
Above Higher Secondary	N	5	8	7	20	7	8	5	20
	Min.	93	95	90	90	99	104	100	99
	Max.	128	129	141	141	120	130	127	130
	Mean	110.50	117.00	115.42	113.95	109.50	112.55	112.88	112.40
	C.V.	-	10.38	12.47	11.83	15.77	6.95	7.34	7.29

Source: Computed.

higher level of education. Even though they are illiterates, they are highly empowered as compared to others. It is found that the unemployed respondents are empowered with low level of female savings at the higher level of education and the employed respondents are empowered with the high level of female savings at the lower level of education.

It is interesting to note from Table 16 that when the accounts are kept by both men and women, the employed illiterates are empowered as compared to the unemployed respondents. On the contrary the employed respondents are empowered at the secondary education when the female alone maintains the accounts. The employed respondents are empowered when female alone keeps the accounts at the high school education level; whereas the unemployed respondents are empowered when female alone keeps the accounts alone at the higher secondary and above higher secondary level of education.

Level of Borrowing and Empowerment

FromTable 12 it is observed that when the borrowing is high, the empowerment is high among the employed respondents at all levels of education (excluding higher secondary); when the borrowing is low, the empowerment is high only at the higher secondary education level. It is interesting to note that the maximum score value is obtained by the employed illiterates when there is no borrowing.

It is clear from Table 13 that when there is female borrowing, the employed respondents are empowered at the middle level education, and the unemployed respondents at the higher level of education. When there is no female borrowing, the employed illiterates are empowered, and the minimum score value is obtained by the unemployed respondents. Thus, it is found that female borrowing is one of the determinant factors for empowerment.

Levels of Asset and Empowerment

Table 17 reveals that when the total asset is Rs.50,000 to Rs.2,00,000, the unemployed respondents are empowered at the primary and the higher secondary levels of education,

Table 16

Score Value of Empowerment According to Account Holder, Levels of Education and Employment

Employment Status		Unemployed (120)					Employed (120)				
Account Holder		*No Account*	*Male*	*Female*	*Both*	*Total*	*No Account*	*Male*	*Female*	*Both*	*Total*
Levels of Education											
Illiterates	N	6	5	6	3	20	3	3	5	9	20
	Min.	75	77	88	72	72	73	70	90	84	70
	Max.	96	105	117	101	117	113	101	124	137	137
	Mean	84.83	90.20	98.83	86.00	90.55	94.67	84.00	104.60	106.33	100.80
	C.V.	10.79	12.87	10.17	16.88	12.80	21.35	18.71	12.85	16.88	17.50
Primary	N	4	8	3	5	20	3	2	5	10	20
	Min.	92	65	104	87	65	67	97	95	89	67
	Max.	96	112	111	107	112	117	113	118	123	123
	Mean	93.50	91.88	107.33	101.20	96.85	93.33	105.00	102.80	105.40	102.90
	C.V.	1[[.85	19.56	3.27	8.99	13.45	26.90	10.7	9.01	8.99	11.97
Secondary	N	3	7	6	4	20	3	2	6	9	20
	Min.	69	80	97	90	69	82	94	107	100	82
	Max.	115	104	117	100	117	121	109	132	121	132
	Mean	97.00	93.14	108.00	96.00	98.75	104.00	101.50	120.83	110.44	111.70
	C.V.	25.34	8.40	6.47	6.94	11.96	19.21	10.45	8.87	6.94	10.97

Contd.

High School	N	2	7	6	5	20	4	2	7	7	20
	Min.	84	93	94	98	84	86	84	91	94	84
	Max.	112	121	112	126	126	108	93	130	128	130
	Mean	98.00	108.00	100.17	106.80	104.35	98.00	88.50	105.14	114.57	105.35
	C.V.	20.20	8.74	6.60	11.76	9.71	9.57	7.19	12.19	11.76	13.35
Higher Secondary	N	3	11	2	4	20	7	2	6	5	20
	Min.	92	98	110	97	92	68	91	87	84	68
	Max.	103	114	119	111	119	118	97	106	124	124
	Mean	97.00	104.73	114.50	103.00	104.20	93.14	94.00	96.16	104.20	96.90
	C.V.	5.74	5.27	5.56	15.80	6.55	17.38	4.51	7.57	15.80	13.65
Above Higher Secondary.	N	-	5	2	13	20	2	5	3	10	20
	Min.	-	93	112	90	90	99	104	113	100	99
	Max.	-	114	128	141	141	120	117	130	127	130
	Mean	-	104.20	120.00	116.76	113.95	109.50	110.80	119.00	111.80	112.40
	C.V.	-	8.40	9.43	7.43	11.83	13.56	4.30	8.02	7.43	7.29

Source: Computed.

Table 17
Score Values of Empowerment According to Total Property, Levels of Education and Employment

Employment Status		*Unemployed (120)*					*Employed (120)*				
Total Property		*Below 50,000*	*50,000 to 200000*	*200000 to 400000*	*Above 400000*	*Total*	*Below 50,000*	*50,000 to 200000*	*200000 to 400000*	*Above 400000*	*Total*
Levels ofEducation											
Illiterates	N	4	3	7	6	20	9	1	-	10	20
	Min.	75	77	72	95	72	70	124	-	84	70
	Max.	100	100	105	117	117	112	124	-	137	137
	Mean	87.25	90.00	87.00	97.17	90.55	91.56	124.00	-	106.80	100.80
	C.V.	14.42	13.10	13.24	11.38	12.80	15.30	-	-	16.16	17.50
Primary	N	6	4	3	7	20	10	2	2	6	20
	Min.	69	94	93	65	65	67	93	89	104	67
	Max.	99	107	107	112	112	118	104	105	123	123
	Mean	88.50	102.50	101.33	98.86	96.85	100.40	98.5	97.00	110.50	102.90
	C.V.	12.60	5.99	7.27	17.27	13.45	14.67	7.90	11.66	6.10	11.97
Secondary	N	7	2	2	9	20	2	3	2	13	20
	Min.	69	97	93	80	69	82	102	109	94	82
	Max.	117	100	95	115	117	121	129	109	132	132
	Mean	102.00	98.50	94	97.33	98.75	101.50	113.67	109.00	113.23	111.70
	C.V.	15.82	2.15	1.50	11.18	11.96	27.17	12.20	-	9.70	10.97

Contd.

High School	N	3	4	3	10	20	5	5	1	9	20
	Min.	112	93	99	84	84	86	97	93	84	84
	Max.	121	103	112	126	126	112	108	93	130	130
	Mean	115.00	98.00	105.33	103.40	104.35	97.00	101.20	93.00	113.67	105.35
	C.V.	4.52	4.86	6.18	11.32	9.71	10.21	4.16	-	14.21	13.35
Higher Secondary	N	7	3	5	5	20	14	-	3	3	20
	Min.	96	92	100	97	92	68	-	95	96	68
	Max.	113	119	114	106	119	118	-	99	124	124
	Mean	104.57	107.00	104.80	101.40	104.20	93.36	-	97.67	112.67	96.90
	C.V.	6.46	12.85	5.20	3.46	6.55	13.14	-	2.36	13.08	13.65
Above Higher Secondary	N	-	3	3	14	20	7	4	3	6	20
	Min.	-	93	122	90	90	104	99	106	100	99
	Max.	-	111	141	129	141	130	117	116	127	130
	Mean	-	103	130.33	112.79	113.95	114.29	107.00	111.33	114.33	112.40
	C.V.	-	8.90	7.45	10.75	11.83	7.40	6.99	4.52	8.42	7.29

Source: Computed.

whereas the employed respondents are empowered at the secondary level of education; and it is noted that the employed respondents are empowered even if they are illiterate. At the higher level (above Rs.4,00,000) of total asset, the empowerment is low among the respondents at all levels of education. When the total asset is Rs.2,00,000 to Rs.4,00,000, the unemployed respondents are empowered at the above higher secondary education level. At the lower level of asset (below Rs.50,000), the unemployed respondents are empowered at the high school education level. Thus, it is inferred that majority of the unemployed respondents are empowered at various levels of education as compared to the employed respondents.

The female asset is the most important determinant of empowerment. Women are highly empowered in Kerala as they have asset rights. At the highest levels of asset, the employed respondents are empowered at the lower level of education, whereas in the case of unemployed respondents, the empowerment is low at high levels of asset. When there is no asset, the unemployed respondents are empowered at the higher secondary education level. When the asset is low, the unemployed respondents are empowered at the above higher secondary and high school education level. Thus, it is found from Table 18 that when the asset is high, the employed respondents are empowered at the lower level of education, whereas when the asset is low, the unemployed respondents are empowered at the higher level of education.

It is surprising to note that though the unemployed respondents are not educated [illiterates], empowerment is high as they have assets. At the primary education level, the employed respondents are empowered when the asset holders are both males and females. The secondary educated employed respondents are empowered when the asset holders are female alone. Among the unemployed respondents, the respondents are empowered at the high school and above higher secondary education level, when the asset holders are females, and at the higher secondary education level when the asset holders are male.

Table 18

Score Values of Empowerment According to Female Property, Levels of Education and Employment

Employment Status		*Unemployed (120)*				*Employed (120)*			
Female Property		*No Property*	*50000 to 100000*	*Above 100000*	*Total*	*No Property*	*50000 to 100000*	*Above 100000*	*Total*
Levels of Education									
Illiterates	N	2	5	13	20	4	6	10	20
	Min.	75	77	72	72	70	73	87	70
	Max.	80	117	101	117	113	124	137	137
	Mean	77.50	93.60	91.38	90.55	91.25	100.33	104.90	100.80
	C.V.	4.56	18.53	9.70	12.80	21.22	20.39	14.79	17.50
Primary	N	-	9	11	20	-	7	13	20
	Min.	-	65	69	65	-	67	93	67
	Max.	-	111	112	112	-	117	123	123
	Mean	-	97.00	96.73	96.85	-	98.43	105.31	102.90
	C.V.	-	14.09	13.61	13.45	-	16.88	8.73	11.97
Secondary	N	-	7	13	20	4	6	10	20
	Min.	-	95	69	69	82	100	102	82
	Max.	-	115	117	117	118	129	132	132
	Mean	-	104.00	95.92	98.75	100.75	112.83	115.40	111.70
	C.V.	-	7.83	13.32	11.96	15.83	9.63	8.56	10.97

Contd.

High School	N	-	5	15	20	1	6	13	20
	Min.	-	100	84	84	93	91	84	84
	Max.	-	113	126	126	93	128	130	130
	Mean	-	107.00	103.47	104.35	93.00	108.33	104.92	105.35
	C.V.	-	5.08	10.92	9.71	-	13.40	13.75	13.35
Higher Secondary	N	1	7	12	20	3	4	13	20
	Min.	110	92	97	92	68	83	84	68
	Max.	110	114	119	119	106	118	124	124
	Mean	110.00	102.57	104.67	104.20	88.33	95.00	99.46	96.90
	C.V.	-	7.65	6.18	6.55	21.67	16.51	11.37	13.65
Above Higher Secondary	N	3	6	11	20	-	8	12	20
	Min.	114	103	90	90	-	106	99	99
	Max.	128	141	122	141	-	120	130	130
	Mean	121.33	122.50	107.27	113.95	-	113.50	111.67	112.40
	C.V.	5.79	10.92	10.90	11.83	-	3.91	9.06	7.29

Source: Computed.

It is found from Table 19 that when the asset holders are both male and female, the empowerment is low among unemployed respondents. Empowerment is low when the asset holders are male alone at all levels of education. The unemployed respondents are highly empowered, when the asset holders are female alone at the various levels of education.

A diverse set of indicators sheds light on women status and reflects the extent of gender quality and empowerment. Many aspects of women's lives help us to understand their status, but these are not adequately quantifiable. Statistical information for deriving indicators for such aspects is either not available, or not very reliable. There is a necessity to identify the indicators of empowerment. There is no upper limit on the number of variables used or indicators constructed. The number of indicators may need to be limited in the context of composition into indices, as a large number of indicators can make the index incomprehensible (Krishnaraj 1997; Rajivan 1998; Rustagi 2000).

INTEGRATED ANALYSIS FOR WOMEN EMPOWERMENT: PATH ANALYSIS

Most fundamental reasons for promoting the empowerment of women is the fact that failing to empower women to reach their potential is a violation of their basic human rights. There is a growing concern over women empowerment in India. The reason is that women in Indian society are subjected to various social and economic disabilities for many centuries. However, their social status began to change during the early part of the twentieth century by the efforts of various social movements, nationalist movements, and reform movements. After independence, the government of India enacted various legislations to safeguard the rights and privileges of women, and also made provision for adequate means of livelihood like that of men. Despite many efforts, majority of women in India suffer due to suppression, oppression and socio-economic exploitation. In order to uplift women, our state and central government have introduced various development

Table 19
Score Values of Empowerment According to Asset Holders, Levels of Education and Employment

Employment Status		Unemployed (120)				Employed (120)			
Asset Holder		Male	Female	Both	Total	Male	Female	Both	Total
Levels of Education									
Illiterates	N	3	1	16	20	3	6	11	20
	Min.	75	117	72	72	70	73	84	70
	Max.	105	117	101	117	101	137	123	137
	Mean	86.67	117.00	89.63	90.55	84.00	107.50	101.73	100.80
	C.V.	18.85	-	10.31	12.80	18.71	20.84	13.15	17.50
Primary	N	-	8	12	20	-	7	13	20
	Min.	-	69	65	65	-	67	89	67
	Max.	-	111	112	112	-	118	123	123
	Mean	-	95.75	97.58	96.85	-	102.14	103.31	102.90
	C.V.	-	13.61	13.89	13.45	-	17.33	8.83	11.97
Secondary	N	-	5	15	20	3	4	13	20
	Min.	-	95	69	69	82	109	100	82
	Max.	-	113	117	117	118	129	132	132
	Mean	-	105.60	96.47	98.75	98.00	122.00	111.69	111.70
	C.V.	-	6.41	12.87	11.96	18.70	17.33	7.88	10.97

Contd.

High School	N	-	2	18	20	-	6	14	20
	Min.	-	112	84	84	-	86	84	84
	Max.	-	121	126	126	-	130	128	130
	Mean	-	116.50	103.00	104.35	-	102.50	106.57	105.35
	C.V.	-	5.46	9.37	9.71	-	15.73	12.72	13.35
Higher Secondary	N	1	4	15	20	4	5	11	20
	Min.	110	96	92	92	68	91	84	68
	Max.	100	110	119	119	106	118	124	124
	Mean	110.00	103.00	104.13	104.20	87.00	102.80	97.82	96.90
	C.V.	-	5.55	7.02	6.55	18.22	9.81	12.89	13.65
Above Higher Secondary	N	-	4	16	20	-	5	15	20
	Min.	-	114	90	90	-	105	99	99
	Max.	-	141	129	141	-	120	130	130
	Mean	-	126.25	110.88	113.95	-	112.60	112.33	112.40
	C.V.	-	9.02	11.19	11.83	-	5.71	7.94	7.29

Source: Computed.

programmes. The present study examines the role of women in the context of gender equality, to control the resources and their empowerment at the household level.

It is the area in which one could see a gap in the existing literature. The present study is vital to fill this gap. Moreover, the present chapter is initiated to perform a general model for the study, whereas the individual aspects have been examined in the previous sections. Moreover, this model is very important to identify the factors which are responsible for maintaining gender equality, control over the resources and empowerment of women at the household level.

To find out the influence of various socio-economic and institutional factors on dependent variable of empowerment of women, the step-wise regression model is applied. It is an obvious fact that all the independent factors are not at all significant in the determination of empowerment. Therefore, the Step-Wise Regression Approach is used to filter significant independent variables, which influence the dependent variables of the empowerment of women.

The results of relationship between the given independent variable and the dependent variable on women empowerment through Step wise Regression analysis indicate that out of eighteen independent factors, only seven factors are found to be statistically significant in determining the women empowerment.

The significant factors in the determination of women empowerment are, *total years of schooling in the family, income earner, account holder, respondent's employment status, and proportion of female income, proportion of female assets and levels of education*. The adjusted coefficient of multiple determinations (R^2) through regression analysis indicates 0.30. It means that out of 100 per cent variation on women empowerment of the respondents, about 30 per cent of variation is explained by the specified seven independent factors. The balance 70 per cent is attributed to "the other factors" which are not included in the given analysis.

Table 8.a.
Step wise Regression Analysis of Explanatory variables with Women Empowerment Index as Dependent Variable

Explanatory Variables	*Regression Co-efficient*	*'t' value*	*'p' level*
Total years of schooling in the family	0.11	1.94	0.053
Income earner	-0.24	-0.28	0.005
Account Holder	0.35	6.01	0.000
Employment Status	-0.31	-2.13	0.034
Proportion of Female income	0.23	3.44	0.001
Proportion of Female Assets	0.20	3.55	0.000
Levels of Education	0.48	6.78	0.000
($\bar{R}^2$) = 0.30; df = 7.232;	'F' value = 15.350.000		

df = degrees of freedom
Source: Computed.

The 'F' test based on $\bar{R}^2$ indicates 15.35, which is found to be statistically significant at 5 per cent level with 7, 232 degrees of freedom. It implies that all the selected seven independent factors are statistically significant to justify the selection of this model and suitability to verify the parameters of the general population.

The path analysis of the explanatory factors with the women empowerment as dependent variable is given in Table 21. The factors like education (0.48), account holder (0.30), proportion of female income (0.23), proportion of female asset structure (0.20), and literacy of family members (0.11) have positive direct effect with the dependent factors on women empowerment. Education has more significant influence than the other factors. Education has a positive relation with empowerment. Summers (1992) says that letting girls go to school, learn to read and experience more of the world beyond their homes make them better-off immediately and enrich their families. Over the time, getting girls into school can transform societies as their sons and daughters and grand sons and grand daughters reap the benefits and thereby they will be empowered.

The two factors viz., the employment (-0.31) and the income earner (-0.24) have negative effects on women empowerment. It means that these factors are negatively related to women empowerment. Due to low levels of literacy, skill training and bargaining capacity, in several countries of the south, women are more often compelled to resort to jobs that are low paid, monotonous, seasonal, labour intensive, and carry considerable occupational risk. As a result poverty among women is more intractable. Coupled with household poverty that women have to deal with, they also face enormous disadvantage that is embedded in gender relations, for example - the domestic of social reproduction under adverse conditions and lack of access to empowerment (Lingam 2006).

In addition to the direct impact of the related factors on empowerment, each variable has indirect effect on empowerment through the other related factors. It has been observed from Table 8.b that employment status has a positive indirect effect (0.44), as against the negative direct effect caused by proportion of income (0.17), levels of education (.02), and income earner (-0.18) on women empowerment. Next to this, the status of being an income earner has its positive indirect effect as against the negative direct effect, caused by proportion of female income (0.10), levels of education (0.30) and employment status (-0.23). Total years of schooling also positive influences individuals on women empowerment.

The indirect impact on women empowerment by proportion of female assets is very meager (0.03) and it is almost nil by account holder and proportion of female income to total income. However, the level of education has indirect effect as against positive direct effect, by proportion of female income (0.09), income earner (-0.15) and employment status (-0.27). On the whole, income earner indirectly influences women empowerment through account holder, employment status and levels of education. The factor proportion of female income has positive influence on women empowerment through total years of schooling, income earner, employment status and proportion of female asset structure. An income that women contribute provides them space to negotiate for greater say in the decision making within the family and relations with their men (Mukhopadhyay and Sundaram 2003). It is surprising to note that the factor employment has made

Table 8.b

Path Analysis of explanatory variables with Empowerment of women as Dependent Variabl

Explanatory Variables	*Regression co-efficient* *Direct Effect*	*Total indirect effect*	*Substantial indirect effect channeled through significant variables*		*Correlation with IYm*
Total Years of Schooling in the Family	0.11	0.11	0.02	Proportion of Female Income	0.22*
			0.05	Levels of Education	
			0.09	Account Holder	
Income Earner	-0.24	0.27	0.10	Proportion of Female Income	0.03
			0.30	Levels of Education	
			-0.23	Employment Status	
Account holder	0.35	0.00	0.06	Levels of Education	0.30*
			-0.04	Employment Status	
			-0.05	Income Earner	
Employment Status	-0.31	0.44	0.17	Proportion of Income	0.13*
			0.02	Levels of Education	
			-0.18	Income Earner	
Proportion of Female Income to Total Income	0.23	0.00	0.21	Levels of Education	0.23*
			-0.11	Income Earner	
			-0.15	Employment Status	
Proportion of Female Assets	0.20	0.03	0.06	Levels of Education	0.23*
			0.05	Proportion of Female Income	
			-0.05	Employment Status	
Levels of Education	0.48	-0.07	0.09	Proportion of Female Income	.35*
			-0.15	Income Earner	
			-0.27	Employment Status	

Source: Computed

- Significant at 5% level

negative effect through income earner, proportion of female income, proportion of female asset structure and levels of education. The factor account holder has positive effect through total years of schooling on women empowerment. The effect of explanatory factors on women empowerment, the independent factor viz., levels of education exerts a higher contribution to the tune of 0.35, followed by account holder education (0.30), proportion of female income (0.23), proportion of female assets (0.23), total years of schooling in the family (0.22), employment status (0.13) and it is the least for Income earner (0.03).

The direct and indirect effects and their relationships in terms of positive and negative are illustrated through path diagram Fig. 1.

Fig. 1. Direct and Indirect Effect of Significant Exogenous Variables on Women Empowerment

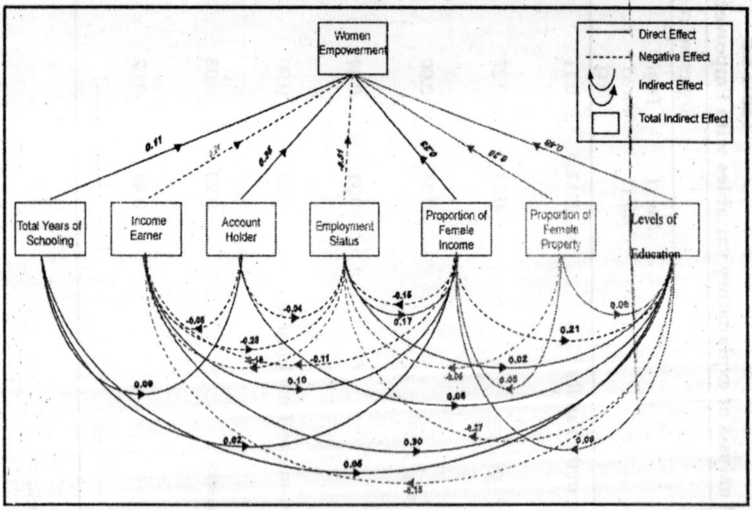

KEY FINDINGS

Employed women are empowered as compared to unemployed women at all levels of education.

- Lower age, employed cohorts are empowered even at primary levels of education and at higher age, the unemployed women are empowered at higher levels of education.

- The employed women who belong to OC and MBC are empowered at lower levels of education and the unemployed women who belong to SC and BC are empowered at higher levels of education.
- The employed women who belong to nuclear families are empowered at lower levels of education and the employed women who belong to joint families are empowered at the higher levels of education.
- The employed women who belong to small and medium sized families are empowered at the lower levels of education and the unemployed women at higher levels of education.
- The unemployed women who have lower age difference with their spouse are empowered at higher levels of education.
- Higher share of female income to the total income of the family leads to empowerment of employed women at lower levels of education
- Higher share of female income to the total expenditure of the family leads to empowerment of women at lower level of education only.
- When the expenditure is controlled by female alone, the employed women are empowered even at lower levels of education
- Higher contribution of female savings to the total savings leads to empowerment of employed women at lower levels of education.
- When the saving accounts are kept by female alone, women are empowered irrespective of levels of education and employment status.
- The rural employed women are empowered at the lower as well as higher education when the assets are kept by female alone.

- Total years of schooling in the family, income earner, account holder, employment status, proportion of female income, and levels of education are the important factors in deciding the level of empowerment.
- Among the selected variables, level of education tops the list in determining the empowerment of rural women.
- Employment status has a negative effect corresponding to all the significant factors of empowerment.

The intensive analysis of field data collected from the two districts of Tamil Nadu have amply provided evidence to the fact that both GEDM and PARM are needed for the empowerment of women. Having discussed the influence of intervening factors at length, through the preceding three chapters, the next chapter takes up an integrated discussion of all results from a policy angle.

9

INTEGRATED DISCUSSION AND FINDINGS

This chapter brings the results obtained in the analysis and integrates them.

INTEGRATED DISCUSSION

Empowerment as a concept was introduced at the International Women's Conference in 1985 at Nairobi. The conference defined empowerment as a redistribution of social power and control of resources in favour of women. Empowerment is a process, not a product. The outcome of empowerment would then be a redistribution of power (Batliwala 1993). The main aim of empowerment is to change subordination and subjugation, transform the structures, systems and institutions which support inequality such as the family, caste and class system, religion, top down development models, etc. It is obvious that rural women are almost as powerless as compared to urban women in terms of access to and control over resources and hence, have no decision-making power. Yet, the decision made by others affects their lives every day.

Women are considered the most disadvantaged group, as they have low consumption, low knowledge and low status, and they are treated as under-utilized resource as they do not possess land or any other property with them (Collier 1991). It is seen that the distribution of power from men to women is required to bring equality between sexes. Further, no country can sustain its development, if it underutilises its women as a productive resource. When women are considered a utilized resource, the goal of empowerment will be fulfilled by achieving gender equality. Therefore one may notice that empowerment is a process aimed at changing the nature and direction of systematic forces, which marginalize women and other disadvantaged sectors in the given contexts. The Ninth Five Year Plan, committed to 'Empower Women' by creating and enabling environment where women can freely exercise their rights both within and outside homes as equal partners along with men, spelt out a major strategy for the empowerment of women.

In many cases, women are unaware of their legal rights, unable to take decision and are greatly influenced by the family ideology that emphasizes the dominance of the male. Though it has become a popular buzzword over the last decade and a half, there has been little informed discussion on the term 'empowerment', says Beteille (1999). Most of the analysis around it so far has been more context-driven than theory-driven. It is important then to look at the context in which discussions over empowerment and indeed women's empowerment have arisen. Wieringa (1998) opines that empowerment of women is an identification of right to determine choices in life and to influence the direction of change, through the ability to gain control over material and non-material resource.

Empowerment is a much-discussed subject, but sensitization about this issue is grossly neglected at the grass root level. Keeping in view of this, the government of India celebrated the year 2001 as the Women's Empowerment Year with the launching of new programmes for the development of women. Empowerment of women means enhancing the self-respect and self-dignity of women, recognizing women's contribution, becoming economically independent and self-reliant and women controlling resources like land and property (Abraham 2003).

Empowerment is not about power over others (a feature of domination) but power to achieve goals and ends. By conceptualizing empowerment in terms of power to the definition, explicitly recognizes that the process of empowerment involves not only changes in access to resources, but also an understanding of one's rights and entitlements and the "conscientisation" that gender roles can be changed and gender equality is possible (Kishor and Gupta 2004).

UNDP (2004) stresses empowerment with gender equality. The present study focuses on empowerment not only with gender equality but also with power of autonomy. That is the researcher identifies two indicators viz., GEDM and PARM to measure empowerment. Gender equality in Decision Making (GEDM) and Power of Autonomy over Resources and Mobility (PARM) are the two sides of a same coin. Both cannot be separated. One cannot get empowerment by eliminating either GEDM or PARM. Thus, empowerment depends on GEDM and PARM or either.

In discussions women's empowerment, emphasis is placed on women's decision making roles, their economic self-entrance and their legal rights to equal treatment, inheritance and protection against all forms of discrimination in addition to the elimination of barrier to their access to resources such as education and employment opportunities. The need to empower women economically and socially and make them self-reliant is keenly felt.

It is heartening for women to be treated as equal partners along with men in the development process. Recent experiences have shown a strong link between education and empowerment. Literacy levels and nature of education, employment access and productive earnings are the concerns regarding women's empowerment. Education plays a positive interventionist role in creating gender equality, or acts as an agent of basic change in the status of women. Education confers empowerment, and empowerment facilitates education. Women's low status and subordination are ascribed to their lack of education, low economic status, lack of access to resources and low decision-making power-expressed by many as having no voice. Strengthening women's economic status, and thus- raising their status in the family and community, is seen as an important component of empowerment. Enabling women to gain access to resources will not only improve their status materially, but also bring about an increased self-esteem and self-confidence. Economic strength is considered the basis of social, political and psychological power in society, and women's low status is seen to stem from their low economic status, and consequent dependence and lack of decision-making power.

After having had a perusal of the literature in the domain of women empowerment, it may be brought out that a large number of scholars within women studies as well as the U.N. agencies have articulated the shift from 'women' to 'gender within development discourse as an advance towards recognizing the power relations within institutional structures that subordinate women and therefore, need to be transformed for the elimination of prevailing gender inequalities (Kabeer and Subramaniam 1999). It is also pertinent to mention that studies on empowerment of rural women are few. Moreover, the scholars have not integrated empowerment with gender equality.

In view of this, the study has made an attempt to interlink empowerment not only with gender equality in decision making but also with power of autonomy over resources and mobility. For this study, two districts viz., Salem and Tiruvarur in Tamil Nadu have been selected on the basis of rural female literacy derived from Tamil Nadu Human Development Report. In the same way, two blocks are selected from each district. Based on the block report, few villages are selected to identify the sample respondents. Totally 240 samples were selected and they were grouped under twelve heads according to levels of education and employment status. The present study was undertaken with the following objectives:

1. To juxtapose the socio economic characteristics of the respondents and the corresponding levels of empowerment and its indicators namely, Gender Equality in Decision- Making and Power of Autonomy over Resources and Mobility (GEDM and PARM)
2. To assess the Gender Equality in Decision-Making and Power of Autonomy over Resources and Mobility

(GEDM and PARM) of the respondents with reference to educational levels and employment status.

3. To examine the empowerment status of rural women in the context of educational levels and employment status.
4. To find out the most influential factors that determine the rural women empowerment and its indicators (GEDM and PARM)
5. To suggest policy measures to empower the rural women.

Around the objectives, the study has framed four hypotheses and tested them with appropriate tools: (i) There is a significant association between rural women income and empowerment, since the financial autonomy of women will enhance empowerment (ii) PARM excels over GEDM in influencing the empowerment of women since women's earnings in the family provide them the more power of autonomy over resources than gender equality in decision making (iii) There exists a significant positive correlation between education and empowerment, employment and empowerment; the correlation between education and empowerment is relatively stronger than the correlation between employment and empowerment (iv) The social factors are more dominant than economic factors in deciding the extent of GEDM, PARM and empowerment; the social factor education plays an important role in deciding the extent of PARM and empowerment and not in deciding the extent of GEDM.

TESTING OF HYPOTHESES

The first hypothesis of the study emphasizes that *there is an association between rural women's income and empowerment; rural women's income and GEDM; rural women's income and PARM.* It is observed from the analysis that the association between rural women's income and GEDM, PARM and empowerment is significant. The chi-square values also confirm that there exists a significant association between these variables. The chi-square value for the association between rural women income and empowerment is higher (47.640) than the association between GEDM and rural women's income (12.268), and PARM and rural women's income (30.982). Besides, it is found that there exists a positive association between rural women's income and empowerment rather than between GEDM and rural women's income and between PARM and rural women's income (Table 16).

From the field data it is found that the levels of income and that of empowerment have inverse relationship. However, on analyzing women's income, one finds a positive association between women's contribution to family income and the levels of empowerment. When women contribute more, they have control over expenditure, and contribute more towards total savings of the family (Table 5.4) and so PARM is enhanced. Hence, the chi–square value for the association between women's income and PARM is higher than the chi–square value for the association between women's income and GEDM.

The second hypothesis states that *PARM excels over GEDM in influencing the empowerment of rural women.* It is seen from the results that the relation between PARM and empowerment is relatively stronger than the relation between GEDM and empowerment. In the study, the PARM is dominating GEDM; PARM exists among rural women due to higher share in the total income of the family: the total expenditure of the family, the total savings of the family and the total asset structure of the family. Economic independence of women leads them to move towards the path of empowerment. Moreover, the rural women are living in the patriarchal society and hence their equality in decision making with their counter parts is affected irrespective of the level of education and the employment status. Hence, PARM excels over GEDM (Table 1).

The third hypothesis brings out the fact that *there exists a significant positive correlation between education and empowerment; employment and empowerment.* It may be inferred from the results that there exists a significant correlation between education and empowerment at 1% level (r = 0.242) and there exists a significant correlation between employment and

Table 1
Correlation between GEDM, PARM and Empowerment

	Empowerment	
Variables	*R*	*'p' value*
GEDM	0.744	0.000
PARM	0.813	0.000

Source: Computed.

empowerment (r = 0.121) at 5% level. The correlation between education and employment is relatively stronger than the correlation between employment and empowerment. Education and gainful employment are the potential sources of women's empowerment. Not only all these sources of modernizing influence, but each two can be a channel for information and a catalyst for behaviours associated with increasing women's access and control over resources. Another aspect of women's employment as a potential source of empowerment is the extent to which households are dependent on women's earnings. Women whose earnings are critical to the sustainability of their households are likely to have greater control over resources. But it is found that compared to employment, education is central to the process of empowerment. Education plays a dominant role in reinforcing social and gender hierarchies. It is education that gives employment opportunities to women (Table 2).

Table 2
Correlation between Education, Employment and Empowerment

	Empowerment	
Variables	*R*	*'p' value*
Education	0.242	0.000
Employment	0.129	0.045

Source: Computed.

The fourth hypothesis reads that *'Social factors are more dominant in deciding the extent of empowerment'* than economic and institutional factors. The result of stepwise regression analysis for GEDM, PARM and Empowerment shows that social factors are more dominant in deciding the extent of empowerment, and one of its indicators is PARM. But for GEDM the institutional factor namely being an account holder dominates the other factors. The regression co-efficient value for the levels of education is highest among the variables of PARM and Empowerment. The regression co-efficient for levels of education is 0.42 and its 't' value is 3.54 and its significance level is 1%. It is clear from Table 7.a that social factor–levels of education dominate the other factors in deciding PARM of the rural women (Table 7.a, 8.a). The value of regression co-efficient is 0.48 for the levels of education. It shows that education plays a vital role as a social factor in deciding the levels of empowerment. Its 't' value is 4.09 and it is significant at 1% level.

The result shows that the institutional factor namely being an account holder dominates the other factors in deciding GEDM in the family. The regression co-efficient value is 0.42, its 't' value is 7.35 and it is significant at 1% level. Thus, it is inferred that the level of education has less significant influence as compared to account holder in deciding GEDM. In the present study, the relation between PARM and empowerment is stronger than the relation between GEDM and empowerment. The most significant factor in deciding PARM is the level of education and hence the level of education plays an important role in determining the empowerment status. Level of education determines the other factors such as employment status, proportion of female income, asset structure, account holder income, asset structure, account holder, etc. (Table 6.a)

It is surprising to note that it is not the level of education that determines the GEDM in the family, but the institutional factor namely being an account holder decides the GEDM in the family. When both male and female keep more and more accounts, the power of autonomy over resources of women is increased. This will bring GEDM in the family. With financial autonomy, women will have more decision-making power and she can bargain equally with their counterparts. Thus the account holder plays a predominant role in deciding GEDM.

FINDINGS

- It may be inferred from the result of the study that women's income plays a significant role in women empowerment. The analysis shows that higher level of women's income results in an increase in women empowerment. As against this, the lower level of income leads to lower level of women empowerment. Therefore one may notice that women's income is vital for women empowerment.
- It may be concluded from the analysis of the study that PARM is dominating GEDM. Further, it is highly heartening that rural women have a high power of autonomy over resources and mobility. It shows a remarkable and encouraging trend in rural women empowerment.
- The study has found that education and employment are the main sources of women empowerment. It is highly interesting to find out that education plays a more vital role than employment does, since education is the base for women employment and higher-level earnings. It is also seen from the result that women, whose earning is substantially high in the rural household, have a greater control of resources and in turn a higher level of empowerment.
- As far as the factors influencing women empowerment are concerned, it may be concluded that education as a social factor plays a dominant role as compared to the role of others Institutional and Economic factors. It may be made clear from the results that education is more potential than other factors. Next to education, the institutional factor plays a significant role in women empowerment.
- By and large, it may be inferred that among the social factors, education records the first place in rural women empowerment and it is found to be the leading factor. Similarly among the economic factors, employment is the potential factor, and it leads to a higher level of income and in turn to women empowerment.

– Further the institutional factor namely being an account holder entitles women to greater power in GEDM in rural families. Therefore it may be concluded that in order to strengthen women empowerment; formal education of women should be strengthened in all possible ways in the rural areas.

POLICY SUGGESTIONS

The following suggestions directly emerge from the study which will be of use for the policy makers and planners:

- The present study brings to focus the need on the part of women to renegotiate gender relation and patriarchal institutions. This can be enabled by achieving their access to earnings and income through education.
- In this context, the study reiterates that adequate resources should be allocated for women's empowerment and activities directed towards gender equality.
- Further, all the empirical findings of the thesis suggest that the provision of employment opportunities for rural women may be enhanced all the more to utilize them productively according to their educational qualification.
- There should be gender equality in recruiting staff members in all industries, irrespective of their scale of operation.
- Women should be selected not only for traditional work but also for non-traditional work, which is a male dominant one.
- Awareness among rural women should be created in getting employment outside the home. They should be entitled to freedom of mobility to the places, away from home, in matters of employment, etc.
- Awareness of higher education should be created among rural women and the family members to enable the freedom of mobility to rural women.

SCOPE FOR FURTHER RESEARCH

- Education and power of autonomy over resources of women provide scope for further research in women studies.
- Employment and gender equality require still deeper probe in many micro settings. Researchers may find this as having a rich potential for further research.
- The relation between education and employment and how employment with education promotes empowerment constitute another theme for a separate study.
- The present study has focused on rural women and GEDM and PARM which have been subjected to a close scrutiny. However, this research has not made any attempt to juxtapose the rural women with their urban counterparts and thereby make any comparative assessment. As there are many economic and social factors which obtain and accentuate the process of empowerment in urban areas, it is suggested that researchers may direct their attention towards this area in future.

BIBLIOGRAPHY

Acker, Joan (1988), *Class, Gender and Relations of Distribution*, In: Signs, 13: 473 – 497.

Agarwal, Bina (1994), *A Field of One's Own Gender and Land Rights in South Asia,* Cambridge University Press, U.K.

_________ (1997), 'Bargaining and Gender Relations; Within and Beyond the Household', *Feminist Economics,* 1(5): 1-5.

Agarwal. D.(2001), 'Education for Empowerment – Meaningful and Relevant' *Social Welfare,* 48, (2): 6-8.

Agnihotri. S.B. (1999), 'Inferring Gender Bias from Mortality Data – A Discussion Note' *'Journal of Development studies,* 35 (4): 175-200.

Andre Beteille (1999), 'Empowerment' *Economic and political Weekly,* 34(10 - 11): 589-97.

Appleton, S., J. Hoddinolt, P. Krishnan (1999), 'The Gender Wage Gap, Three African Countries', *Economic Development and Cultural Change* 47(2) : 289 – 312.

Aromolaran, A. (2002), *Private Wage Returns to Schooling in Nigeria:* 1996-1999. New Q Haven: Yale University.

Arvind K Sharma (1996), 'People's Empowerment' *The Indian Journal of Public Administration,* July – September 1996. 42 (3): 255 – 260.

Assistant Director of Statistics (2005), *District Statistical Handbook,* Salem.

Assistant Director of Statistics (2005), *District Statistical Handbook,* Tiruvarur.

Balk, Deborah (1997), "Defying Gender Norms in Rural Bangladesh: A Social Demographic Analysis." *Population Studies* 51(2): 153-172.

Banerji Anita (2000), 'Gender and the Law – An Economic Dimension' *Women and Economic Development*, New Delhi, Deep and Deep Publications: p-217.

Barua, P.K. (2002), Women Power: The Vast Human Resources Vikasini, 17(4)

Basu, Alaka Malwade (1992), *Culture, the Status of Women, and Demographic Behaviour*. Oxford: Clarendon Press.

Batliwala, S, B K Anitha, A Gurumuthy and CS Wali (1998), *Status of Rural Women in Karnataka*, National Institute for Advanced Studies: Bangalore.

Batliwala, S. (1993), *Empowerment of Women in South Asia* – FFHC, FAO: New Delhi.

_________(1994), 'The Meaning of Women's Empowerment', New Concepts from Action' In : Gita Sen et al (eds) *Popular Policies Reconsidered; Health, Empowerment and Rights*, Harward; Centre of Population and Development Studies.

Becker, G. (1981), *A Treatise on the Family*, Cambridge, Mass: Hardward University Press.

_________(1971), *The Economics of Discrimination*, Chicago, Chicago University Press.

Beegle, Kathleen (2001), "Bargaining power within couples and Use of Prenatal and Delivery Care in Indonesia." *Studies in Family Planning*, 32(2): 130-46.

Beer, Ursula (1990), *Geschlecht, Structure, Geschichte – Soziale Konstituierung des' Geschlechterver haltnisses*. Frankfurta, M: New York.

Behrman, Jere R and Anil Deolalikar (1995), "Arc There Differential Returns to Schooling by Gender? The Case of Indonesian Labour Markets." *Oxford Bulletin of Economics and Statistics* 57(1): 97-117.

Behrman, Jere R and Barbara L Wolfe (1989), "Does more Schooling Make Women Better / Nourished and Healthier?: Adult Sibling Randowm and Fixed Effects Estimates for Nicaragua." *The Journal of Human Resources* 24(4): 644-663.

Bhasin Kamala (1985), *Towards Empowerment, Report of FAO-FFHC/ AD South Asia Training for Women Development Workers*, New Delhi and Rome; Freedom from Hunger campaign/Action for development (FAO).

Bhat Shan K. and Nirmala V. (2002), 'Female Empowerment; Occupational Scales in Kerala' In: Renje Reddy A (ed). 'Empowerment of Women and Ecological Development', Serial publications, New Delhi', pp.172 – 189.

Bloch, Francis and Vijayendra Rao (2000), *'Terror as a Bargaining Instrument: A Case Study of Dowry Violence in Rural India.'* Washington, DC, World Bank, Development Research Group.

Bloom, Shelah S. (2001), "Dimensions of Women's Autonomy and the Influence on *Maternal* Health Care Utilization in a North Indian City." *Demography* 38(1): 67-78.

Bourne, Katherine L and George M Walker (1991), "The Differential Effect of Mothers\Education on Mortality of Boys and Girls in India." *Population Studies 5(2):* 203-219.

Buch, Nirmala (2000), *Women's Experience in New Panchayat: The Emerging Leadership of Rural Women.* Center for Women's Development Studies Occasional, New Delhi: Paper No.35.

Cameron, L.A, J. Malcolm Dowling, and Christopher Worswick (2001), "Education and Labor Market Participation of Women in Asia: Evidence from Five Countries." *Economic Development and Cultural Change* 49(3): 459-77.

Cart, Martha Chen and Renana Jhabvala (1997), Speaking out: Women's Empowerment in South Asia. London: IT Publications.

Census of India (1991 and 2001), Provisional Population Totals. Registrar General of India. New Delhi: Government of India.

Chandra (1997), 'Women and Empowerment', *Indian journal of public Administration*-July-Sep. 13 (3).

Choudry Anand Meenaxi (1996), 'Empowering Strategies for Rural Women in India' *Kurushetra,* 44 (6). 18-23.

Coker, Ann L and Donna L Richter (1998), "Violence Against Women in Sierra Leone: Frequency and Correlates of Intimate Partner Violence and Forced Sexual Intercourse." *African Journal of Reproductive Health* 2(1): 61 -72.

Collier (1991), 'Women in Development: Defining the Issues' Oxford Economic Papers.

Devadas R.P., L.S Rajagopal and Rama Thilagam G. (1989), 'Home science Education and Women's Empowerment' paper presented at the Conference on Global Empowerment of Women by Association for Women in Development at Washington D.C.

November Pp.1-12. (1999) 'Empowerment of Women through Self Help Groups: An Indian Experience' In: Sharma R.K. (ed) *Empowering Women key to third World Development*, MD publications, New Delhi: pp.119-135.

Dixon-Muller, Ruth (1989), 'Patriarchy, Fertility and Women's Work in Rural Societies' in *International Union for the Scientific Study of Population*, International Population Conference, New Delhi, 1989, Vol.2, 291-304, IUSSP, Liege, Belgium.

_________ (1993), *'Population Policy and Women's Rights: Transforming Reproductive Choice'*, Praeger, New York.

Dreze, J. and A. Sen (1991), *Hunger and Public Action*, Oxford: Clarendon Press.

Duraisamy, P. (2002), "Changes in Returns to Education in India, 1983-94: By Gender, Age- cohort and Location." *Economics of Education Review* 21 (6): 609-22.

Duvvury, Nala and Keera Allendorf (2001), *Domestic Violence in India: The Roles of Education and Employment*. Sixth Women's Policy Research Conference, "The Status of Women: Facing the Facts, Forging the Future", Washington, D.C.

Dyson, Tim and Mick Moore (1983), On Kinship Structure Female Autonomy and Demographic Behaviour in India, *Population and Development Review*, 9 (1). 35-60.

Empowerment of Women (2001), *A Background Paper for the Task Force on Gender Equality of the Millenium Project*. Washington, DC, International Center for Research on Women.

Esim, S. (2001), Why Women Earn Less. Gender-Based Factors Affecting the Earnings of Self-Employed Women in Turkey. *The Economics of Women and Work in the Middle East and North Africa*. E. M. Cinar. Amsterdam, Elsevier.

Fapohonda, Eleanor (1988), 'The Non-pooling Household – A Challenge to Theory' in *Home Dividend, Women and Income in the Third Word*, (ed.) Dairy Dwyer and Judith Bruce, Stanford University: Stanford, Press.

Fiere P. (1972), The Pedagogy of the Oppressed' London: Harmonds worth, *Frontline*, December 24. 70 – 72.

Folbre, Nansy (1996), Hearts and Spades: Paradigms of Household Economics. *World Development*, 14(2): 245-55.

Gail Omvedt (2005), 'Women in Governance in South Asia'. *Economic and Political Weekly*, 40 (44&45), : 4746.

Ghambhir, S.G. (2000), 'Economics of Gender Discrimination: A Case Study of Rural India' in *Women and Economic Development* (Ed.) Anita Banerji and Rajkumar Sen, New Delhi: Deep and Deep Publications.

Giriappa. S. (1998), *The Role of Women in Rural Development*, Delhi: Daya publishing house.

Gladis Abraham (2003), Female Workforce Participation: Need for empowerment. *Yojana* May 47(5) 31-34.

Gopalan, Sarala (2002), *Towards Equality–The Unfinished Agenda: Status of Women in India* – 2001'. National Commission for Women, New Delhi: Government of India.

Government of India, Ministry of *Human Resource Development*, Dept. of Education, September (1991:) "Mahila Samakhy-Education for Women's Equality", pp.1-2.

Govindasamy, Pavalavalli and B.M. Ramesh (1996), *Maternal education and gender bias in child care practices in India.* Annual Meetings of the Population Association of America, New Orleans.

Govindasamy, Pavalavalli (2000), Poverty, Women's Status, and Utilization of Health Services in Egypt. *Women, Poverty, and Demographic Change.* B, Garcia. Oxford, Oxford University Press: 263-285.

Greenhalgh, Susan (1985), "Sexual Stratification: The Other Side of "Growth with Equity" in *East Asia." Population and Development Review* 11(2): 265-314.

Hartmann, Heidi. (1981), Capitalism, Patriarchy, and Job Segregation by Sex. In: Blaxall, Martha; Barbara, eds. *Women and the Workplace.* Chicago: London Press pp.137-169.

Hindin, Michelle J. (2000), "Women's Autonomy, Women's Status and Fertility-related Behavior in Zimbabwe." *Population Research and Policy Review* 19(3): 255-282.

Hollos, Marida (1998), The Status of Women in Southern Nigeria: is Education a Help or a Hindrance? *Women and education in sub-Saharan Africa: power, opportunities, and constraints.* M. Bloch, J. A. Beoku-Betts and B. R. Tabachnick. Boulder, Colorado, Lynne Rienner Publishers: pp. 247-276.

Human Development Report (2001), New York: United Nations Development Program. http://www.undp.org/ hdr2001/ indicator/pdf /hdr-2001-table-5.pdf.

Iyyampillai S. and Kulandai Theresa S. (2001), 'Status Inside and Outside the Home Co-related' *Social Welfare*, November

Jain, Shoblinta (2006), 'Women's Agency in the context of Family overworks in Indian Diaspora' *Economic and Political Weekly* 41 (23): 2312-2315.

Jasbir Singh (2004), 'Plans for an Asian University for Women' *The Bulletin*, May (159).

Jayanthi, C. (2001), 'Catching up with Education' *Yojana*, August.

Jeffery, Patricia and Roger Jeffery (1994), Killing my Heart's Desire: Education and Female Autonomy in Rural North India. *Women as subjects: South Asian histories*. N. Kumar. Charlosttesville, University Press of Virginia.

Jeffrey, J. and A. Basu (Eds.) (1996), Girls' Schooling, Women's Autonomy and Fertility Change in South Asia, New Delhi: Sage Publications.

Jejeebhoy, Shirccn (1996), *Women's Autonomy and Reproductive Behaviour in India: Linkages and Influence of Socio Cultural Context*. Seminar on Comparative Perspectives on Fertility Transition in South Asia, Islamabad-Rawalipindi, Pakistan, IUSSP.

Jejeebhoy, Shireen and Zeba Sathar (2001), "Women's Autonomy in India and Pakistan: the Influence of Religion and Region." *Population and Development Review* 27(4): 687-712.

Jo Rowlands (2000), What is Empowerment, in *Empowering Women for Development*, (ed). Haleh Afshar & Fatima Aiikhan, Hyderabad. Booklinks Corporation,

Jyothi Rani (1991), *Exclusion of Domestic Work in the Market Model*, Indian Economic Association Conference, Anantapur.

Kabeer, Naila (1994), *Reversed Realities–Gender Hierarchies in Development Thought*, New Delhi, Kali for women.

_________(2001), *Reflections on the Measurement of Women's Empowerment* in Discussion Women's Empowerment–Theory and practice, Sida studies No.3 Novum Grafiska AB, Stockholm.

Kabeer, Naila and Ramya subrahmaniam (eds). (1999), *Institutions, Relations and Outcomes*- A Framework and Case Studies for Gender- Aware Planning. New Delhi: Kali for Women.

Kalpagam, U. (1999), Women Work and Domestic Duties: Income Planning for Housewives' *The India Journal of Labour Economics,* Vo1.42(4).

Karl Marliee (1995), *Women and Empowerment; Participation and Decision Making;* London and New Jersy; Zed Books Ltd.

Kei Kawabata (1995), *'Toward Gender Equality–The Role of Public Policy,'* The World Bank–Washington DC.: 2-3.

Khandekar, Shahidur R. (1988), "Determinants of Women's Time Allocation Rural Bangladesh." *Economic Development and Cultural Change* 37(1): 111-126.

Kingdon, Geeta G. (1998), "Does the Labor Market Explain Lower Female Schooling in India?" *Journal of Development Studies* 35(1): 39-65.

Kingdon, Geeta G and Jeemol Unni (1998), "Education and Women's Labour Market Outcomes in India: An analysis using NSS household data." *unpublished Report.*

Kishor, Sunita (1995), *Autonomy and Egyptian Women: Findings from the (1988) Egypt Demographic and Health Survey.* Calverton, MD, ORC Macro.

Kishore Sunita and Kamala Gupta (2004), 'Women's Empowerment in India and Its States – Evidence from the NFHS'. *Economic and Political Weekly,* 39 (7) : 694-712.

Koenig, Michael A. (2003), "Women's Status and Domestic Violence in Rural Bangladesh: Individual- and Community-level Effects." *Demography* 40(2): 269-288.

Kreckel, Reinhard. (1992), Politische Soziologie der soialen Ungleichheit. Frankfurt a. M., New York.

Krishna Ahooja Patel (1993), 'Gender Distance Among Countries', *Economic and Political Weekly* 28(7): 295-305.

Krishnaji (1987), 'Poverty and Sex Ratio' Some Data and Speculation' *Economic and Political Weekly* 22 (3), June 6.

Krishnaraj, Maithreyi (2001), 'How Gender Figures in Economic Theorizing and Philosophy' *Economic and Political Weekly* 36 (17): 1425- 1434.

Kritz, MM and P Makinwa-Adebusoye (1999), "Determinants of Women's Decision-Making Authority in Nigeria: the Ethnic Dimension." *Sociological Forum* 14(3): 399-424.

Lakshmi Devi (ed) (1998), *'Women Empowerment and Societal Improvement'* New Delhi: Anmol Publications.

Lakshmi, S. (2000), 'Occupational Distribution of Women Workers in Tiruchirapalli District Tamil Nadu' In: *Women and Economic Development*, (ed.), Anita Banerji and Rajkumar Sen) Deep & Deep: New Delhi.

Lalitha Devi (1982), Status and Employment of Women in India, Delhi B.C. Publishing corporation.

Lalitha N. (1997), *'Rural Women Empowerment and Development Banking*, New Delhi: Kanishka Publishers.

Lawrance H. Summers (1992), 'Investing in all the People. Educating Women in Developing Countries, Policy and Research Series, *World Bank Report* 356(45): 1-24.

Lingam Lakshmi (2006), Gender, Households and Poverty, *Economic and Political Weekly*. 41(20) : 1989-98.

Mahmud Simeen and Anne M Johnston (1994), "Women's Status, Empowerment and Reproductive Outcomes' Gitasen, Adrine Germain and Lincoln, C. Chen (eds.). *Population Policies Reconsidered Health Empowerment and Rights*, Botson, MA; Harvard School of Public Health.

Malathy, R. (1994), "Education and Women's Time Allocation to Nonmarket Work in an Urban Setting in India." *Economic Development and Cultural Change* 42(4): 743-760.

Malhotra, Anju and Mark Mather (1997), "Do Schooling and Work Empower Women in Developing Countries? Gender and Domestic Decisions in Sri Lanka." *Sociological Forum* 12(4): 599-630.

Malhotra, Anju, Sidney Ruth Schuler and Carol Boender (2002), 'Measuring Women's Empowerment as a Variable in International Development'. *Unpublished* paper prepared for the World Bank.

Malhotra, Anju (1991), "Gender and Changing Generational Relations: Spouse Choice in Indonesia." *Demography* 28(4): 549-70.

Malinisur (2004), 'Women's Right to Education– A Narrative on International Law *'Indian Journal of Gender Studies*, 11(3) New Delhi: Sage Publications.

Mammen, Kristin and Christina Paxson (2000), "Women's Work and Economic Development." *The Journal of Economic Perspectives* 14(4): 141-164.

Manonmoney N. (2000), 'Emerging Technologies in Mass Media of Communication and Its Impact on Women's Culture and Development' Anita Banerji and Rajkumar Sen *Women and Economic Development*, (ed.), New Delhi: Deep & Deep Publications.

Margret Cormack (1976), *'The Hindu Women*, Bombay: Asia Publishing House, p.12.

Mark H. Keller, in David McConkey (1992), *"Aiming at the Future"*, Education Dept., United Mission to Nepal, Kathmandu.

Marshall, Alfred (1907), 'The Social Possibilities of Economic Chivalry', *Economic Journal*, 17, March, 7-29.

Mason, Karen (1986), "The Status of Women: Conceptual and Methodological Issues in Demographic Studies." *Sociological Forum* 1(2): 284-300.

Mazumdar, V., K. Sharma, N. Buch and C.P. Sujaya. (2001). 'Gender and Government–A Country Paper–India'. Study Commissioned by UNDP, New Delhi: Centre for Women's Development Studies.

Meena Acharya and Puspha Ghimire (2005), 'Gender Indicators of Equality, Inclusion and Poverty Reduction–Economic and Political Weekly, 40 (44, 45): 4719-4727.

Metcalfe, Bevely Dawn and Afanassieva, Marianne (2005), 'Gender, Work and Equal Opportunities in Central and Eastern Europe', *Women in Management Review'*, 20(6) : 397-411.

Mill, John Stuart (1879), The Subjection of Women' reprinted in Essays on Sex Equality (ed) Alice Rossi, Chicago: University Press.

Millennium Development Goals. http://www.developmentgoals.org/.

Ministry of Human Resource Development, Educational Statistics (Various years). http://www.education.nic.in.

Morley, Louise (1995), 'Theorizing Empowerment in the U.K. Public Services', *Empowerment in Organisations'*, 3(3): 35-41.

Moser, O.N., Caroline (1994), *Gender, Planning and Development: Theory, Practice and Training*, London: Routledge.

Mukhopadhyay, Swapna and Ratna M Sudarshan (eds) (2003), *Tracking Gender Equity under Economic Reforms: Continuity and Change in South Asia*, New Delhi: Kali for Women.

Mukul Mukherjee (2004), 'Women and Work in the Shadow of Globalisation' *Indian Journal of Gender Studies '* 11(3) New Delhi : Sage Publications.

Nair. K.R., and Siddagangamma (2000), 'Women Workers-Still Exploited, Still Underapit', *Social Welfare,* May.

Nandini Azad (1998), 'Gender and Equity: Experience of the Working Women's Forum, India'. *The Journal of Human Resources,* 33(4).

Narashimhan (2000), 'Empowering Women' An Alternative Strategy from Rural India' New Delhi: sage publications.

Neelima and T. Shyam Swaroof (2000), 'Putting the Girl Child in School', *Social Welfare,* September.

Newman, Constance (2001), *Gender, time use, and change: Impacts of agricultural export employment in Ecuador.* Washington DC, The World Bank, Development Research Group/ Poverty Reduction and Economic Management Network.

Niraula, Bhanu B. and S. Philip Morgan (2000), Gender Inequality in Two Nepali Settings. *Women, Poverty, and Demographic Change,* B. Garcia. New York: Oxford University Press: pp. 42-72.

Nisha Singh (2001), Technology Education and the Indian Women' *University News,* 39(10), March 5.

Nussbaum, C., Martha (2000), *Women and Human Development,* London: Cambridge University Press.

Pande, Rohini and Nan Marie Astone (2001), *Explaining son preference in rural India: The independent role of structural vs. individual factors.* Annual Meeting of the Population Association of America, Washington DC.

Pigon, AC (1952), *'Men's and Women's Wages'* reprinted in Essays in Economics, London: MacMillan.

Psacharopoulos, G and H Patrinos (2002), *Returns to Investment in Education: A Further Update.*

Rainuka Dagar (1998), Issues in Women's Development and Gender Justice. *N.S.S. Manual on Women's Development and Gender Justices,* Punjab: Brijesh Printers.

Rajivan, Anuradha K. (1998), 'Engendering Official Data Systems– At State and District Levels'. Department of Women and Child Development, New Delhi: Government of India.

Ramachandran (2002). 'Education and the Status of Women' in R.Govinda (ed), *India Education Report*, New Delhi: Oxford University Press.

Ranjana Kumari (1992), (ed.) *Women in Decision-Making*, New Delhi: Vikas Publishing House.

Rao, Vijendra (1997), "Wife-beating in Rural South India: a Qualitative and Econometric Analysis." *Social Science & Medicine* 44(8): 1169-80.

Ravi Prakesh Yadav (2001), The Working Women of India' *Social Welfare*, May.

Rustagi Preet (2000), 'Identifying Gender Backward Districts Using selected Indicators', *Economic and Political Weekly*, 35(48): 4276-86.

__________(2004), 'Significance of Gender related Development Indicators: An Analysis of Indian States', *Indian Journal of Gender Studies*, New Delhi, Sage Publications, 291-343.

Satish B. Agnihotri (2002), 'High Female Literacy, Low Child Population is there a Threshold effect' *Economic and political Weekly*, September 28.

Satya Sundaram, I. (2001), 'Education and Empowerment of Village Women' *Social Welfare*, May 2001.

Schuler Sidney Ruth and Syed M Hashemi (1993), Defining and Studying Empowerment of Women. 'A Research Note from Bangladesh. *JSI working paper* No.3. Arlington, VA'JSI Research and Training Institute, April 1993.

Schuler, Sidney Ruth and Syed M Hashemi (1994), "Credit Programs, Women's Empowerment, and Contraceptive use in Rural Bangladesh." *Studies in Family Planning* 25(2): 65-76.

__________ (1996), "Credit Programs, Patriarchy and Men's Violence against Women in Rural Bangladesh." *Social Science & Medicine* 43(12): 1 729-42.

Sen, Amartya (1983), Economics and the Family,' *Asian Development Review*, 1(2).

__________ (1990), 'Gender and Co-operative Conflicts' in Persistent Inequalities; Women and Development (ed) Irene Tinker, U.K: Oxford University, Press.

__________ (1992), 'Class, Gender and other groups an 'Inequality Reexemened' Oxford: Claredon press.

________ (1995), 'Gender Inequality and Theories of Justice' in *Women, Culture and Development* (ed) Martha Nussbaum and Jonathan Glover, Oxford: Claredon Press.

Sen, Amartya (2001), 'Many Faces of Gender Inequality, *Frontline* 18(22) Oct.27-Nov. 09, 2001.

Sen, Purna (1999), "Enhancing Women's Choices in Responding to Domestic Violence in Calcutta: A Comparison of Employment and Education." *European Journal of Development Research* (2): 65-86.

Sengupta, Manisha and Nan E Johnson (2003), Does Educational Superiority Autonomize Daughters-in-law Who Live With their Mothers-in-law in India? A Test of Caldwell's Thesis Annual Meeting of the Population Association of America. Minneapolis, Minnesota.

Seth Mira (2001), *Women and Development. The Indian Experience*, New Delhi: Sage Publications.

Sethuraman S.V. (1989), '*Gender, Informality and Poverty: A Global Review*' Bardhan: PP-242-45.

Shanmugasundaram Yasodha (1993), "*Women Employment in India*", Chennai: Allied Publishers.

Shanthi, K. (2005), *Women in India: Retrospect and Prospect*, New Delhi: Anmol Publications.

Sharma Kumud (1991), 'Grassroots Organization and Women's Empowerment; Some Issues in the Contemporary Debate' *Samya Shakti* Vol.(6): 28-44,

Shelley P.B. (2004), Empowerment of Women-emerging Opportunities and Potential Threats: *The Hindu* May 11.

Singh O.R. (2001), 'Education and Women's Empowerment', *Social Welfare*, April 2001.

Smith, Adam (1776), '*An Inquiry into the Nature and Causes of Wealth of Nations*, reprint 1976, Oxford: Clarendon Press.

Suguna, B. (2002), "Self Help Groups (SHGs): New Women's Movement. *Vikasini*, 17(4)

Suguna, R. (2001), 'Women's Empowerment: Concept and Framework' *Social Welfare*, December.

Suman Krishna Kant (2001), 'Women's Empowerment and Mutual Cooperation in the Family' *Social Welfare*, April 2001.

Sumitra Mahajan (2001), 'Philosophy Goals and Achievements' *Yojana*, August 2001.

Suroor Hasan (2005), 'Gender Equality Still a Distant Dream; *The Hindu* May 20 p.11.

Tamil Nadu Human Development Report (2003), Government of Tamil Nadu, Delhi: Social Science Press.

Tansel, Aysit (1994), "Wage Employment, Earnings, and Returns to Schooling for Men and Women in Turkey." *Economics of Education Review* 13(4): 305.

Tapen Neeta (1998), *'Need for Women Empowerment'* New Delhi: Rawat Publications.

Tripa and Kaushik (2002), 'Impact of Financial Assistance Schemes on the Economic Empowerment of Women', *Indian Journal of Social Research*, 43(2) : 93-96.

U.N.Fourth World Conference on Women. Beijing, China 4-15th September, 1995. A/CONF.177/20.gopher://gopher. undp.org/00/unconfs/women/off/a-20.en.

UNDP (1995), The Human Development Report, New Delhi: Oxford University press.

UNDP (2004), Human Development Report, UNDP, Washington, DC.

UNESCO Education for All: Global Monitoring Report 2003/2004: *'Gender and Education for All The Leap to Equality'*. http://portal. unesco.org/education/ efa.

UNESCO. General Comment. 18th Session, 19 November (1974). Recommendations Concerning Education for International Understanding, Co-operation, Peace and Education related to Human Rights and Fundamental Freedoms.

UNICEF (2002), *Progress of the World's Women 2002*, New York.

United Nations Development Programme (1995), *Human Development Report*. New Delhi: Oxford University Press.

United Nations Educational, Scientific and Cultural Organisation (UNESCO) (1981), Women and development : Indicators of Changing Role. *Socio-economic Studies* 3. Paris: UNESCO.

Venkatasubramanian K. (2001), Women! Be Courageous, Other Things Follow' *University News*, 39(42), October 15-21.

Visaria, Leela (1993), Regional Variations in Female Autonomy and Fertility and Contraception in India. *Working Paper* No.50. Ahmedabad : Gujarat Institute of Development Research.

Visaria, Leela (1999), Violence Against Women in India: Evidence from rural Gujarat. *Domestic Violence in India.* B.B, D.N, R.A and V.N. Washington, DC, ICRW: 9-17.

Vishwanathan, N. (1997), Theories of Women, Gender Development: Introduction' in Nalint Viswanathan, Lynn Dugger, Laurier Nisonoff and Nan Wiegersma (eds.), *The Women, Gender and Development Reader,* **12-27.** London, Zed Books.

Vlassoff, Carol (1994), "From Rags to Riches: The Impact of Rural Development on Women's Status in an Indian Village." *World Development* 22(5): 707-719.

Walby, Silvia (1990), *Theorizing Patriarchy.* Oxford: Cambridge/ Mass.

Waldron, Ingrid (1983), "Sex Differences in Human Mortality: The Role of Genetic Factors." *Social Science and Medicine* 17(6): 321-333.

Waller, William and Ann Jenneng's (1990), 'On the Possibility of Feminist Economics; The Convergence of Institutional Economics and Feminist Methodology, '*Journal of Economic Issues,* 24(2), June.

Wieringa S. (1994), Women's Interests and Empowerment: Gender Planning Reconsidered, *Development & Change* vol.25 (4), The Huge: Blackivell publishers.

_________(1999), Women's Empowerment in Japan: Towards an Alternative Index on Gender Equality, Unpublished, Institute of Social Studies, The Hague.

World Bank (1991), World Development Report, Washington.

World Bank (1992), World Development Report, Washington.

World Bank (2001), *Engendering Development – Through Gender Equality in Rights, Resources, and Voice,* World Bank and Washington, DC and New York: Oxford University Press.

World Development Indicators. 2000. World Bank, Washington DC. http://www.worldbank.org/data/wdi2000/pdfs/tab2-13.pdf.

World Development Report. 1998. New York: Oxford University Press. http://www.world bank.Org/wdr/wdr98/index.htm.

www.emeraldinsight.com/ 0964-9425.htm.

Youssef, Naida H. (1982), 'The Interrelationship between the Division of Labour in the Household, Women's Roles and Their Impact on Fertility' in R Anker, M Buvinic and N H Youssef (eds), Women's Roles and Population Trends in the Third World, Croom Helm, London.

APPENDICES

Appendix – I

Education, Employment and Empowerment of Rural Women in Tamil Nadu

Interview Schedule
(For Doctoral Programme)

I. GENERAL INFORMATION

a. Name of the Respondent :
b. Name of the District :
c. Name of the Block :
d. Name of the Village :
f. Age of the Respondent :
g. Years of Education :
h. Marital Status :
— Married ( )
— Unmarried ( )
— Single ( )
i. Religion
— Hindu ( )
— Muslim ( )
— Christian ( )
— Others ( )

j. Community
- — Others ( )
- — OC ( )
- — BC ( )
- — MBC ( )
- — SC/ST ( )

k. Type of Household :
- Joint ( )
- Nuclear ( )

l. Size of the Household
- — Small 1-4 ( )
- — Medium 5-6 ( )
- — Large 7 & above ( )

m. Head of the Household :
- — Male ( )
- — Female ( )

II. EDUCATIONAL AND EMPLOYMENT STATUS OF THE HOUSEHOLD

Name	*Age / Sex*	*Relationship to the Respondent*	*Literacy Level*	*Employment Status*

1. Sex ratio :
2. No. of Earners :
   - Male ( )
   - Female ( )
3. No. of Dependants :
   - Male ( )
   - Female ( )
4. E/D Ratio :
5. Age difference between husband & wife :
6. Child–Adult Ratio :

III. INCOME BY SOURCES (IN RS.)

Source	*Owner of the Sources*			*Value (Rs.)*
	Male	*Female*	*Both*	
Total Income				

Proportion of female income to total income :

IV. HOUSEHOLD EXPENDITURE

	Whose money is allocated			
	Male	*Female*	*Both*	*Expenditure per month*
Food items				
Cereals Pulses Oil Miscellaneous Beverages Fuel & Other things				
Non food items				
Clothing House rent/repair Cosmetics Education Medical expenses Recreation Religious & festival Social ceremonies				
Other major expenditure				
Marriage Higher education Donation Others (specify)				
Total expenditure				

Proportion of Female income to total expenditure :

V. ANNUAL HOUSEHOLD SAVINGS

Item	*Account Holder*			*Savings (Rs.)*
	Male	*Female*	*Both*	
LIC				
Chit funds				
Post office				
SHGs				
Finance Bank				
Cash in hand				
Total Savings				

Proportion of female savings to total savings :

VI. BORROWINGS

Source	*Amount borrowed*	*Borrowed person*	*Amount repaid*	*Repaid person*	*R. I.*
		M F B		*M F B*	

Total Borrowings =

Proportion of female borrowing to total borrowings

VII. OWNERSHIP OF PROPERTY - HOUSEHOLD ASSET STRUCTURE

Item	*Relationship to the respondent*	*Value (Rs)*
Land		
House		
Jewels		
Cash in hand		
Durable goods		
Non-durable goods		
Bank deposits		
Live stock Others		
Total Asset Structure =		

Proportion of female ownership to total asset structure :

VIII. OCCUPATIONAL PATTERN:

Self-employed in organized sector ( )
Self-employed in unorganized sector ( )
Wage-employed in organized sector ( )
Wage-employed in unorganized sector ( )

IX. DAILY ACTIVITIES OF THE HOUSE (HOME MAKER)

Task	*Time*
Waking	
Sleeping	

Working hours :
Rest hours :

X. EMPOWERMENT INFORMATION

a. Gender Equality in Decision Making (GEDM)

1. Who is the decision-maker in your family?
   Male ( ) Female ( ) Both ( )
2. Who manages financial resources in the family?
   Male ( ) Female ( ) Both ( )
3. Who has savings in your family?
   Male ( ) Female ( ) Both ( )
4. Who withdraws money from the bank?
   Male ( ) Female ( ) Both ( )
5. Who makes decision in respect of your children's education?
   Male ( ) Female ( ) Both ( )
6. Who makes decisions in your children's marriage?
   Male ( ) Female ( ) Both ( )
7. Who has power to employ servants in your house?
   Male ( ) Female ( ) Both ( )
8. Who got \ who will get property in your family?
   Male ( ) Female ( ) Both ( )
9. Who has the highest level of education in your family?
   Male ( ) Female ( ) Both ( )
10. Who decides the spacing of child in your family?
    Male ( ) Female ( ) Both ( )

11. Who has undergone medical intervention for family planning?
Male ( ) Female ( ) Both ( )

12. Which child gets preferential treatment in your family?
Male ( ) Female ( ) Both ( )

13. Who will assist you in your house hold activities?
Male ( ) Female ( ) Both ( )

14. Who decides on the purchase of groceries & vegetables?
Male ( ) Female ( ) Both ( )

15. Who decides on the purchase of land and other properties?
Male ( ) Female ( ) Both ( )

16. Which physical resources are used for liquidity in your family?
Male's assets ( ) Female's assets ( ) Both ( )

17. Who assumes child care responsibility in your family?
Male ( ) Female ( ) Both ( )

18. Who gets preference in getting professional education?
Male ( ) Female ( ) Both ( )

19. Who decides the family budget?
Male ( ) Female ( ) Both ( )

20. Who decides the leisure activities?
Male ( ) Female ( ) Both ( )

21. Who decides the gift made to others?
Male ( ) Female ( ) Both ( )

22. Who will have more rest hours?
Male ( ) Female ( ) Both ( )

23. Who will have more working hours?
Male ( ) Female ( ) Both ( )

24. Who helps your children in their academic work?
Male ( ) Female ( ) Both ( )

25. Who will get preference in reading magazines and newspapers?
Male ( ) Female ( ) Both ( )

b. Power of Autonomy over Resources and Mobility (PARM)

1. Are you able to spend money for your personal needs?
WOP ( ) WP ( ) NA ( )

2. Do you buy on your own durable goods like T.V., fridge, washing machine, etc.?
   WOP ( ) WP ( ) NA ( )

3. Do you buy jewellary according to your own wish?
   WOP ( ) WP ( ) NA ( )

4. Are you allowed to spend for your mothers' side?
   WOP ( ) WP ( ) NA ( )

5. Are you able to cultivate crops according to your wish?
   WOP ( ) WP ( ) NA ( )

6. Are you entitled to purchase land / buildings according to your wish?
   WOP ( ) WP ( ) NA ( )

7. Could you express your desire in your studies?
   WOP ( ) WP ( ) NA ( )

8. Do you have power to pledge/mortgage it for raising funds?
   WOP ( ) WP ( ) NA ( )

9. Are you able to vote according to your wish?
   WOP ( ) WP ( ) NA ( )

10. Did you have the privilege of giving your opinion as to the choice of spouse for your marriage?
    WOP ( ) WP ( ) NA ( )

11. Do you decide on your work schedule each day?
    WOP ( ) WP ( ) NA ( )

12. Are you allowed to watch T.V / listen to radio according to your own wish?
    WOP ( ) WP ( ) NA ( )

13. Are you allowed to cook the items according to your wish?
    WOP ( ) WP ( ) NA ( )

14. Are you allowed to keep money with you for the daily expenses of your home?
    WOP ( ) WP ( ) NA ( )

15. Do you have power to sell your land / buildings which are in your name?
    WOP ( ) WP ( ) NA ( )

16. Do you have power to spend / invest the income from the sale of crops of income from other sources?
    WOP ( ) WP ( ) NA ( )

17. Has your property been disposed by your family members?
    WOP ( ) WP ( ) NA ( )

18. Are you allowed to borrow from others?
    WOP ( ) WP ( ) NA ( )

19. Are you allowed to sell the property to others?
    WOP ( ) WP ( ) NA ( )

(Freedom of Mobility)

20. Are you allowed to visit your friends' or relatives' house?
    WOP ( ) WP ( ) NA ( )

21. Are you allowed to attend your friends' and relatives' marriages and other functions?
    WOP ( ) WP ( ) NA ( )

22. Are you allowed for shopping?
    WOP ( ) WP ( ) NA ( )

23. Do you enjoy the privilege to entertain your friends / relations in your home?
    WOP ( ) WP ( ) NA ( )

24. Do you enjoy the privilege to obtain higher education in other places away from house?
    WOP ( ) WP ( ) NA ( )

25. Do your family members allow you to move over to other places, by virtue of your employment?
    WOP ( ) WP ( ) NA ( )

II. CRITERIA OF EMPOWERMENT

1. Have you been aware of empowerment of women?
   Fully ( ) Partially ( ) Not at all ( )

2. Is there any improvement in your awareness in response to present survey?
   Fully ( ) Partially ( ) Not at all ( )

3. To what extent does T.V. bring awareness?
   Fully ( ) Partially ( ) Not at all ( )

4. To what extent do magazines bring awareness?
   Fully ( ) Partially ( ) Not at all ( )

5. To what extent does education bring awareness?
   Fully ( ) Partially ( ) Not at all ( )

6. To what extent does employment bring awareness?
   Fully ( ) Partially ( ) Not at all ( )

7. Are you aware of women's rights? (Property rights)
   Fully ( ) Partially ( ) Not at all ( )

8. Does income of women bring empowerment?
   Fully ( ) Partially ( ) Not at all ( )

9. How do you assure yourself in terms of gender empowerment awareness after marriage?
   Fully ( ) Partially ( ) Not at all ( )

10. Does type of family (joint) affect women's empowerment?
    Fully ( ) Partially ( ) Not at all ( )

11. Do women development programmes bring empowerment to women?
    Fully ( ) Partially ( ) Not at all ( )

XII. OPEN ENDED QUESTIONS

1. Give your views on need for educating women
2. Give your views on women taking to employment
3. Give your views on empowerment of women
4. Personal Information
   Home violence – Specify the reason for home violence
5. Why are you not employed?
6. Why are you not educated?[not getting higher education also]
7. Why are you employed?

Appendix – II

District Ranked As Per Female Literacy Rate in Rural Area-2001

Rank in Literacy Rate	*State/District*	*Percentage of Female Literates*
1.	Kanniyakumari	84.11
2.	Thoothukkudi	70.66
3.	The Nilgiris	67.18
4.	Nagapattinam	65.70
5.	Thiruvarur	65.47
6.	Tirunelveli	64.04
7.	Thanjavur	61.13
8.	Tiruchirappali	59.27
9.	Virudhunagar	57.54
10.	Ramanathapuram	58.65
11.	Pudukkottai	57.04
12.	Thiruvallur	57.96
13.	Madurai	56.05
14.	Vellore	57.26
15.	Kancheepuram	58.25
16.	Sivaganga	55.34
17.	Theni	54.26
18.	Cuddalore	53.36
19.	Thiruvannamalai	52.80
20.	Coimbatore	56.16
21.	Dindigal	52.85
22.	Perambalur	51.41
23.	Namakkal	51.63
24.	Ariyalur	49.63
25.	Karur	50.27
26.	Villupuram	49.72
27.	Erode	46.70
28.	Salem	46.11
29.	Dharmapuri	44.79
30.	Chennai	-
31.	Tamilnadu	55.84

Source: Census Report 2001, Government of India.

Appendix j III

Distribution of the Respondents According to Levels of GEDM, PARM and Empowerment by the Earners and Dependents

	Categories	N	Levels of GEDM			Levels of PARM			Levels of Empowerment		
			Low	*Medium*	*High*	*Low*	*Medium*	*High*	*Low*	*Medium*	*High*
Total Earners	1 j 3	147	86(61.9)	29(54.7)	32(66.7)	85(63.4)	25(51.0)	37(64.9)	65(62.5)	53(57.0)	29(67.4)
	Above 3	93	53(38.1)	24(45.3)	16(33.3)	49(36.6)	24(49.0)	20(35.1)	39(37.5)	40(43.0)	14(32.6)
	N	240	139(100)	53(100)	48(100)	134(100)	49(100)	57(100)	104(100)	93(100)	43(100)
Female Earners	Nil Earners	95	60(43.2)	20(37.7)	15(31.2)	53(39.6)	19(38.8)	23(40.3)	46(44.2)	38(40.9)	11(25.6)
	1 - 3	145	79(56.8)	33(62.3)	33(68.8)	81(60.4)	30(61.2)	34(59.7)	58(55.8)	55(59.1)	32(74.4)
	N	240	139(100)	53(100)	48(100)	134(100)	49(100)	57(100)	104(100)	93(100)	43(100)
Total Depen-dents	1 j 3	13	8(5.8)	4(7.6)	1(2.0)	6(4.5)	4(8.2)	3(5.3)	29(27.9)	28(30.1)	23(53.5)
	Above 3	227	131(94.2)	49(92.4)	47(98.0)	128(95.5)	45(91.8)	54(94.7)	75(72.1)	65(69.9)	20(46.5)
	N	240	139(100)	53(100)	48(100)	134(100)	49(100)	57(100)	104(100)	93(100)	43(100)
Female Depen-dents	No dependents	34	20(14.4)	10(18.9)	4(8.3)	19(14.2)	6(12.3)	9(15.8)	14(13.5)	13(14.0)	7(16.3)
	1 - 3	169	98(70.5)	33(62.2)	38(79.2)	88(65.7)	40(81.6)	41(71.9)	71(68.3)	66(70.9)	32(74.4)
	Above 3	37	21(15.1)	10(18.9)	6(12.50)	27(20.1)	3(6.1)	7(12.3)	19(18.2)	14(15.1)	4(9.3)
	N	240	139(100)	53(100)	48(100)	134(100)	49(100)	57(100)	104(100)	93(100)	43(100)

Source: Computed.

Figures in parentheses are percentage to column total.

N - Number of sample respondents, GEDM plus PARM equals Empowerment

Appendix j IV

Distribution of the Respondents According to Levels of GEDM, PARM and Empowerment by proportion of Savings Borrowings and Property

	Categories	N	Levels of GEDM			Levels of PARM			Levels of Empowerment		
			Low	*Medium*	*High*	*Low*	*Medium*	*High*	*Low*	*Medium*	*High*
Proportion of Savings	Upto 25%	86	56(40.3)	14(26.4)	14(29.2)	47(35.1)	19(38.8)	20(35.1)	40(38.5)	35(37.6)	11(25.6)
	25 j 50%	40	12(8.6)	12(22.6)	18(37.5)	19(14.2)	9(18.3)	12(21.1)	8(7.7)	21(22.6)	11(25.6)
	Above 50%	114	71(51.1)	27(51.0)	16(33.3)	68(50.7)	21(42.9)	25(43.8)	56(53.8)	37(39.8)	21(48.8)
	N	240	139(100)	53(100)	48(100)	134(100)	49(100)	57(100)	104(100)	93(100)	43(100)
Proportion of Borrowing	Below 25%	87	53(38.1)	18(34.0)	16(33.3)	58(43.3)	14(28.6)	15(26.3)	49(47.1)	26(28.0)	12(27.9)
	Above 25%	153	86(61.9)	35(66.0)	32(66.7)	76(56.7)	35(71.4)	42(73.7)	55(52.9)	67(72.0)	31(72.1)
	N	240	139(100)	53(100)	48(100)	134(100)	49(100)	57(100)	104(100)	93(100)	43(100)
Proportion of Property	Upto 25%	89	58(41.7)	20(37.7)	11(22.9)	58(43.3)	17(34.7)	14(24.6)	49(47.1)	33(35.5)	7(16.3)
	25 j 50%	54	31(22.3)	14(26.4)	9(18.8)	31(23.1)	9(18.4)	14(24.6)	24(23.1)	20(21.5)	10(23.3)
	Above 50%	97	50(36.0)	19(35.9)	28(58.3)	45(33.6)	23(46.9)	29(50.8)	31(29.8)	40(43.0)	26(60.4)
	N	240	139(100)	53(100)	48(100)	134(100)	49(100)	57(100)	104(100)	93(100)	43(100)

Source: Computed.

Figures in parentheses are percentage to column total.

N - Number of sample respondents, GEDM plus PARM equals Empowerment

Appendix j V

Distribution of the Respondents According to Levels of GEDM, PARM and Empowerment by Proportion of Income and Expenditure

	Categories	N	Levels of GEDM			Levels of PARM			Levels of Empowerment		
			Low	*Medium*	*High*	*Low*	*Medium*	*High*	*Low*	*Medium*	*High*
Proportion of Female Income	Upto 25%	154	94(67.6)	31(58.5)	29(60.4)	92(68.7)	30(61.2)	32(56.1)	76(73.1)	61(65.6)	17(39.6)
	25 j 50%	65	32(23.0)	17(32.1)	16(33.3)	38(28.3)	16(32.7)	11(19.3)	24(23.1)	28(30.1)	13(30.2)
	Above 50%	21	13(9.4)	5(9.4)	3(6.3)	4(3.0)	3(6.1)	14(24.6)	4(3.8)	4(4.3)	13(30.2)
	N	240	139(100)	53(100)	48(100)	134(100)	49(100)	57(100)	104(100)	93(100)	43(100)
Proportion of Expenditure	Upto 25%	156	94(67.6)	35(66.0)	27(56.3)	95(70.9)	31(63.3)	30(52.6)	78(75.0)	60(64.5)	18(41.9)
	25 j 50%	51	28(20.2)	10(18.9)	13(27.1)	28(20.9)	11(22.4)	12(21.1)	19(18.3)	22(23.7)	10(23.2)
	Above 50%	33	17(12.2)	8(15.1)	8(16.6)	11(8.2)	7(14.3)	15(26.3)	7(6.7)	11(11.8)	15(34.9)
	N	240	139(100)	53(100)	48(100)	134(100)	49(100)	57(100)	104(100)	93(100)	43(100)

Source: Computed.

Figures in parentheses are percentage to column total.

N - Number of sample respondents, GEDM plus PARM equals Empowerment

Appendix – VI

A Zero Order Correlation Matrix Among X_1's variables and GEDM

Variables	*Total Years of Schooling in the Family* (X_1)	*Age Difference between husband and wife* (X_2)	*Account Holder* (X_3)	*Levels of Education* (X_4)	*Employment Status* (X_5)	*Proportion of female assets* (X_6)	*GEDM (Y)*
Total Years of Schooling in the Family (X_1)	1.00	0.02	0.25*	0.10	0.01	-0.02	0.28*
Age Difference between husband and wife (X_2)	0.02	1.00	-0.01	-0.19*	-0.11	- 0.15*	-0.13*
Account Holder (X_3)	0.25*	-0.01	1.00	0.13*	0.13*	0.06	0.47*
Levels of Education (X_4)	0.10	-0.19*	0.13*	1.00	0.88*	0.47*	0.18*
Employment Status (X_5)	0.01	-0.11	0.13*	0.88*	1.00	0.53*	0.10
Proportion of female assets (X_6)	-0.02	- 0.15*	0.06	0.47*	0.53*	1.00	0.10
GEDM (Y)	0.28*	-0.13*	0.47*	0.18*	0.10	0.10	1.00

Source : Computed.

* indicates significant correlation relation between variables at 5% level.

Appendix j VII

A Zero Order Correlation Matrix Among X_1m variables (Independent Variables) PARM

Variables	*Level of Education* (X_1)	*Employment Status* (X_2)	*Proportion of Income* (X_3)	*Proportion of Borrowings* (X_4)	*Account Holder* (X_5)	*Proportion of Female Assets* (X_6)	*Income Earner* (X_7)	*Control over Expenditure* (X_8)	*PARM (Y)*
Level of Education (X_1)	1.00	0.89*	0.44*	0.14*	0.13*	0.13*	0.63*	0.60*	0.20*
Employment Status (X_2)	0.89*	1.00	0.52*	0.13*	0.13*	0.17*	0.76*	0.71*	0.1
Proportion of Income (X_3)	0.44*	0.52*	1.00	0.06	0.06	0.26*	0.44*	0.45*	0.31*
Proportion of Female Borrowings (X_4)	0.14*	0.13*	0.06	1.00	0.01	0.17*	0.03	0.02	0.20*
Account Holder (X_5)	0.13*	0.13*	0.06	0.01	1.00	-0.03	0.22*	0.15*	0.11
Proportion of Female Assets (X_6)	0.13*	0.17*	0.26*	0.17*	-0.03	1.00	0.11	0.15*	0.26*
Income Earner (X_7)	0.63*	0.76*	0.44*	0.03	0.22*	0.11	1.00	0.88*	-0.03
Control over Expenditure (X_8)	0.60*	0.71*	0.45*	0.02	0.15*	0.15*	0.88*	1.00	0.05
PARM (Y)	0.20*	0.10	0.31*	0.20*	0.11	0.26*	-0.03	0.05	1.00

Source : Computed.

* indicates significant correlation relation between variables at 5% level.

Appendix j VIII

A Zero order Correlation Matrix Among X_1's Variables and Empowerment

Variables	*Total Years of Schooling in the Family (X_1)*	*Income Earner (X_2)*	*Account Holder (X_3)*	*Employment Status (X_4)*	*Proportion of Female Income (X_5)*	*Proportion of Female Assets (X_6)*	*Levels of Education (X_7)*	*Empowerment (Y)*
Total Years of Schooling in the Family (X_1)	1.00	0.04	0.25*	0.01	-0.08	0.01	0.1	0.22*
Income Earner (X_2)	0.04	1.00	0.22*	0.76*	0.44*	0.11	0.63*	0.03
Account holder (X_3)	0.25*	0.22*	1.00	0.13*	0.06	-0.03	0.13*	0.35*
Employment Status (X_4)	0.01	0.76*	0.13*	1.00	0.52*	0.17*	0.88*	0.13*
Proportion of Female Income (X_5)	-0.08	0.44*	0.06	0.52*	1.00	0.26*	0.44*	0.23*
Proportion of Female Assets (X_6)	0.01	0.11	-0.03	0.17*	0.26*	1.00	0.13*	0.23*
Levels of Education (X_7)	0.10	0.63*	0.13*	0.88*	0.44*	0.13*	1.00	0.24*
Empowerment (Y)	0.22*	0.03	0.35*	0.13*	0.23*	0.23*	0.24*	1.00

Source: Computed.

* indicates significant correlation relation between variables at 5% level.

Appendix VIII

A Zero order Correlation Matrix Among X_i's Variables and Empowerment

Variables	Total Years of Schooling in the Family (X_1)	Income Earner (X_2)	Account Holder (X_3)	Employment Status (X_4)	Proportion of Female Income (X_5)	Proportion of Female Assets (X_6)	Levels of Education (X_7)	Empowerment (Y)
Total Years of Schooling in the Family (X_1)	1.00	0.04	0.25*	0.01	-0.08	-0.01	0.1	0.22*
Income Earner (X_2)	0.04	1.00	0.22*	0.76*	0.44*	0.11	0.43*	0.03
Account holder (X_3)	0.25*	0.22*	1.00	0.13*	-0.06	-0.03	0.13*	0.35*
Employment Status (X_4)	0.01	0.76*	0.13*	1.00	0.52*	0.17*	0.88*	0.13*
Proportion of Female Income (X_5)	-0.08	0.44*	-0.06	0.52*	1.00	0.26*	0.44*	0.23*
Proportion of Female Assets (X_6)	-0.01	0.11	-0.03	0.17*	0.26*	1.00	0.13*	0.23*
Levels of Education (X_7)	0.10	0.43*	0.13*	0.88*	0.44*	0.13*	1.00	0.24*
Empowerment (Y)	0.22*	0.03	0.35*	0.13*	0.23*	0.23*	0.24*	1.00

Source: Computed

* Indicates significant correlation relation between variables at 5% level